CONTENTS

CONTENTS

iv

THE ELEMENTS OF
NEW TESTAMENT GREEK

J.W.WENHAM

BASED ON THE EARLIER WORK BY

H.P.V.NUNN

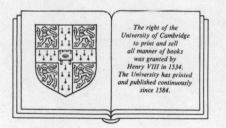

The right of the
University of Cambridge
to print and sell
all manner of books
was granted by
Henry VIII in 1534.
The University has printed
and published continuously
since 1584.

CAMBRIDGE UNIVERSITY PRESS

CAMBRIDGE

NEW YORK   NEW ROCHELLE

MELBOURNE   SYDNEY

Published by the Press Syndicate of the University of Cambridge
The Pitt Building, Trumpington Street, Cambridge CB2 1RP
32 East 57th Street, New York, NY 10022, USA
10 Stamford Road, Oakleigh, Melbourne 3166, Australia

ISBN 0 521 09842 4

First published 1965
Reprinted 1967 1970 1973 1975 (twice) 1976
1977 1979 1981 1982 1985 1987 1988

Printed in Great Britain at the
University Press, Cambridge

CONTENTS

PREFACE

This started as a radical revision, it ended as a new book. The author has long been impressed with the fundamental soundness of Nunn's *Elements* as a book for beginners, regarding it as incomparably the best book of its type published in this country. The subject is introduced gently and unhurriedly. The ground to be covered is sensibly chosen, representing a good year's work for the average student. Nunn's discursive lucidity is admirably suited to those who have to work on their own, and the exercises are well conceived. Yet thirteen years of teaching from this book have revealed many possibilities of improvement. The owners and publishers have kindly given me permission to revise it completely, using what material I like and omitting or changing what I like. I have been in the happy position of being allowed, if necessary, to write a new book, leaning heavily on Nunn, yet without risking the charge of plagiarism.

As work on the book progressed, so the possibilities of improvement seemed to multiply. The result in the end has been literally thousands of changes, many very small but many quite considerable. The guiding principle throughout the work of rewriting has been to try to conform the book as closely as possible to its title. That is to say, to try to present the elements (and only the elements) of New Testament Greek as simply and completely as possible. The learning of a language is an enormous task. The secret of success is to gain a thorough grasp of the elements. If the elements are known, the rest will come bit by bit easily enough. But if the elements are not known, the student will flounder and make no progress. The student should be protected from all avoidable toil which does not directly further this end.

In the case of the New Testament it is possible to discover with remarkable precision just what the elements are. We are dealing with a limited body of literature containing about 137,500 words, of which the vocabulary has been statistically analysed and the grammar has been minutely examined. I have taken a great deal of trouble so to select the material that the student may know that everything he is learning is really useful, and that if he can learn all that the book contains he will have mastered the complete elements of New Testament Greek. I have also tried to simplify the presentation in every possible way.

The results may be summarised under the headings of omissions, additions and rearrangements.

Omissions include the Reading Exercises from the *Shepherd of Hermas* and the *Second Epistle of Clement* (the student needs rather the encouragement of actual New Testament study); most of the references to Latin and Classical Greek; various points of overlapping; and a number of rare (or non-existent!) forms and constructions. These include future participles, most of the optative, several comparatives and superlatives, ἡμϲτερος, γνωθι, προς with genitive and dative, μειζω. These, though useful in their place, are relatively unimportant and should not load the beginner's memory. They may of course be met at an early stage in the study of a New Testament book and will be sought for in vain in the *Elements*. But this work is not intended as a reference book from which to elucidate unusual points of Greek grammar, but as a textbook of the elements, which is to be systematically learnt. A great saving of labour has been effected by a radical simplification of the third declension, of conditional sentences, and of the -μι verbs. I shall consider that I have done the student a great service if I have succeeded in robbing the -μι verbs of their terror. I have omitted altogether about 170 of the less common words from the vocabularies and have reduced the number of principal parts from 73 to 42.

The most obvious omission to strike the eye is the disappearance of accents. We are indebted to D. F. Hudson's *Teach Yourself New Testament Greek* for pioneering this revolution. The accentual tradition is so deeply rooted in the minds of classical scholars and of reputable publishers that the sight of a naked unaccented text seems almost indecent. Yet from the point of view of academic integrity, the case against their use is overwhelming. The oldest literary texts regularly using accents of any sort date from the first century B.C. The early uncial manuscripts of the New Testament had no accents at all. The accentual system now in use dates only from the ninth century A.D. It is not suggested that the modern editor should slavishly copy first-century practices. By all means let us use every possible device that will make the text easier and pleasanter to read; but the accentual system is emphatically not such a device. Accurate accentuation is in fact difficult. Most good scholars will admit that they sometimes have to look their accents up. To learn them properly consumes a great deal of time and effort with no corresponding reward in the understanding of the language. When ingrained prejudice has been overcome, the clean unaccented text becomes very pleasant to the eye. In Hellenistic Greek the value of accents is confined to the distinguishing of pairs of words otherwise the same. In this whole book it means only four groups of words: $\epsilon\iota$ and $\epsilon\hat{\iota}$; the indefinite and interrogative pronouns; parts of the article and the relative pronoun; and parts of the present and future indicative active of liquid verbs. I have adopted the practice of retaining the circumflex in $\mu\epsilon\nu\hat{\omega}$, $-\epsilon\hat{\iota}s$, $-\epsilon\hat{\iota}$, $-o\hat{v}\sigma\iota\nu$ and in $\epsilon\hat{\iota}$; of always using a grave accent for the relatives $\grave{\eta}$, $\grave{o}$, $o\grave{\iota}$ and $a\grave{\iota}$, and an acute for the first syllable of the interrogative pronoun ($\tau\acute{\iota}s$, $\tau\acute{\iota}\nu a$, etc.). These forms are then at once self-explanatory, and the complications of enclitics are avoided. All other accents have been omitted.

I should dearly love to take the reform one stage further, by the abolition of the useless smooth breathing. Judged by the criterion of antiquity, breathings have no right to inclusion. Judged by the criterion of utility, ' should be used as an indication of elision or crasis, and nothing else, and the rough breathing would then stand out clearly as the equivalent of *h*. The fear that examinees might be penalised for the omission of the smooth breathing has alone deterred me from trying to effect this reform. I should like to know if other examiners would support this proposal.

As far as additions are concerned, I have steadily resisted the temptation to add much, believing the old *Elements* to err if anything on the side of over-fulness. I have made good certain deficiencies, e.g. guidance in writing the script, expressions for time, the forms of the Second Future Passive, the use of τov with the infinitive, the use of $\iota\nu a$ in noun clauses and the use of $o\grave{v}$ and $\mu\eta$ in questions. The vocabulary I have completely revised with the help of Morgenthaler's *Statistik des Neutestamentlichen Wortschatzes*, replacing the 170 uncommon words by about 110 very common ones. The number of New Testament occurrences of each word is now given in the vocabularies. There are now very few words included which occur less than 20 times in the New Testament and very few omitted which occur more than 30 times. This will make the systematic memorising of the vocabularies more rewarding. If the words in the vocabularies are learnt, nearly 85 per cent of the words of the New Testament will be familiar and many of the rest will be within reach of an intelligent guess. In order to facilitate the mastery of this basic word list, considerable care has been taken to see that the words are used not only in the exercises in which they first appear, but also in later exercises and tests.

Most of the other additions contain no new material, but are simply aids to assimilation; e.g. in the vocabularies there is a great increase in the number of English words derived from the Greek. In this I acknowledge considerable help from B. M. Metzger's *Lexical Aids for Students of New Testament Greek*. I have included periodical revision test papers. (These come usually two at a time and have been composed with a certain cunning so as to hold an even balance between student and teacher! The student knows exactly the possible range of questions to prepare for, but he does not know which paper the teacher will set, and so must cover the whole ground when revising.) It is believed that the summaries of morphology and syntax will be a great help in revision. As a further aid to assimilation I have adopted various visual devices, e.g. the use of heavy type to emphasise new forms, tables of contractions, and a graphic representation of the notion of tense. The lessons contain many new illustrative examples, taken from the New Testament and as far as possible containing only grammatical forms already known. I have also provided some guidance on further reading, and fuller indices.

Most important of all are the rearrangements. The English grammar has been completely revised and co-ordinated with the rest of the book. In the interest of those who have never been taught English grammar properly and who have never tackled a foreign language, I have retained the elementary grammatical explanations in the early lessons. Nevertheless, the student is advised to study some such work as R. B. Morgan's *Junior English Grammar* (Murray)—to which I am much indebted in the revision—in addition to this summary statement. The student who has some Latin will find little to learn in the first dozen lessons, except alphabet and vocabulary.

The vocabularies have been entirely rearranged, so that all the words of one type are now grouped together in one (or at most two) vocabularies. Much material has been moved from one part of the book to another, so that each subject can be systematically mastered, e.g. the scattered references to prepositions have been concentrated into two lessons and the two lessons on the infinitive have been brought together. Matter in footnotes has been transferred to the proper place in the text. (See, for example, the article.) The verbal system now has a logical arrangement, being built up progressively in the order of the six principal parts. All of this of course has meant an almost complete rewriting of the exercises. (The author will be most grateful for corrections to the *Elements* or to the *Key*,[1] and for suggestions for improving later editions.) All in all it may be said that the present book represents a slightly more limited field, sown with more carefully selected seed and cultivated more intensively. It is confidently expected to give a heavier yield.

This book may be criticised for its incompleteness. Some fairly common forms which were not included in the old *Nunn* will still be looked for in vain, and some rare forms which could be tracked down are now no longer to be found at all. But this is the price (and a very small one) which has to be paid for limiting the book to the elements of the language. Suggestions are given on pp. 191–2 for further reading.

Stress has been laid on the need for mastering the elements before beginning serious work on the New Testament text. This is self-evidently true, but there is no reason at all why, for interest's sake, translation should not be attempted long before the whole book has been learnt. An acquaintance with all the important forms can be gained from the summaries.

A word on the vexed question of pronunciation. There is a considerable diversity of practice in this country. This is a pity, as it is a great help to learn by ear as well as by eye. The system recommended here is as close an approximation to the Revised Pronunciation advocated by the Classical Association as seems practicable for an English-speaking

[1] J. W. Wenham, *Key to the Elements of New Testament Greek* (Cambridge, 1965).

PREFACE

student, and corresponds fairly closely to that in general use on the
Continent and in America.

Finally a word of thanks to the many who have helped in the produc-
tion of this book, only a few of whom I can mention by name. I owe
much of course to many previous writers. I am particularly indebted to
J. G. Machen's *New Testament Greek for Beginners* and to E. G. Jay's
New Testament Greek, and most of all to A. T. Robertson's *A Grammar
of the Greek of the New Testament in the Light of Historical Research* and
A New Short Grammar of the Greek Testament. I should like to thank
the Dean and Chapter of Ely (who are the proprietors of the book) and
the syndics and staff of the Cambridge University Press for their help
and encouragement. I should like to express my personal gratitude to
Professor C. F. D. Moule, to Professor K. Grayston, to the Rev. I. H.
Marshall and to my sons, Gordon, Peter and Michael, for valuable help
at various stages, and to Mr H. C. Oakley, whose scrutiny of almost the
whole manuscript has been invaluable. Last, but not least, I owe a great
debt to the generations of students at the London College of Divinity
and Tyndale Hall, who have kept alive my zest for elementary Greek
and who have continually provoked me to strive for forcefulness and
simplicity of presentation.

J.W.W.

NOTE TO THE STUDENT

While the student's steadfast aim should be the mastery of the essentials
of the language step by step, it will greatly add to his enjoyment to refer
to the actual text of the Greek New Testament as he goes along. This
can begin at the very first lesson. By the time Lesson 12 has been
reached (and given a little guidance from the teacher with the forms
which have not been dealt with) he will find himself getting on quite
well with (say) the First Letter of John. (It might be well to start at
verse 5.)

It has been suggested that the bulkiness of this book, resulting from
the fullness of its exercises and its explanatory matter, makes it look
rather formidable to the beginner. It may cheer those who are starting
on the course to know how *little* there is to learn. Almost everything is
contained in the 26 pages: 227–235; 242–258; together with a dozen
rules on pp. 236–241.

J.W.W.

xi

INTRODUCTION: ENGLISH GRAMMAR

1. SENTENCES, CLAUSES AND PHRASES

A **sentence** is a group of words which makes complete sense. Clauses and phrases make sense, but not complete sense.

A **clause** is a group of words which has a finite verb (see Section 15), but is only part of a sentence, e.g. 'We do not know *where they have laid him*'.

A **phrase** is a group of words without a finite verb, e.g. 'under the fig-tree'.

2. SUBJECT AND PREDICATE

Every sentence has two parts: the subject and the predicate. The **subject** names the person or thing uppermost in mind when the sentence is formed. The **predicate** makes an assertion about the subject.

Subject	Predicate
I	die
The glorious gospel	is sent into all the world

Or the predicate may take the form of a question, e.g. 'Must I die?', or a command, 'Go into the world'. In the latter case the subject is often 'understood', i.e. it is not expressed.

Subject	Predicate
I	must die
You (understood)	go into the world

3. PARTS OF SPEECH

By parts of speech we mean the various classes under which all words used in speaking and writing may be arranged. There are eight parts of speech:

(1) A **noun** is the name of anything (Latin *nomen*, 'name'), e.g. 'John', 'brother', 'love'.

I

(2) A **pronoun** is a word used instead of a noun (Latin *pro*, 'for'; *nomen*, 'name'), e.g. 'I', 'you', 'they', 'him', 'who'.

(3) An **adjective** is a word joined to a noun to qualify (that is, add something to) its meaning (Latin *adjectum*, 'a thing thrown to'), e.g. 'good', 'many'.

(4) A **verb** is a word by means of which we can make a statement, ask a question, or give a command about some person or thing (Latin *verbum*, 'word', so called as being the principal word in the sentence), e.g. 'I write', 'Do you see?', 'Depart'.

(5) An **adverb** is a word joined to a verb to qualify its meaning (Latin *ad*, 'to'), e.g. 'immediately', 'well', 'very'. (Adverbs sometimes qualify an adjective or another adverb: '*very* good', '*very* well'.)

(6) A **preposition** is a word joined to, and generally placed before, a noun (or pronoun) to show the relation of the person or thing denoted by the noun to something else (Latin *praepositum*, 'placed before'), e.g. 'of', 'with', 'by'.

(7) A **conjunction** is a word that joins together sentences, clauses or words (Latin *conjungo*, 'I join'), e.g. 'and', 'but', 'because'.

(8) An **interjection** is a word thrown into a sentence to express a feeling of the mind (Latin *interjicio*, 'I throw in'), e.g. 'Oh!', 'Alas!', 'Woe!'

The **article**, which is in fact a kind of adjective, is also sometimes classed as a separate part of speech. In English we have both the *definite article* ('the') and the *indefinite article* ('a'), but in Greek there is no indefinite article.

The first principle to be remembered in determining the parts of speech is that a word must be carefully examined with reference to the function which it performs in the sentence. In English many words having exactly the same form must be regarded as entirely different parts of speech, according to the place which they occupy in the sentence, and must be translated by wholly different words in Greek, according to their meaning.

Many words may be nouns or verbs, according to the place which they occupy in the sentence, e.g. 'judge', 'love', 'work', 'glory'.

Other words may be adjectives or verbs, e.g. 'clean', 'free'.

Others may be nouns, adjectives or verbs, e.g. 'last', 'stone'.

A more difficult example is 'that', which (as we shall see later) can be:

(1) A **demonstrative pronoun**: *That* is the man.

(2) A **demonstrative adjective**: Give me *that* book.

(3) A **relative pronoun**: This is the book *that* I want.

(4) A **conjunction**: He said *that* this was the book.

Try your hand at determining the parts of speech of the word 'that' in the following sentence: 'He said that that "that" that that man used was incorrect.'

Remembering then always to consider the word in connection with its sentence, the student should ask himself the following questions to help him find out what part of speech a word is:

(1) Is it the name of anything? If so, then it is a noun.

(2) Can a noun which is mentioned or thought of before be substituted for the word without altering the sense? Then it is a pronoun.

(3) Does it answer any of the questions: 'What kind?', 'How many?', 'Which?', with regard to some noun? Then is it an adjective.

(4) Does it make a statement, ask a question, or give a command? Then it is a verb.

(5) Does it answer the questions: 'How?', 'When?', 'Where?' Then it is an adverb. ('How?', 'When?' and 'Where?' are also themselves adverbs.)

(6) Does it stand before a noun or pronoun to show its relation to something else? Then it is a preposition. (Another test of a preposition is that it is a word which is not a verb but which can stand before 'him' and 'them', but not before 'he' or 'they'.)

(7) Does it join sentences, clauses or words? Then it is a conjunction.

Consider the following sentence: 'The man went quickly down the narrow street and did not stop, alas!'

THE	Adds something to the meaning of 'man', tells us which man it was, i.e. some man already known.	Therefore it is a kind of adjective. In this case of course the definite article.
MAN	Is the name of something.	Therefore it is a noun.
WENT	Makes a statement about the man.	Therefore it is a verb.

QUICKLY	Qualifies the verb 'went'; tells us how he went.	Therefore it is an adverb.
DOWN	Stands before the noun 'street', showing the relation between the street and the man's movement.	Therefore it is a preposition.
THE	See above.	
NARROW	Adds something to the meaning of 'street'.	Therefore an adjective.
STREET	The name of something.	Therefore a noun.
AND	Joins together two clauses.	Therefore a conjunction.
DID STOP	Make a statement about the man.	Therefore verbs.
NOT	Qualifies the verb 'did stop' because it tells us how he stopped, i.e. not at all.	Therefore an adverb.
ALAS	Expression of a feeling.	Therefore an interjection.

4. NOUNS

There are four kinds of nouns:

(1) A **proper noun** is the name appropriated to any particular person, place or thing (Latin *proprius*, 'belonging to a person'), e.g. 'John', 'Jerusalem', 'Passover'.

(2) A **common noun** is the name which all things of the same kind have in common (Latin *communis*, 'belonging to all'), e.g. 'brother', 'town', 'country'.

(3) A **collective noun** is the name of a number of persons or things forming one body, e.g. 'crowd', 'church', 'flock'.

(4) An **abstract noun** is the name of some quality, state or action considered apart from the person or thing in which it is embodied (Latin *abstractus*, 'withdrawn'), e.g. 'wisdom', 'peace', 'baptism'.

5. PRONOUNS

There are nine kinds of pronouns:

(1) **Personal pronouns:** 'I', 'you', 'we', 'they'.

(2) **Demonstrative pronouns:** 'this', 'that'.

(3) **Possessive pronouns:** 'mine', 'yours', 'ours', 'theirs'.

(4) **Interrogative pronouns:** 'who?', 'whose?', 'whom?', 'which?', 'what?'

(5) **Indefinite pronouns:** 'anyone', 'someone', 'something', 'a certain one', 'some'.

(6) **Reflexive pronouns** are used when a pronoun in the predicate and the subject of the sentence refer to the same person or thing, e.g. 'The man hates *himself*', 'It did it by *itself*'.

(7) **Emphasising pronouns** simply mark emphasis, e.g. 'You *yourselves* have heard', 'I saw the man *himself*'.

The **emphasising pronoun** and the word which it emphasises *both* belong to either subject or predicate, whereas the reflexive pronoun is always in the predicate and so is separated from the subject. The emphasising pronoun usually immediately follows the word emphasised, though there are sometimes words in between, as in 'John did it *himself*'. In this case 'himself' is still part of the subject.

(8) **Reciprocal pronoun:** 'one another'.

(9) **Relative pronouns** ('who', 'whom', 'whose', 'which', 'that') are used to connect a subordinate clause with the main clause in such sentences as: 'The Spirit *who* gives life is promised', 'He *whom* the Father promised is here', 'The words *that* I speak are life'. These pronouns refer (or 'relate') back to a noun or pronoun which is called the **antecedent**: '*The Spirit* who...', '*He* whom...', '*The words* that...'.

6. ADJECTIVES

A. There are six kinds of adjectives:

(1) **Adjectives of quality,** which answer the question 'What kind of?', e.g. '*narrow* street', '*good* men'.

(2) **Adjectives of quantity,** which answer the questions 'How many?', 'How much?', e.g. '*two* disciples', '*much* fruit', '*no* food'.

(3) **Demonstrative adjectives,** which answer the question 'Which?', e.g. '*these* women', '*that* house'.

(4) **Possessive adjectives,** which indicate possession, e.g. '*my* master', '*our* Father'.

(5) **Interrogative adjectives,** which ask questions, e.g. '*whose* image is this?'

5

(6) **The identical adjective**: 'same', e.g. 'The *same* men came back.'

B. There are three **degrees of comparison: positive, comparative** and **superlative.** The regular forms of comparison are:

hard	harder	hardest
just	more just	most just

An example of irregular comparison is:

good	better	best

The forms 'very hard', 'very just', 'very good' are called **elative superlatives.**

C. An adjective can be used either attributively or predicatively.

(1) **Attributive use.** In the phrase 'the blind beggar', the word 'blind' merely qualifies the word 'beggar'. That is to say, it defines him more exactly by mentioning one of his attributes. There is no complete sentence; nothing has yet been predicated of the man.

(2) **Predicative use.** 'The beggar is blind', however, predicates something of him. It constitutes a complete sentence.

7. VERBS

A. There are two kinds of verbs:

(1) **Transitive verbs** are so called because they denote an action which necessarily affects or passes over to some person or thing other than the subject of the verb (Latin *transire*, 'to pass over'), e.g. 'I throw', 'I take'. These statements are not complete; we ask immediately, 'What do you throw or take?' The name of the person or thing affected by the action must be supplied in order to make a complete sentence: 'I throw a ball', 'I take an apple'. The person or thing affected by the action of the verb is called the **direct object.**

(2) **Intransitive verbs** denote an action which does not affect any person or thing besides the subject of the verb, e.g. 'I remain', 'the sun shines'. These sentences are complete statements in themselves.

B. There are also **verbs of incomplete predication.** These verbs require another word to make a complete predicate. The commonest is the verb 'to be'. 'He is' by itself is incomplete. A sentence can be completed by the addition of:

(*a*) a **predicative noun**: He is the shepherd;
(*b*) a **predicative pronoun**: He is mine;
(*c*) a **predicative adjective**: He is good.

The completing word or group of words is known as the **complement**.

Other verbs of incomplete predication, which can be either transitive or intransitive, include:

Intransitive   become, seem, appear
Transitive   declare, choose, call, think, consider

It is important to distinguish carefully between the object and the complement of a verb, because (as we shall see later) this will affect the case to be used. The complement always refers to the same person (or thing) as the subject, the object to someone (or something) different:[1]

e.g. God became man (complement).   I remain faithful (complement).
     God made man (object).   I chose faithful men (object).

The difference in case can sometimes be seen quite clearly even in English. We say:

I am *he* (complement: nominative case).
God made *him* (object: accusative case).

8. ADVERBS

A. There are five kinds of adverbs:

(1) **Adverbs of manner**, which answer the question 'How?', e.g. 'He thinks wisely, well, truly'.

(2) **Adverbs of time**, which answer the question 'When?', e.g. 'I went yesterday, later, afterwards'.

(3) **Adverbs of place**, which answer the question 'Where?', e.g. 'She goes here, there'.

(4) **Adverbs of degree**, which qualify an adjective or another adverb, e.g. '*quite* quick', '*very* slowly', '*almost* at once'. (Some adverbs of degree can also qualify a verb, e.g. 'I *quite* like it'.)

(5) **Interrogative adverbs**: 'How?', 'Why?', 'Where?', 'When?'

---

[1] Except of course in the case of the reflexive pronoun (p. 5).

B. Degrees of comparison are expressed thus:

(regular)	wisely	more wisely	most wisely
(irregular)	well	better	best

9. INFLECTION

Nouns, pronouns, adjectives, verbs and some adverbs are capable of undergoing certain changes in form. The part of the word which contains the basic idea is known as the **stem**. The stem remains unchanged, but modifications of this basic idea are introduced by means of changes of form, which are known as **inflections**.

The study of the form of words is known as **morphology** (or *accidence*). The study of the arrangement of words in the sentence is known as **syntax**.

Inflection is important in English, but it is far more important in Greek. English has comparatively few inflections, whereas in the early stages of Greek the learning of the inflections is the student's main task.

Nouns, pronouns and (in Greek) adjectives may have inflections for number, gender, and for case (see Section 10).

(1) Number, e.g.

Singular:	heart,	church,	child,	I
Plural:	hearts,	churches,	children,	we

(2) Gender. In English we distinguish four genders: *masculine* (to denote males), *feminine* (to denote females), *neuter* (to denote things), *common* (for words which can denote either males or females, e.g. 'child'). Sometimes the feminine may be formed from a masculine stem by inflection, e.g. 'priestess' from 'priest'.

In Greek, gender has to do with the form of the words and has little to do with sex. There are *masculine*, *feminine* and *neuter* forms, but 'bread' is masculine, 'head' is feminine, and 'child' is neuter.

8

10. CASES

Case is the form or function of a word which shows its relation to some other word in the sentence. Five cases are to be distinguished: nominative, vocative, accusative, genitive and dative. In English, case inflection is usual only in the genitive. *'s* in such phrases as 'the apostle's brother' is a case ending, and 'apostle's' is an inflected form. A somewhat fuller inflection survives in the pronoun 'he' (nominative), 'him' (accusative), 'his' (genitive). In New Testament Greek all five case forms are still to be found.

But although English virtually has only two case *forms*, the five case *functions* are still to be distinguished.

(1) **Nominative**: (*a*) The *subject* of the verb is in the nominative case.

  (*b*) The *complement* to an intransitive verb is in the nominative case.

Note. When one noun follows another to explain or describe it more fully, the two words are said to be **in apposition**, and are in the same case. Thus in 'John the Baptist was fasting', 'John' (the subject) and 'the Baptist' (in apposition to 'John') are both nominative.

(2) **Vocative** is the case of *address*, e.g. '*Master*, I am coming', '*O Lord*, save me'.

(3) **Accusative** is the case of the *direct object* of a transitive verb.

(4) **Genitive** is the case of *possession*, e.g. 'The *apostle's* brother', 'the brother *of the apostle*'. (This account of the accusative and genitive will need some modification when we come to study their uses in Greek.)

(5) **Dative** is the case of the *indirect object*. Consider the sentence: 'The owner gave him the donkey.' That which is directly affected by the action of the verb is the donkey; it was the donkey that the owner *gave*. So 'the donkey' is the direct object and is accusative. 'Him' is the person *to whom* or *for whom* it was given. This is the indirect object and is dative. It could equally well have been expressed: 'The owner gave the donkey *to him*.'

9

11. INFLECTION OF THE VERB

Greek verbs are set out according to this pattern:

> I loose
> Thou loosest (Modern English: You loose)
> He looses
> We loose
> You loose
> They loose

The first three are of course singular and the last three plural.

Person

'I' and 'we' denote that the person *who is speaking* is doing the action, and they are said to be in the **first person**.

'Thou' and 'you' denote that the person *spoken to* is doing the action, and they are said to be in the **second person**.

'He' (also 'she' and 'it') and 'they' denote that the person *spoken about* is doing the action, and they are said to be in the **third person**.

It will be observed that in the older English there were two inflected forms, 'loosest' and 'looses', whereas in modern English the separate forms for the second person singular have almost disappeared. In Greek there are usually six distinct forms.

Verbs which are not used in the first and second persons, but only in the third, are known as **impersonal verbs**, e.g. 'it is lawful', 'it is necessary'.

12. TENSE

Tense is concerned with two things:

(1) The time at which an action takes place.
(2) The state or nature of the action.

The English tenses may be set out as in Table 1 (opposite).

Except for the future tense, the tenses in Greek are concerned almost wholly with the nature and state of the action, and not with time.

It will be noticed that the English tense system is built up by the use of the verbs 'to be' and 'to have', which act as **auxiliary verbs**: 'I *was* loving', 'I *had* loved'. In Greek the verb 'to be' is used, but only for the comparatively uncommon *periphrastic* tenses. (See Lesson 37.)

Table 1. *The English tenses*

| | Time | | |
	Past	Present	Future
State Continuous	IMPERFECT I was loving I used to love	PRESENT CONTINUOUS I am loving	FUTURE CONTINUOUS I shall be loving
Simple	PAST SIMPLE I loved	PRESENT SIMPLE I love	FUTURE SIMPLE I shall love
Complete	PLUPERFECT I had loved	PERFECT I have loved	FUTURE PERFECT I shall have loved
Continuous-complete	PLUPERFECT CONTINUOUS I had been loving	PERFECT CONTINUOUS I have been loving	FUTURE PERFECT CONTINUOUS I shall have been loving

13. VOICE

Voice is an inflection of the verb which denotes whether the subject does the action or is acted upon.

> **Active:** They loose the colt.
> **Passive:** The colt is loosed by them.

It will be observed that when a sentence in the active is put into the passive, the direct object of the active verb becomes the subject of the passive verb.

A complete table of tenses in the passive voice can of course be constructed to correspond with the table of active tenses in the previous section: 'I was being loved', 'I am being loved', etc.

14. MOOD

Mood is the form of the verb which indicates the *mode* or *manner* in which the action is to be regarded. There are four moods:

(1) The **indicative** makes a statement or asks a question: 'He goes', 'were you listening?'

11

(2) The **imperative** gives a command, entreaty or exhortation: 'Go', 'make haste', 'let him come'.

(3) The **subjunctive** expresses a thought or wish rather than an actual fact. It is the mood of doubtful assertion, e.g. 'God *save* the king', 'thy will *be done*', 'if I *were* you, I *would* not go', 'so that I *may* arrive', 'in order that I *might* succeed'.

> Contrast the Indicative: I *shall* be at home (certainty)
> with the Subjunctive: I *should* be at home (uncertainty).

(4) The **infinitive** expresses an action generally, i.e. without reference to a particular person or thing. It is normally prefaced by the word 'to', e.g. 'he wanted *to stay*'. Sometimes, however, 'to' is not found, e.g. 'he can *stay* (i.e. he is able *to stay*)', 'he saw me *come*'.

The infinitive is a **verbal noun**. As a verb it will have tense and voice, and it may have an object or a qualifying adverb, e.g. '*to love* (Present Infinitive Active) *animals* (object) *greatly* (adverb)'.

As a noun it can itself be the subject or object of another verb, e.g.

> As **subject**: *To err* is human ('to err' is virtually equivalent to the noun 'error').
> As **object**:   They desire *to live* (i.e. they desire 'survival').

'To err' and 'to live' are short **noun phrases**. Such phrases, which do the work of a noun, can be of any length, e.g. They desire *to live in the castle happily ever after*.

15. PARTICIPLES

Participles are **verbal adjectives**. Being verbs they have tense and voice and they may have an object. Being adjectives they can qualify nouns. There are two participles in English—the **Active Participle** ending in *-ing* and the **Passive Participle** which usually ends in *-ed*, e.g. 'loving', 'loved'.

Participles can be formed by the use of auxiliaries:

> e.g. having loved (Past Participle Active)
> having been loved (Past Participle Passive), etc.

The principal use of the participles in English is to form (with the help of auxiliary verbs) the continuous and complete tenses of the verb, e.g. 'I am loving', 'I have loved'. Its simple adjectival use may be seen in an expression like 'his loving wife'. In Greek the participle has a wide range of uses which will be studied in due course.

The Indicative, Imperative and Subjunctive make up the **finite verb**, while the Infinitive and Participle belong to the **verb infinite**.

16. SIMPLE, MULTIPLE AND COMPLEX SENTENCES

A **simple sentence** is a sentence which contains a single subject and a single predicate.

A **double** (or **multiple**) **sentence** is a sentence which contains two (or more) statements of equal value; that is to say, neither is subordinate to, or dependent upon, the other, e.g. 'he went out and he wept'. In this case 'he went out' and 'he wept' are of equal status and are said to be **co-ordinate**.

A **complex sentence** is a sentence which contains a **main clause** and a **subordinate clause** which is dependent upon it, e.g. 'he wept (main clause), because he had been faithless (subordinate clause)'.

There are three classes of subordinate clauses: **noun, adjective** and **adverb clauses**.

17. NOUN CLAUSES

Noun clauses are subordinate clauses which do the work of a noun in relation to some part of another clause:

e.g. **as subject:**   *That he is coming* is certain.
   as object: He said *that he was king*.
                  He asked *how it happened*.
                  He told him *that he must go*.
   as complement: My hope is *that you may succeed*.
   in apposition to a noun: I had no idea *that you would oppose me*.

With verbs of saying, what is said may either be given in **direct speech**, i.e. the very words of the speaker are recorded and put within inverted commas, e.g. 'He said, "I am going away"', or they may be given in **indirect speech**, in which case the meaning is preserved but the form of the words is altered, e.g. 'He told them *that he was going away*'.

13

CLAUSES [E.G. 17–19]

The same principle applies to a whole range of *verbs of saying or thinking* and includes such verbs as 'to feel', 'to learn', 'to know', 'to see'.

The three examples of object clauses given above represent three types of indirect speech:

When a noun clause which is the object of a verb states a fact, it is called a **dependent** (or **indirect**) **statement**: 'He said *that he was king.*'

When it begins with an interrogatory word, it is called a **dependent** (or **indirect**) **question**: 'He asked *how it happened.*'

When it gives the words of a command, it is called a **dependent** (or **indirect**) **command**: 'He told him *that he must go.*'

18. ADJECTIVE CLAUSES

Adjective clauses are subordinate clauses which do the work of an adjective in relation to some part of another clause.

They are introduced either by a relative pronoun or by a word which is equivalent to a relative pronoun, e.g. 'when', 'where' in such expressions as: 'the time *when* (at which) we meet', 'the town *where* (in which) I was born'.

19. ADVERB CLAUSES

Adverb clauses are subordinate clauses which do the work of an adverb in relation to some part of another clause.

There are eight classes:

(1) **Purpose** (often called **final**) **clauses**: 'He ran *that he might get home soon.*'

(2) **Time** (or **temporal**) **clauses**: 'He ran *when he reached the road.*'

(3) **Place** (or **local**) **clauses**: 'He ran *where the road was level.*'

(4) **Causal clauses**: 'He ran *because he was late.*'

(5) **Consequence** (or **consecutive**) **clauses**: 'He ran *so that* (i.e. with the result that) *he got home early.*'

(6) **Conditional clauses**: 'He ran *if he was late.*'

(7) **Concessive** (or **adversative**) **clauses**, which denote contrast: 'He ran *although he was early.*'

(8) **Comparative clauses**: 'He ran *faster than she could.*'

14

20. PARSING

To parse a word completely is to say the following things about it.

If it is a **noun**, it is necessary to give its number, gender, case and part of speech:

e.g. He gave it to the *women*.

women: plural, feminine, dative, noun.

If it is a **pronoun**, the person must be added and the kind of pronoun:

e.g. He gave it to *them*.

them: third person, plural, feminine, dative, personal pronoun.

If it is a **verb**, it is necessary to give, person, number, tense, mood, voice and part of speech:

e.g. He *gave* it to the women.

gave: third person, singular, Past Simple, Indicative, Active of the verb 'to give'.

In the case of a **participle** which is a **verbal adjective**, gender and case will have to be given in addition to its characteristics as a verb. Thus:

λυων (luōn) 'loosing': singular, masculine, nominative of the Present Participle Active of the verb λυω, 'I loose'.

ENGLISH GRAMMAR TEST PAPER A

1. Set out the words of the following sentence in a vertical column and determine the part of speech of each, giving your reasons: 'Alas! You have never truly repented of your wicked sins because you are proud.'

2. Give examples of the four kinds of nouns.

3. Write two sentences illustrating the difference between the reflexive and the emphasising pronoun.

4. Explain the difference between the attributive and predicative uses of the adjective.

5. Explain the function of the four moods, illustrating by short sentences, using the verb 'to loose'.

6. Give the names of the tenses in past time which represent the following states: continuous, simple, complete, continuous-complete. What is the first person singular of the verb 'to loose' in each tense?

7. Give an example of a final, a consecutive and a concessive clause.

8. What do you understand by the following terms: syntax, impersonal verb, auxiliary verb, finite verb, dependent question?

ENGLISH GRAMMAR TEST PAPER B

1. What are the nine kinds of pronouns? Give one example of each.

2. Explain the terms transitive and intransitive, active and passive.

3. Describe the functions of the five cases.

4. Give the names of the tenses in present time which represent the following states: continuous, simple, complete, continuous-complete. What is the first person singular of the verb 'to loose' in each tense?

5. Give two examples of the verb infinite.

6. What are the characteristics of verbs of saying and thinking?

7. Give an example of a local, a conditional and an adversative clause.

8. What do you understand by the following terms: predicate, verb of incomplete predication, antecedent, elative superlative, morphology?

LESSON 1

The Greek Language
The alphabet, pronunciation and writing

THE GREEK LANGUAGE

Greek is a living language with an immensely long history. Its emergence from the parent stock of the Indo-European languages is lost in antiquity. But its written history may be traced from the time of Linear B (c. thirteenth century B.C.); through the period of the great classical writers, like Homer (c. eighth century B.C.), Plato (fourth century B.C.) and many others; through the Hellenistic Age, when the

Old Testament was translated into Greek (the so-called Septuagint version comes probably from the second and third centuries B.C.) and the New Testament was written; through the Byzantine period (beginning *c.* sixth century A.D.), right into modern times. In spite of many changes Greek has been recognisably one language for more than 3000 years. In the classical period different dialects, such as Attic, Ionic and Doric, existed side by side. Of these, Attic became the foremost literary dialect, and it was adopted as the official language of the Macedonian Empire after the conquests of Alexander the Great. Alexander himself ardently desired to propagate Hellenistic culture throughout his domains, and in time Greek became the *lingua franca* of the civilised world. This 'common' (κοινη) language, the so-called *Koiné* or *Hellenistic Greek*, developed somewhat simpler (and sometimes less precise) forms than the purest Attic Greek and it incorporated some forms from other dialects. But in the days of St Paul it was a medium through which he could communicate his message freely throughout the length and breadth of the Mediterranean world. He wrote to the Christians in Rome, not in Latin, but in Koiné Greek.

THE ALPHABET

The *Greek Alphabet* consists of 24 letters, a good many of which are identical with the corresponding letters of the Latin alphabet which we still employ. Both alphabets were derived from the Phoenician alphabet, from which the Hebrew alphabet also took its origin.

The letters given in the second column on pages 18–19 are now used only as capital letters in printed Greek books, but originally letters like these were used in all Greek writing. They are generally called **uncial** letters, and the early vellum manuscripts of the New Testament are called uncial manuscripts, because they are written throughout in these letters.

About the tenth century A.D. another style of writing was perfected somewhat like the letters in the third column. These were called **cursive** or running letters, because, like our modern handwriting, they could be written without raising the pen from the paper. This type of writing has remained in use ever since, both in manuscripts and printed books.

Nowadays capitals are used in Greek for proper nouns and for the first letter of a paragraph, and to mark the beginning of a direct quotation, where English would use inverted commas. They are not generally used at the beginning of each new sentence. The small letters are, therefore, of far greater importance than the capitals and should be mastered first. The capitals will be left till Lesson 2.

The student should learn by heart the list of the names of the letters down the first column, so that he may be able, when the time comes, to find the words in a lexicon as quickly as possible. ('Lexicon' is the term generally used for a Greek–English dictionary.)

The alphabet

Name of letter	Capital letters	Small letters	English equivalent	Pronunciation	Notes
Alpha	A	α	a	like *a* in French 'à la'	
Bēta	B	β	b	like English *b*	
Gamma	Γ	γ	g	hard *g* as in 'get'	(1)
Delta	Δ	δ	d	like English *d*	
Epsīlon	E	ε	e	like *e* in 'met'	(2)
Zēta	Z	ζ	z	like English *dz* or *z*	(3)
Ēta	H	η	ē	like *ê* in 'fête'	(2)
Thēta	Θ	θ	th	like *th* in 'thin'	
Iōta	I	ι	i	like *i* in 'hit'	(4)
Kappa	K	κ	k	like English *k*	
Lambda	Λ	λ	l	like English *l*	
Mu	M	μ	m	like English *m*	
Nu	N	ν	n	like English *n*	
Xī	Ξ	ξ	x	like English *x*	
Omīcron	O	o	o	like *o* in 'not'	(2)
Pī	Π	π	p	like English *p*	
Rhō	P	ρ	r	like English *r*	
Sigma	Σ	σ, ς	s	like *s* in 'house'	(5)

18

Tau	T	τ	t	like English *t*	(6)
Upsīlon	Υ	υ	u	like *oo* in 'book'	(7)
Phī	Φ	φ	ph	like English *ph* or *f*	
Chī	X	χ	ch	like *ch* in 'loch'	(8)
Psī	Ψ	ψ	ps	like *ps* in 'lips'	
Ōmega	Ω	ω	ō	like *o* in 'tone'	(2)

Notes. (For illustration of the points made, see Vocabularies, pp. 193 ff.)

(1) Before another gamma, γ is sounded like *n*, hence: ἀγγελος, 'angel' (Vocab. 5); εὐαγγελιον 'evangel', 'gospel' (Vocab. 7). (It is also pronounced *n* before κ, χ, ξ, but words of this type are rare.)

(2) Note that there are two letters to represent the English letter *e*, and two to represent the letter *o*. Epsilon and omicron ('little *o*') are short. Eta and omega ('big *o*') are long.

(3) ζ is properly *dz*, e.g. σωζω, 'I save' (Vocab. 3); but when it is the initial letter, it is usually pronounced *z*, e.g. ζητεω, 'I seek' (Vocab. 4).

(4) ι can also be used as a consonant, e.g. in proper nouns like Ἰησους, 'Jesus' (Vocab. 6) or Ἰουδαιος, 'Jew' (Vocab. 5), in which case it is pronounced like *y* in 'yes'.

(5) There are two forms of sigma. σ is used when the letter occurs at the beginning or in the middle of a word, ς when it is the final letter, e.g. Ἰησους.

(6) 'Tau' (the name of the letter) is pronounced as in 'taught'.

(7) In English words derived from Greek, υ becomes *y*, e.g. ὑποκριτης becomes 'hypocrite' (Vocab. 9). (Our capital Y has come from the Greek capital Υ through Latin.) ευ, however, sometimes becomes *ev*, e.g. εὐαγγελιον, 'evangel'.

(8) It is worth making the effort to distinguish the pronunciation of κ and χ, even if one feels self-conscious in aspirating the *ch*, since it is a great help to correct spelling. 'Chi' (the name of the letter) is pronounced as in 'kite'.

THE PRONUNCIATION OF DIPHTHONGS

Diphthongs are sounds produced by two vowels being sounded together. Pronounce

αι	as	*ai*	in	aisle
ει		*ei*		veil
οι		*oi*		oil
αυ		*au*		Faust
ου		*ou*		route
ευ, ηυ		*eu*		feud
υι		*ui*		quit

Note. No distinction in pronunciation is to be attempted between η and ει, or between ευ and ηυ.

WRITING THE SMALL LETTERS

Writing should be practised with the help of two lines. Most letters should be written without removing the pen from the paper. Copy the following example, noticing carefully what parts of the letter are written above and what parts are written below the line. The asterisk denotes the point at which to begin.

α β γ δ ε ζ η θ ι κ λ μ ν ξ ο π ρ σ or ς τ υ φ χ ψ ω

Distinguish carefully ν with the pointed base and υ with the rounded base. Note that ι is not dotted.

EXERCISE I

Having learnt the names of the letters in their proper order fluently:

(1) Write out the small letters of the Greek alphabet with the English equivalent for each letter.

(2) Write out the English alphabet and give the Greek small letter equivalent for each letter as far as possible.

These exercises should be repeated until perfect.

20

LESSON 2

Capital letters, breathings and other signs

Most of the capital letters are very like either their small equivalents, or the equivalent English capital. When the small letters have been mastered, there are only ten capital letters that require notice.

Δ can be easily remembered since a river delta is so called from its resemblance in shape to Δ.

P and X are very like the small letters ρ and χ, but need to be distinguished from the English P and X.

H and Υ are η and υ, not the English H and Y.

Γ Λ Ξ Σ Ω have forms unlike any English letters and different from their small equivalents.

Capital letters are all of the same height, and all rest upon the line.

BREATHINGS

It will be noticed that there is no sign for the letter *h* in the Greek alphabet. The want of such a sign is made up by the marks called breathings, one of which is written over every vowel or diphthong that begins a word. The **rough breathing** ʽ (turned like the opening comma in inverted commas) is sounded like our letter *h*; ὁ is pronounced *hŏ*, ἁ is pronounced *ha*. The **smooth breathing** ʼ (turned like the closing comma in inverted commas) indicates that the vowel is to be sounded without the *h* sound. If the word begins with a diphthong, the breathing is placed over the second vowel, and not over the first. Thus in Vocab. 3 it is εὑρισκω, I find, not ἑυρισκω. ρ at the beginning of a word has a rough breathing, e.g. ῥημα (Vocab. 29); cf. our English word 'rhododendron' (Vocab. 7). No attempt should be made to

21

pronounce the rough breathing when used with ρ. With vowels, however, breathings must be written and the rough breathing pronounced carefully.[1]

IOTA SUBSCRIPT

A small ι is often written under the letters α, η, ω, especially when one of these letters ends a word. It is called the iota subscript and is a relic of an ancient diphthong. It is not pronounced, but it must always be written. Several examples may be seen in the opening verses of St John's Gospel, which is used in Exercise 2.1 below, e.g.

$$ἀρχῃ \quad αὐτῳ \quad σκοτιᾳ.$$

PUNCTUATION

The comma	,	as in English
The full-stop	.	as in English
The semi-colon	·	(above the line)
The question-mark	;	

ELISION AND DIAERESIS

An apostrophe (the same sign as the smooth breathing) is used to show that a vowel has been elided, i.e. dropped out, before a vowel or diphthong at the beginning of the next word. In Exercise 2.1 (which is taken from John 1. 1–14) there are examples of

$$δι' \quad \text{written for } δια \text{ (verse 3)}$$
$$\text{and } ἀλλ' \quad \text{written for } ἀλλα \text{ (verse 8).}$$

In both English and Greek a diaeresis (··) is occasionally placed over the second of two vowels to show that they do not form a diphthong, but are to be pronounced separately, e.g. 'naïve'. There is an example in Exercise 2.2, where (at John 1. 23) the word Ἠσαΐας (the Greek form of 'Isaiah') occurs. This is four syllables: Ἠ-σα-ι-ας, not three: Ἠ-σαι-ας.

---

[1] In the case of words which begin with a capital letter, the breathing is placed in front of the word. Thus: Ἰησους, 'Jesus'; Ἰουδαιος, 'Jew'; Ῥωμη, 'Rome'. With a diphthong, the breathing is written over the second vowel as usual. Thus: Υἱος, 'Son'.

ACCENTS

In modern printed texts the great majority of words have at least one accent; either acute ('), grave (`) or circumflex (˜ or ⌢). As stated in the preface, these are to be completely ignored, except on the rare occasions (which will be mentioned as they arise) when differences in accent are useful for distinguishing differences of meaning.

STRESS

There are different systems in use for deciding which syllable of a word is to be stressed. It is best simply to take care to pronounce each syllable clearly (particularly to be careful to distinguish the long and short vowels), and then let stress take care of itself.

EXERCISE 2

1. Write out the following in small Greek letters, inserting breathings where necessary. The English letter *h* at the beginning of a word denotes a rough breathing. The vowels *e* and *o* are marked with a stroke over the line when they are long; when not marked they are short. Care must be taken to use the proper Greek letter for them. The letter *i* in brackets denotes that an iota subscript is to be written under the preceding vowel. An apostrophe (denoting elision) should be reproduced by an apostrophe in Greek.

en archē(i) ēn ho logos, kai ho logos ēn pros ton theon, kai theos ēn ho logos. houtos ēn en archē(i) pros ton theon. panta di' autou egeneto kai chōris autou egeneto oude hen. ho gegonen en autō(i) zōē ēn, kai hē zōē ēn to phōs tōn anthrōpōn. kai to phōs en tē(i) skotia(i) phainei, kai hē skotia auto ou katelaben. egeneto anthrōpos, apestalmenos para theou, onoma autō(i) iōannēs· houtos ēlthen eis marturian, hina marturēsē(i) peri tou phōtos, hina pantes pisteusōsin di' autou. ouk ēn ekeinos to phōs, all' hina marturēsē(i) peri tou phōtos. ēn to phōs to alēthinon, ho phōtizei panta anthrōpon, erchomenon eis ton kosmon. en tō(i) kosmō(i) ēn, kai ho kosmos di' autou egeneto, kai ho kosmos auton ouk egnō. eis ta idia ēlthen, kai hoi idioi auton ou parelabon. hosoi de elabon auton edōken autois exousian tekna theou genesthai, tois pisteuousin eis to onoma autou, hoi ouk ex haimatōn oude ek thelēmatos sarkos oude ek thelēmatos andros all' ek theou egennēthēsan. kai ho logos sarx egeneto kai eskēnōsen en hēmin, kai etheasametha tēn doxan autou, doxan hōs monogenous para patros, plērēs charitos kai alētheias. The student may correct his exercise by comparing it with John 1. 1–14 in the Bible Society's Greek Testament (2nd edn., Nestle–Kilpatrick text). There are a few capital letters in the Nestle–Kilpatrick text. In correcting the exercise the corresponding small letter may easily be checked from the alphabet table. This exercise should be done several times until perfect.

2. Write out the Greek of John 1. 19–28 in English characters. (Be careful to give the correct English equivalents of · and ;.)

3. Write out the following in small Greek letters. (Do not try to insert breathings.) The exercise may be corrected from Matthew 6. 21–4. (It will be seen that iota subscripts have also been ignored.)

ΟΠΟΥ ΓΑΡ ΕΣΤΙΝ Ο ΘΗΣΑΥΡΟΣ ΣΟΥ, ΕΚΕΙ ΕΣΤΑΙ ΚΑΙ Η ΚΑΡΔΙΑ ΣΟΥ. Ο ΛΥΧΝΟΣ ΤΟΥ ΣΩΜΑΤΟΣ ΕΣΤΙΝ Ο ΟΦΘΑΛΜΟΣ. ΕΑΝ ΟΥΝ Η Ο ΟΦΘΑΛΜΟΣ ΣΟΥ ΑΠΛΟΥΣ, ΟΛΟΝ ΤΟ ΣΩΜΑ ΣΟΥ ΦΩΤΕΙΝΟΝ ΕΣΤΑΙ. ΕΑΝ ΔΕ Ο ΟΦΘΑΛΜΟΣ ΣΟΥ ΠΟΝΗΡΟΣ Η, ΟΛΟΝ ΤΟ ΣΩΜΑ ΣΟΥ ΣΚΟΤΕΙΝΟΝ ΕΣΤΑΙ. ΕΙ ΟΥΝ ΤΟ ΦΩΣ ΤΟ ΕΝ ΣΟΙ ΣΚΟΤΟΣ ΕΣΤΙΝ, ΤΟ ΣΚΟΤΟΣ ΠΟΣΟΝ. ΟΥΔΕΙΣ ΔΥΝΑΤΑΙ ΔΥΣΙ ΚΥΡΙΟΙΣ ΔΟΥΛΕΥΕΙΝ· Η ΓΑΡ ΤΟΝ ΕΝΑ ΜΙΣΗΣΕΙ ΚΑΙ ΤΟΝ ΕΤΕΡΟΝ ΑΓΑΠΗΣΕΙ, Η ΕΝΟΣ ΑΝΘΕΞΕΤΑΙ ΚΑΙ ΤΟΥ ΕΤΕΡΟΥ ΚΑΤΑΦΡΟΝΗΣΕΙ· ΟΥ ΔΥΝΑΣΘΕ ΘΕΩ ΔΟΥΛΕΥΕΙΝ ΚΑΙ ΜΑΜΩΝΑ.

4. Read as much as possible of the Greek Testament aloud, paying great attention to the breathings and the length of the vowels. Students who are working alone and who have no one to whom they can read aloud are recommended to put portions of the Greek into English letters, and to put them back into Greek letters after an interval. It is most important to be able to read the characters accurately and quickly before proceeding further.

The Present Indicative Active of λυω
Questions

THE PRESENT INDICATIVE ACTIVE OF λυω

Re-read carefully Introduction: English Grammar, Sections 9, 11, 12, 13, 14.

The **present indicative active** of the verb λυω 'I loose' is as follows:

1st singular	λυω	I am loosing *or* I loose
2nd singular	λυεις	you are loosing *or* you loose
3rd singular	λυει	he, she *or* it is loosing *or* looses
1st plural	λυομεν	we are loosing *or* we loose
2nd plural	λυετε	you are loosing *or* you loose
3rd plural	λυουσι(ν)	they are loosing *or* they loose

Movable ν

The so-called 'movable ν' at the end of the third person plural is found as a termination of several Greek forms, which will be noticed as they are reached. The student is advised always to include it, though he will sometimes find it omitted in the New Testament.

Inflection

Each of the Greek words in the table above may be divided into two parts:

(1) A *stem* λυ, which never changes and which denotes the fundamental meaning of the verb, i.e. 'loose'.

(2) An *ending* ω, εις, ει, etc., which changes with every person. As nearly every Greek verb has the same endings in the present tense, it is easy to conjugate the present tense of any other verb by first taking off the final ω of the 1st person singular to find the stem, and then adding the endings to this stem.

The words in the table above, when compared with their English equivalents, furnish a good example of one of the principal differences between Greek and English, namely that one word may be sufficient to make a statement in Greek, where two or three words are necessary in English. This is because the endings of words are changed in Greek to denote changes in the meaning of the words, while in English these variable endings have almost entirely disappeared.

For example, in the English Present Simple tense the only form which retains its personal ending is the third person singular 'looses'. Consequently it is necessary to insert a personal pronoun 'I', 'you', 'they', etc., before the verb, to avoid confusion and to show the person and number of the subject of the verb. But in Greek the person and number of the subject of the verb are already made sufficiently clear by the variable ending, and so there is no need to add a personal pronoun unless special emphasis is required.

The second person singular

In spoken English we do not now use the old second person singular 'thou' in addressing a single person, but we use the form 'you'. In Greek the second person singular is *always* used in addressing a single person, and the second person plural is kept for addressing more than one person.

The old English use could make important distinctions very concisely. For example, at Luke 22. 31, 32 our Lord declared: 'Satan hath desired to have you (plural: the twelve disciples)....But I have prayed for thee (singular: Simon Peter).' But, as one of the purposes of learning Greek is to enable the student to get behind the well-known phraseology of his English version, it seems best to abandon 'thou' and 'thee' altogether. In the early exercises the distinction between singular and plural is always to be clearly indicated. Where 'you' is to be translated into Greek, the number required ('sing.' or 'pl.') will be shown. In rendering Greek into English, the student must similarly say whether 'you' is singular or plural. This practice will be followed as far as Exercise 6, after which the student may use, in ambiguous cases, whichever form he likes.

26

TRANSLATING THE PRESENT TENSE

It will be noticed that two English equivalents are given for one Greek form of the Present tense. This is because there are more tenses in English than in Greek, and one Greek tense has to do the work of two English tenses. *The Greek Present corresponds more closely in meaning to the English Present Continuous than to the Present Simple.*

The forms of the Present Continuous tense illustrate another difference between English and Greek, namely that in English we freely employ auxiliary verbs to form our tenses (in this case the Present tense of the verb 'to be' is used) while in Greek a single word is used. Another form of the English Present uses the verb 'to do' as an auxiliary, e.g. 'I do know'. In a statement this is emphatic, but in questions it is often the normal use, e.g. we say, 'Do I know?' not 'Am I knowing?' or 'Know I?' Similarly 'do' is frequently used with the negative, e.g. 'I do not know', 'he does not go'.

QUESTIONS

In Greek there is no difference whatever in the form of a statement and the form of an ordinary question. The existence of a question is indicated solely by the presence of the question-mark (;). The student will need therefore to look at the punctuation-mark at the end of a sentence before deciding how to translate it.

EXERCISE 3

Learn Vocabulary 3 on p. 193. The words given in this and the following vocabularies are words which occur frequently in the New Testament. The number written after each word is the approximate number of times that the word is used in the New Testament. It is hoped that the student will be encouraged to learn the words diligently by realising that when he has learnt the first vocabulary he will be familiar with about 4259 words in the Greek New Testament! The words given in brackets after the English meanings are memory aids. Most of them are derived directly from the Greek words.

For the sake of clarity and simplicity the English equivalents of the

verb are given in their Present Simple form, despite the fact that the
Present Continuous is nearer to the fundamental meaning of the Greek
Present tense.

A

Translate into English: Λυει. λυομεν, λυουσιν, λυετε, λυεις. εὑρισκ-
ομεν, γραφει, βαλλετε· βλεπεις, ἐγειρουσιν. λεγουσιν; κρινετε,
βαλλομεν, ἐσθιω, πεμπουσιν, λαμβανετε, σωζομεν, μενει. ἐχεις;
γινωσκω; θεραπευετε.

B

Give the Greek for: We loose, they loose, you loose (sing.), you loose
(pl.), he looses, they are loosing, she is loosing. Do you have (pl.)? He
is saving; are they healing? I am throwing; she raises, we judge, you
remain (sing.), you judge (pl.); does he send? You are writing (pl.),
you are eating (sing.), he finds, we are taking, they see. Do you say
(sing.)?

LESSON 4

-εω verbs

There are many verbs whose stems end in ε. When endings are added
to such stems, certain contractions take place:

    ε combines with ε to give ει
    ε combines with o to give ου
    ε coming before a long vowel or a diphthong drops out.

    Thus the Present Indicative Active of φιλεω 'I love' is conjugated as
follows:

φιλω	for	φιλεω	I am loving *or* I love
φιλεις		φιλεεις	you are loving *or* you love
φιλει		φιλεει	he, she *or* it is loving, loves
φιλουμεν		φιλεομεν	we are loving *or* we love
φιλειτε		φιλεετε	you are loving *or* you love
φιλουσι(ν)		φιλεουσι(ν)	they are loving *or* they love

These three very important **rules of contraction of -εω verbs** may
be represented diagrammatically thus:

$$\epsilon + \epsilon \rightarrow \epsilon\iota$$
$$\epsilon + o \rightarrow ov$$
$$(\epsilon) + \text{long or diphthong.}$$

EXERCISE 4

Learn Vocabulary 4 on pp. 193-4. *Note*. With verbs of this type the
vocabularies (or a lexicon) will always give the first person singular in
its uncontracted (-εω) form, so that its method of conjugation may be
recognised at once. This is the form in which these verbs should be
learnt. But in the New Testament the first person singular will of
course always be found in its contracted (-ω) form.

A

Λαλουμεν, αἰτεις, τηρουσιν, ποιειτε. μετανοει; μαρτυρουσιν, ζητειτε,
καλω· θεωρουμεν, τηρεις, μισω. βλασφημει; εὐλογουσιν, φιλουμεν,
βαλλετε, γινωσκω, ἐγειρεις. ἐχουσιν; θεραπευει, κρινετε, μενομεν,
σωζουσιν.

B

They are seeking, he asks, you (sing.) call, we are bearing witness, I
speak; you (pl.) keep, she makes. Do you (pl.) look at? We love, they
are calling, she asks, they do, we are seeking, they bear witness, he is
looking at. Are they blaspheming? She is repenting. We hate; you
(pl.) bless. I call. We write, they eat, she is finding, it judges, you
(sing.) send.

LESSON 5

Second Declension nouns in -oς
The nominative, vocative and accusative cases

Re-read Introduction: English Grammar, Sections 2, 7, 9, 10.

SECOND DECLENSION NOUNS IN -oς

Nouns, like verbs, are much more fully inflected in Greek than in English. λογος (stem λογ), meaning 'word', is typical of a large class of nouns (mostly masculine) which make up the Second Declension in -oς. It is declined as follows:

Singular	Nominative	λογος	a word (subject)
	Vocative	λογε	O word
	Accusative	λογον	a word (object)
	Genitive	λογου	of a word
	Dative	λογῳ	to or for a word
Plural	Nominative	λογοι	words (subject)
	Vocative	λογοι	O words
	Accusative	λογους	words (object)
	Genitive	λογων	of words
	Dative	λογοις	to or for words

(Note the iota subscript which is always found in the dative singular of the first and second declension. It is not sounded.)

There is no indefinite article in Greek. When, therefore, a word like λογος stands alone, it usually means 'a word'. But it can mean simply 'word'. The right translation is nearly always obvious from the context.

NOMINATIVE AND ACCUSATIVE: SUBJECT AND DIRECT OBJECT

In English if we want to show that a word is the subject of a sentence, we nearly always put it before the verb, while the word which is the (direct) object of the sentence is placed after the verb. If we invert the order of the words, we invert the meaning of the sentence. In the sentence 'An angel finds a man', 'an angel' is the subject of the sentence, and 'a man' the object. On the other hand in the sentence 'A man finds an angel', 'a man' is the subject of the sentence, and 'an angel' the object. We have inverted the order of the words, and, in doing so, we have also inverted the meaning of the sentence.

The first of these two sentences would be, in Greek: ἄγγελος εὑρίσκει ἄνθρωπον. *We show that* ἄγγελος *is the subject by putting it in the nominative case, and that* ἄνθρωπον *is the object by putting it in the accusative case.*

In Greek the meaning of the sentence is still the same if we invert the order of the words and write ἄνθρωπον εὑρίσκει ἄγγελος, because in Greek it is not the order of the words, but the case form, which decides which word is the subject or the object. This means that a Greek writer is much freer than we are in the arrangement of words. He can put them down more or less in the order in which they come into his head. When a writer wishes to emphasise a word, he will often either bring it forward to the beginning of the sentence or leave it till the end of the sentence.

Before translating an English sentence into Greek it is necessary to know which word is the subject of the verb, and which is its direct object, if it has one.

The subject can always be found by putting 'who?' or 'what?' before the verb. In the first sentence given above—'An angel finds a man'— we ask, 'Who finds?' The answer is 'an angel'. 'An angel' is therefore the subject. In the same way we can easily see that 'a man' is the subject of the second sentence.

We can find the direct object by placing 'whom?' or 'what?' after the verb. In the case of the first sentence we say, 'An angel finds whom?' Answer: 'a man'. Therefore 'a man' is the object of the sentence.

Transitive and intransitive verbs

Many verbs, such as μενω 'I remain', cannot have a direct object. Verbs which cannot have a direct object are called *intransitive verbs*. Verbs which do have a direct object are called *transitive verbs*. Some verbs, such as λαλεω, can be used either transitively or intransitively:

e.g. Transitive: λαλουμεν λογους   We speak words
     Intransitive: λαλουμεν   We talk

(It will be noticed that in the vocabulary only one English equivalent is normally given for each Greek word, e.g. λαλεω, 'I speak'. But in fact two words in different languages are seldom, if ever, precisely equivalent. A word may have several possible translations. λαλεω, for instance, can be translated 'speak', 'talk', 'say', 'utter'. In due course the student will have to learn to use his own judgement in choosing the best rendering. But in the meantime he should adhere to the equivalents given in the vocabularies, in order to impress upon his mind the most generally useful translation.)

Number

Verbs agree with their subject in number.

If the subject of the verb is a noun in the singular, the verb will be in the third person singular; if it is a noun in the plural, or two or more nouns joined together by 'and', the verb will be in the third person plural: e.g.

ἀνθρωπος ἐγειρει λιθον   A man raises a stone
ἀνθρωποι ἐγειρουσιν λιθον   Men raise a stone
ἀνθρωπος και ἀγγελος ἐγειρουσιν   A man and an angel raise a stone
λιθον

VOCATIVE

Vocative is the case of address. As in English, it may be preceded by ὠ, 'O!' (Whether ὠ is used or not is largely a matter of the writer's taste.) Thus:

Κυριε, σωζεις   ⎫   ⎧   O Lord, you save
or   ὠ Κυριε, σωζεις ⎭ = ⎩ *or* Lord, you save.

EXERCISE 5

Learn Vocabulary on p. 194. From now on, attention will not be called
to the new vocabularies. The student should automatically look to see if
there are any new words to learn as soon as he has completed the lesson.

A

1. Ὦ Ἰσραηλ, θανατον ζητειτε; 2. ἀγγελος λαον σωζει. 3. κυριος
γραφει λογους. 4. τηρειτε νομους. 5. Φαρισαιοι φιλουσιν
Χριστον; 6. θεωρειτε ἀγρους. 7. ἐχει θρονον. 8. μισει
κοσμον και ζητει φιλον. 9. λεπρε, βλασφημεις; 10. γινωσκομεν θανατον. 11. βαλλω λιθους. 12. διακονοι μαρτυρουσιν.
13. εὐλογουμεν διδασκαλους. 14. ἀποστολος θεραπευει παραλυτικον; 15. Ἰουδαιοι και Φαρισαιοι αἰτουσιν φιλους. 16. ὀφθαλμους θεραπευει. 17. φοβος λαμβανει ἀδελφους και λαον.
18. ζητεις πρεσβυτερον; 19. ποιουμεν ποταμον. 20. ἐχω
ἐχθρους.

B

1. An angel calls a man. 2. A brother has a field. 3. Lords send
messengers. 4. They are writing words. 5. Are you (pl.) finding
a stone? 6. Christ judges men and angels. 7. Do you (sing.)
keep laws? 8. A man and an angel seek a place. 9. We bear
witness and a people repents. 10. Lord, you remain. 11. Apostles
speak and servants have fear. 12. Do you (sing.) make a throne?
13. They hate Christ and love death. 14. An elder speaks.
15. He saves lepers and paralytics and heals eyes. 16. Do Pharisees
write laws? 17. Jews, we know Christ. 18. Does she judge
words? 19. I am looking at a river. 20. She looses a friend.
21. You (pl.) are seeking a world. 22. Israel says, 'Does Christ
save?'[1]

---

[1] There are no inverted commas in Greek. Simply use a capital letter after
the comma.

LESSON 6

The genitive and dative cases
The definite article
Declension of Ἰησους

THE GENITIVE CASE

The genitive case can generally be translated into English by the use of the preposition 'of', or by adding 's to the noun,

> e.g. οἰκος ἀνθρωπου *means* a house of a man
>
> *or* a man's house.

THE DATIVE CASE

The commonest use of the dative case is to denote the person *to* or *for* whom anything is done, i.e. the *indirect object*,

> e.g. γραφει νομους λαῳ. He writes laws for a people.
>
> μαρτυρει ἀνθρωπῳ. He bears witness to a man.

THE DEFINITE ARTICLE

The definite article ('the') is declined in Greek like a noun. The forms that go with words in the *masculine* gender are as follows:

Singular			Plural		
N.	ὁ		N.	οἱ	
A.	τον		A.	τους	
G.	του		G.	των	
D.	τῳ		D.	τοις	

It will be noticed that the endings, except the nominative singular, are the same as those of λογος. There is, of course, no vocative.

The definite article is always in the same case and number and gender as the noun to which it is joined,

> e.g. του ἀνθρωπου of the man
>
> τοις ἀνθρωποις to the men.

'The man's house' is sometimes written in the following order: ὁ του ἀνθρωπου οἰκος.

34

Special uses of the article

There are four examples of the use of the article in Greek where it is not used in English.

(1) Θεος usually has the article,

    e.g. ὁ Υἱος του Θεου   the Son of God.

(2) ἀνθρωπος, when it refers to men as a whole class, usually has the article, e.g. ὁ υἱος του ἀνθρωπου   the son of Man

    οἱ υἱοι των ἀνθρωπων   the sons of men.

(3) Abstract nouns (e.g. love, truth, peace) often have the article,

    e.g. ἡ ἀγαπη[1] μενει   Love remains.

There is one important exception to this rule. It will be recalled that the function of a noun in Greek (unlike English) is indicated by case ending rather than by word order. When two nouns in the nominative are linked by the verb 'to be', it may not be clear which is subject and which is complement. Thus

    ὁ Λογος ἐστιν ὁ Θεος *could be either* The Word is God.

                        or   God is the Word.

In such cases the complement usually drops the article, and is usually placed before the verb.

    Θεος ἐστιν ὁ Λογος *can only be* The Word is God.[2]

So in the case of abstract nouns we have

    ὁ Θεος ἀγαπη ἐστιν God is love. (1 John 4. 8, 16)

[1] For ἡ, the feminine of the definite article, see Lesson 8. For ἀγαπη, see Vocab. 8.

[2] In ancient manuscripts which did not differentiate between capital and small letters, there would be no way of distinguishing between Θεος ('God') and θεος ('god'). Therefore as far as grammar alone is concerned, such a sentence could be printed: θεος ἐστιν ὁ Λογος, which would mean either, 'The Word is a god', or, 'The Word is the god'. The interpretation of John 1. 1 will depend upon whether or not the writer is held to believe in only one God or in more than one god. It will be noticed that the above rules for the special uses of the definite article are none of them rigid and without exceptions. It is wiser not to use them as a basis for theological argument until the student has reached an advanced stage in the knowledge of the language. For a full treatment, see Blass–Debrunner–Funk, *A Greek Grammar of the New Testament*, Part III, 8, especially para. 273; Moulton–Turner, *A Grammar of New Testament Greek*, III, 182 ff.

(4) The name ’Ιησους prefers the article,

    e.g. ὁ ’Ιησους λαμβανει τον ἀρτον   Jesus takes the bread.

With proper names in general, however, it seems to be largely a matter of the author's whim whether he uses the article or not. Sometimes the article is added, sometimes it is left out.

DECLENSION OF ’Ιησους

’Ιησους follows a slightly modified form of the Second Declension, having no separate form for the vocative and dative, both of which follow the genitive:

N.	’Ιησους
A.	’Ιησουν
G.V.D.	’Ιησου

EXERCISE 6

A

1. Γραφει τον νομον του Κυριου.   2. οἱ ἀνθρωποι ζητουσιν τους ἀγγελους.   3. οἱ δουλοι ποιουσιν ὁδον τῳ Κυριῳ.   4. ὁ ἀδελφος του δουλου βλεπει τον οἰκον.   5. τηρουσιν τον λογον του Θεου.   6. ὁ ’Ιησους εὐλογει τον ἀρτον και τον οἰνον του ἐχθρου.   7. ὁ διαβολος μισει τον του Θεου ναον.   8. ἐσθιετε τον καρπον;   9. ὁ Κυριος σωζει ἁμαρτωλους.   10. οἱ ’Ιουδαιοι ποιουσιν σταυρον τῳ ’Ιησου.   11. παρθενοι γινωσκουσιν τους λογους του ὀχλου.   12. ὁ ἡλιος και ὁ ἀνεμος θεραπευουσιν.   13. ὁ νομος τῳ κοσμῳ ἐστιν.   14. μισθος ἐστιν ὁ οἰνος.

B

1. Does time remain?   2. Are you (pl.) seeking heaven?   3. James has a reward for the son.   4. We see a desert.   5. The angel writes laws for the world.   6. The man's slave is making bread. 7. The devil seeks a time for Christ's temptations.   8. Sinners see the apostles' words and repent.   9. Jesus says to the crowd, 'Do you love God?'   10. The apostles know the Lord.   11. Does the Son of God seek heaven?   12. They hate temptation.   13. Have

you (sing.) a house and fields, bread and wine?   14. We are finding
the place for a temple.   15. A man and a servant take the elder's
fruit.   16. God is the reward and the reward is God.

LESSON 7

Gender
Second Declension neuter nouns

GENDER

Re-read Introduction: English Grammar, Section 9 (2).

In English all nouns denoting men or male animals are masculine; all
nouns denoting women or female animals are feminine; all other nouns
are neuter. But in Greek the rule is not so simple. Nearly all nouns
denoting men or male animals are masculine, and nearly all those
denoting women or female animals are feminine; but other nouns may
be either masculine, feminine or neuter. The gender is usually to be
inferred from the ending. As we have seen, most nouns ending in -ος in
the Second Declension are masculine.

All nouns ending in -ον are neuter. This includes such words
as παιδιον and τεκνον, both of which mean 'child'.

SECOND DECLENSION NEUTER NOUNS

ἐργον 'work' is declined as follows:

Singular			Plural		
	N.	ἐργον		N.	ἐργα
	V.	ἐργον		V.	ἐργα
	A.	ἐργον		A.	ἐργα
	G.	ἐργου		G.	ἐργων
	D.	ἐργῳ		D.	ἐργοις

Note that the nominative, vocative and accusative cases have the same
ending.

37

The **definite article** that goes with neuter nouns is declined as follows:

Singular	N.	το	Plural	N.	τα
	A.	το		A.	τα
	G.	του		G.	των
	D.	τῳ		D.	τοις

That is to say, the definite article follows the endings of ἐργον exactly, except for the nominative and accusative singular, which are το, not τον. (τον is accusative *masculine*.)

Neuter plural subjects

There is one exception to the rule that verbs agree with their subject in number. **Neuter plural subjects are followed by singular verbs.** In other words neuter plural subjects are treated as though they were singular collective nouns,

e.g. τα παιδια εὑρισκει τα βιβλια The children find the books.

This rule is not kept very strictly (especially when the subjects concerned are persons), but it should always be followed by a student when translating into Greek.

EXERCISE 7

A

1. Οἱ Φαρισαιοι του συνεδριου μισουσιν τον Ἰησουν. 2. τα δαιμονια γινωσκει τον Χριστον και ἐχει φοβον. 3. οἱ ἀποστολοι λαλουσιν το εὐαγγελιον κυριοις και δουλοις. 4. τηρουμεν τα σαββατα. 5. οἱ διδασκαλοι λαλουσιν τοις τεκνοις τα μυστηρια των οὐρανων. 6. οἱ ἀνθρωποι ἐχουσιν προβατα και πλοιον. 7. θεωρεις το του Ἰησου προσωπον; 8. οἱ δουλοι λαμβανουσιν τα δενδρα τῳ Ἰακωβῳ. 9. ὁ ἀδελφος ζητει το του παιδιου μνημειον. 10. ποιειτε τα ἐργα του διαβολου. 11. οἱ Ἰουδαιοι γραφουσιν βιβλια. 12. βλεπομεν τα σημεια των καιρων. 13. εὑρισκει ἀργυριον. 14. οἱ διακονοι τηρουσιν τα ποτηρια του ἱερου Ἱεροσολυμων. 15. παρθενος ποιει ἱματιον τῳ Ἰησου; 16. το μυστηριον εὐαγγελιον ἐστιν.

B

In this and subsequent exercises, the student is free to translate 'you' as either singular or plural, unless the number is determined by the context.
1. Christ blesses the cup of wine and the bread.   2. Do you know the signs of the Son of Man?   3. The Lord saves men and children.
4. The children ask the elders for garments.¹   5. Do you see the sheep?   6. We bear witness to the gospel of God.   7. The Jews love the sabbath and Jerusalem.   8. Angels see the face of God.
9. Do the demons love the tombs?   10. The Sanhedrin judges sinners.   11. Children know the mysteries of heaven.   12. Jesus sends the boat.   13. We love the temple's books.   14. We see a place of trees.   15. God hates the works of the devil and of sinners.
16. Have the apostles money?   17. The Sabbath is the sign of God.

¹ 'Ask for' takes a double accusative. The object asked-for and the person from whom it is asked are both put in the accusative case.

LESSON 8

First Declension feminine nouns in -η

There are three closely related forms of the First Declension feminine. An example of the first is ἀρχή 'beginning':

	Singular	N.V.	ἀρχή	Plural	N.V.	ἀρχαι
		A.	ἀρχην		A.	ἀρχας
		G.	ἀρχης		G.	ἀρχων
		D.	ἀρχη		D.	ἀρχαις

The **definite article** which goes with all feminine nouns is declined thus:

	Singular	N.	ἡ	Plural	N.	αἱ
		A.	την		A.	τας
		G.	της		G.	των
		D.	τη		D.	ταις

That is to say, it follows the endings of ἀρχή exactly.

39

We have now had examples of nouns of all three genders and of the forms of the article which go with them. The full declension of the article is as follows:

		M.	F.	N.
Singular	N.	ὁ	ἡ	το
	A.	τον	την	το
	G.	του	της	του
	D.	τῷ	τῇ	τῷ
Plural	N.	οἱ	αἱ	τα
	A.	τους	τας	τα
	G.	των	των	των
	D.	τοις	ταις	τοις

The definite article, of course, agrees in number, gender and case with the noun with which it is connected.

EXERCISE 8

A

1. Γινωσκουσιν οἱ ἀδελφοι την ἀγαπην του Θεου.   2. ἡ ἀρχη του εὐαγγελιου Ἰησου Χριστου, Υἱου Θεου.[1]   3. οἱ ἀποστολοι γραφουσιν τας ἐπιστολας.   4. οἱ Φαρισαιοι της συναγωγης ζητουσιν την δικαιοσυνην.   5. εὐλογουμεν την ὑπομονην του Χριστου.   6. αἱ γραφαι μαρτυρουσιν τῷ Χριστῷ.   7. τηρεις τας ἐντολας;   8. οἱ διδασκαλοι θεωρουσιν την νεφελην.   9. ὁ Ἰησους λαλει τας παραβολας τῷ λαῷ της κωμης.   10. γινωσκομεν την φωνην του ὀχλου.   11. φιλουμεν τον οἰκον της προσευχης.   12. ἡ ὀργη του Θεου μενει.   13. οἱ δουλοι αἰτουσιν την εἰρηνην.   14. ὁ Χριστος ἀρτος της ζωης ἐστιν.   15. σωζεις την ψυχην;   16. ἐσθιομεν τον καρπον της γης.   17. οἱ ἀποστολοι ἐχουσιν την τιμην των ἀνθρωπων;   18. ὁ ἀγγελος εὑρισκει την φυλακην.

[1] For apposition, see Introduction: English Grammar, section 10, subsection (1). References to the introductory English Grammar in the footnotes will in future be abbreviated thus: E.G. 10 (1).

B

1. God is judging the earth.   2. You know the commandments.
3. The apostles love God's covenant.   4. He has money, the price
of a field.[1]   5. The elders of the village throw stones.   6. God
saves men's souls.   7. James sends a letter for the apostle's friend.
8. I see the cup of the wrath of God.   9. God is love and righteousness.   10. You are sending the words of the gospel of peace.
11. The slaves hate the prison.   12. Are the children taking the
books of (the) scripture?   13. God knows the prayers of men.
14. The reward of steadfastness is life.   15. Israel knows the
teaching of the commandments.

LESSON 9

First Declension feminine nouns in -α

The other two forms of the First Declension feminine are:

Singular	N.V.	ἡμερα	day	δοξα	glory
	A.	ἡμεραν		δοξαν	
	G.	ἡμερας		δοξης	
	D.	ἡμερᾳ		δοξῃ	
Plural	N.V.	ἡμεραι		δοξαι	
	A.	ἡμερας		δοξας	
	G.	ἡμερων		δοξων	
	D.	ἡμεραις		δοξαις	

Note. (1) The plural endings are identical with those of ἀρχη.

(2) The singular of ἡμερα is the same as that of ἀρχη, except that α
replaces η.

(3) δοξα follows ἡμερα for nominative, vocative and accusative, and
ἀρχη for genitive and dative singular.

[1] See p. 40, footnote.

41

(4) Nouns with stems ending in

    vowel or ρ follow ἡμερα,

    consonant other than ρ follow δοξα.

EXERCISE 9

A

1. Ἡ βασιλεια των οὐρανων ζωη και ἀληθεια ἐστιν.　2. ὁ Θεος μισει την ἀδικιαν και την ἁμαρτιαν.　3. ἡ γενεα ἁμαρτωλων μετανοει;　4. ὁ Χριστος κεφαλη της ἐκκλησιας ἐστιν.　5. δαιμονια ἐχει ἐξουσιαν;　6. θεωρουμεν την ἀρχην της ἡμερας. 7. ὁ Θεος πεμπει τον λογον της ἐπαγγελιας.　8. οἱ Φαρισαιοι τηρουσιν τας ἐντολας της θυσιας.　9. ὁ καρπος του Θεου ἀγαπη, χαρα και εἰρηνη ἐστιν.　10. οἱ ἀνθρωποι βλεπουσιν το προσωπον και ὁ Θεος βλεπει την καρδιαν.　11. οἱ ἁμαρτωλοι ἐχουσιν μετανοιας τοπον.　12. αἱ χηραι ἐχουσιν ἀρτον τοις παιδιοις; 13. Πετρος εὐλογει τον Κυριον της γης και της θαλασσης.　14. αἱ γλωσσαι των ἀποστολων λαλουσιν λογους της σοφιας του Θεου. 15. ἡ ὡρα της δοξης του Χριστου χαρα ἐστιν τοις ἀγγελοις. 16. ποιουμεν οἰκιαν λιθων.　17. ἡ της ἀγαπης μαρτυρια ὁδον ποιει τῃ του Κυριου παρουσιᾳ.　18. ἡ Γαλιλαια και ἡ Ἰουδαια γινωσκουσιν τας χρειας των χηρων.

B

1. They seek the time of the promise.　2. The angels of heaven have joy.　3. Paul bears witness to the truth of the gospel and the wisdom of God.　4. Repentance is the door of salvation.　5. Do the children repent?　6. The door of the tomb is a stone. 7. God makes the seas, the rocks of the earth and the clouds of heaven.　8. The need of the widow is joy.　9. Christ has the authority of God.　10. Is the church the kingdom of God? 11. God hates the unrighteousness of men.　12. Jesus heals the widow's son.　13. The devil's generation blasphemes.　14. Do you know the hour of temptation?　15. Does Paul eat the sacrifices? 16. He seeks a heart of peace and righteousness.　17. Paul's joy is the cross of Christ.　18. They seek the day of salvation. 19. The apostles' tongues speak words of truth to the people.

REVISION TEST 1

Allow yourself 20 minutes. The number of marks to award for each correct answer is shown in square brackets at the end of each question; total 25.

In writing out declensions and conjugations it is not necessary to repeat stems which do not change.

1. Give the Present Indicative Active of μισεω. [1 mark]
2. Decline the definite article in full. [2]
3. Give the Greek for: I do,[1] I eat, I find, I keep, I raise, I take. [3]
4. Give the Greek for: anger, boat, commandment, covenant, face, field, fruit, garment, honour, joy, people, place, prayer, promise, reward, sacrifice, sign, stone, temple (shrine), tomb, unrighteousness, village, widow, world. [12]
5. Give the Greek for: (1) for the sea, (2) of the desert, (3) of love, (4) for the cup, (5) of the tongue, (6) of the way, (7) for Jesus. [7]

LESSON 10

First Declension masculine nouns
Further uses of accusative, genitive and dative

FIRST DECLENSION MASCULINE NOUNS

Nouns of the First Declension ending in -ης or -ας in the nominative singular are masculine. They are declined as follows:

Singular				
N.	προφητης	prophet	νεανιας	young man
V.	προφητα		νεανια	
A.	προφητην		νεανιαν	
G.	προφητου		νεανιου	
D.	προφητῃ		νεανιᾳ	

[1] With -εω verbs, give the uncontracted form.

43

Plural	N.	προφηται	νεανιαι
	V.	προφηται	νεανιαι
	A.	προφητας	νεανιας
	G.	προφητων	νεανιων
	D.	προφηταις	νεανιαις

Note. The plural endings are identical with those of the feminine nouns; in the singular, only the vocatives and genitives need be noticed.

First Declension nouns in -ας are nearly all proper names. When such nouns have stems ending in ε, ι or ρ, they are declined precisely like νεανιας with the genitive ending -ου, e.g. ’Ανδρεας, -ου 'Andrew'; ’Ηλειας, -ου 'Elijah'. Those with stems ending in other letters have an -α ending in the genitive singular, which is a form found in the Doric dialect. This *'Doric' Genitive* is found in such words as Σατανας, -α 'Satan'; ’Ιουδας, -α 'Judas'.

Note. Because these words in -ης and -ας are masculine, they will take the masculine form of the definite article.

Thus: ζητει τους τελωνας   He seeks the tax-collectors.
Conversely: εὑρισκουσιν την παρθενον   They find the virgin.

FURTHER USES OF ACCUSATIVE, GENITIVE AND DATIVE
The accusative

(1) In Lesson 5 we saw how the accusative is used for the **direct object**.

(2) It is also used to express **motion to**. There are two prepositions meaning 'to', both of which are followed by the accusative: προς meaning 'to' or 'towards', and εἰς meaning 'to' or 'into'. They can be represented diagrammatically thus:

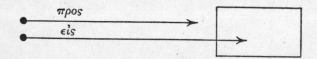

The root idea of the accusative is **extension**. προς and εἰς define more closely the degree of extension.

The genitive

(1) In Lesson 5 we saw the genitive used to translate 'of'. Frequently this indicates **possession**, e.g. 'the people of God' (that is, 'the people who belong to God'). But possession is only a particular instance of a more general idea. The genitive in fact expresses the **genus** (or kind) of the thing specified. Thus 'baptism of repentance', 'son of man', 'coming of Christ' are not possessive, but they all describe in some way the kind of thing specified—the kind of 'baptism', or 'son', or 'coming'. When the genitive expresses the genus of the thing specified we are dealing with an example of the genitive properly so called.

(2) It is also used to express a totally different idea, that of **separation**. This corresponds to the Latin *ablative*[1] (*ablatus* meaning 'carried away'). There are two prepositions meaning 'from', both followed by the genitive: ἀπο meaning 'from' or 'away from'; and ἐκ meaning 'from' or 'out of'. Thus:

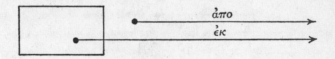

The dative

(1) In Lesson 6 we saw the dative used to express the **indirect object,** the person *to* or *for* whom something is done. (Notice that the idea of 'to' here is not one of motion, which is accusative, but is one of *personal interest*.)

(2) The dative can also be used to indicate a place—the so-called **locative** use. So ἐν, meaning 'in', takes a dative.

---

[1] In the parent Indo-European language from which both Greek and Latin are derived there were separate genitive and ablative cases. The ablative has survived in Latin, but in Greek the separate case forms have disappeared, and the functions of the ablative have been taken over by the genitive. It is useful to retain the technical term 'ablative' as a means of pin-pointing these uses of the genitive. The *locative* and *instrumental*, referred to in the next section, were also separate cases, whose functions have been taken over by the dative. Interestingly, in the present-day Greek of popular speech, the dative itself has now disappeared.

(3) It can also be used for the instrument by which something is done.
An example of the **instrumental** use (which requires no preposition) is:

ὁ ἀγγελος σωζει τον νεανιαν λογῳ.

The angel saves the young man *by a word* (or *with a word*).

EXERCISE 10

A

1. Ὑποκριτα, τηρεις τας ἐντολας ἀλλ᾽ οὐ φιλεις τον Θεον.   2. οἱ
οὖν μαθηται μενουσιν ἐν τῃ οἰκιᾳ.   3. ὁ Ἰησους λεγει την
παραβολην τοις μαθηταις και τῳ τελωνῃ.   4. ὁ ἀρα Χριστος
κριτης ἐστιν των ἀνθρωπων ἐν τῃ ἡμερᾳ της ὀργης.   5. οἱ
ἐργαται βαλλουσιν λιθους εἰς την θαλασσαν;   6. Ἡλειας ὁ
προφητης καλει τον λαον.   7. ἐν τῃ ἡμερᾳ της δοξης βλεπομεν
Χριστον προσωπον προς προσωπον.   8. Ἰησους ἐστιν· σωζει
γαρ τον λαον ἀφ᾽ ἀμαρτιας.   9. ὁ δε ἀγγελος λυει Πετρον ἐκ
της φυλακης.   10. ὁ Ἰουδας οὐ φιλει τον Ἰησουν οὐδε τους
μαθητας.   11. Ἰωανης γινωσκει τον ἀδελφον Ἰουδα.   12. ὁ
δε Ἰησους ἐγειρει τον νεανιαν ἐκ θανατου.   13. μισουμεν οὖν
τα ἐργα του Σατανα.   14. οἱ στρατιωται τηρουσιν τους λογους
του Ἰωανου του βαπτιστου και μετανοουσιν, ἀλλ᾽ οἱ Φαρισαιοι οὐ
μετανοουσιν, οὐ γαρ ἐχουσιν την ἀγαπην του Θεου.

B

1. Jesus therefore says, 'The Son of man is in the clouds of heaven'.
2. The Jews seek the prophet's voice in the desert.   3. Do the sons
of God keep the commandments from (i.e. out of) (the) heart?
4. Do the tax-collectors blaspheme?   5. The disciples then have the
love of God.   6. The workmen do not find the way to the cross,
and they do not see the sacrifice of Jesus.   7. And the hypocrites do not know life but remain in sin.   8. Christ speaks in
parables to the young men; for they seek truth.   9. From the
beginning of the world Christ is Lord.   10. The judge does not take
the money from the elders of the church, nor does he hate the apostles.
11. The soldiers throw Andrew the apostle into prison.   12. You see

with the eyes of love.[1]   13. John the Baptist calls the people to repentance.   14. The Pharisees seek signs from (i.e. out of) heaven. 15. Elijah does not love the sacrifices of sinners, the works of Satan.

LESSON 11

Second Declension adjectives
The attributive use of adjectives
Adjectives used as nouns

Re-read Introduction: English Grammar, Section 6c.

SECOND DECLENSION ADJECTIVES

Adjectives of the Second Declension have endings which we already know. They are of two kinds. Those with stems ending with a **consonant other than ρ** are declined as follows:

ἀγαθος good

		M.	F.	N.
Singular	N.	ἀγαθος	ἀγαθη	ἀγαθον
	V.	ἀγαθε	ἀγαθη	ἀγαθον
	A.	ἀγαθον	ἀγαθην	ἀγαθον
	G.	ἀγαθου	ἀγαθης	ἀγαθου
	D.	ἀγαθῳ	ἀγαθη	ἀγαθῳ
Plural	N.V.	ἀγαθοι	ἀγαθαι	ἀγαθα
	A.	ἀγαθους	ἀγαθας	ἀγαθα
	G.	ἀγαθων	ἀγαθων	ἀγαθων
	D.	ἀγαθοις	ἀγαθαις	ἀγαθοις

It will be seen that the masculine endings are λογος endings,
the feminine endings are ἀρχη endings,
the neuter endings are ἐργον endings.

[1] 'with' is here Instrumental.

47

Those with stems ending in a **vowel or** ρ are precisely the same, except that the feminine singular follows ἡμερα, giving:

$$\text{ἅγιος} \quad \text{holy}$$

	M.	F.	N.
N.	ἅγιος	ἁγια	ἅγιον
V.	ἅγιε	ἁγια	ἅγιον
A.	ἅγιον	ἁγιαν	ἅγιον
G.	ἁγιου	ἁγιας	ἁγιου
D.	ἁγιῳ	ἁγιᾳ	ἁγιῳ

ATTRIBUTIVE USE OF ADJECTIVES

In cases where there is no definite article in English, the Greek adjective can come either before or after its noun.

'a good prophet' *is either* (1) ἀγαθος προφητης
        or (2) προφητης ἀγαθος.

(Adjectives, like the article, of course agree with the nouns which they qualify in number, gender and case.)

When there is a definite article, article and adjective are put in the so-called **attributive position**, which has two forms:

'the good prophet' *is either* (1) ὁ ἀγαθος προφητης
        or (2) ὁ προφητης ὁ ἀγαθος.

Note that in both forms of the attributive position *the adjective is immediately preceded by the article.*

ADJECTIVES USED AS NOUNS

In English we sometimes use an article and an adjective without a noun expressed, e.g. 'the deaf (people)'. In Greek this is quite a common use, giving such expressions as:

ὁ πρωτος the first man   οἱ ἁγιοι   the holy men, the saints
αἱ ἀγαθαι the good women   τα ἐσχατα   the last things

Incidentally there is no Greek word for 'things' used in a general sense. Some such form as this must always be used.

EXERCISE 11

A

1. Οἱ ἄπιστοι Ἰουδαιοι οὐ μετανοουσιν.   2. ἐν ταις ἐσχαταις ἡμεραις ὀλιγοι ἐχουσιν την ἀγαπην.   3. ὁ ἀποστολος ὁ ἀγαπητος πρωτον γραφει καινην ἐπιστολην τῃ ἐκκλησιᾳ.   4. ὁ Ἰησους θεραπευει τους τυφλους και τους λεπρους.   5. οἱ μαθηται ἐσθιουσιν τον καρπον τον ἀκαθαρτον;   6. ὁ Θεος κρινει ἑκαστον νεανιαν.   7. ὁ παραλυτικος ἐστιν ἐν μεσῳ του ἱερου και εὐλογει τα καλα ἐργα του Θεου.   8. οἱ πτωχοι φιλουσιν το εὐαγγελιον.

B

In this exercise, whenever the definite article is used with an attributive adjective, give both the possible translations.

1. Wise virgins.   2. Sufficient steadfastness.   3. The new life. 4. Beautiful thrones.   5. Believing children.   6. Unbelieving prayers.   7. Bad times (accusative).   8. On (in) the third day. 9. The poor man's garment.   10. The first prayer.   11. The only God.   12. The sins of the unbelievers.   13. New books.   14. An unclean sheep and an unclean soul.   15. A good heart.   16. The last hour.   17. Eternal scriptures.   18. A beloved widow.   19. A few boats of the disciples.   20. Powerful angels.   21. In the midst of the river.   22. O blind hypocrite!

C

1. The rest find the only young man in the desert.   2. The bad prophets do not bear witness to the truth.   3. The soldiers first make a new cross for the Son of God.   4. Good words save men from death.   5. Does Paul alone remain faithful?[1]   6. Andrew is Christ's first disciple.   7. The wise do not know God by wisdom, but the poor seek the kingdom of God.   8. Jesus, a man powerful in words and works.   9. The servant is a good soldier for Jesus Christ. 10. The remaining children ask for bread from Jesus' brothers. 11. The friends have sufficient money.   12. Paul sees the third heaven.   13. The last enemy is death.

[1] Complement to intransitive verb: E.G. 7.

LESSON 12

Predicative use of adjectives
Present Indicative of the verb 'to be'

PREDICATIVE USE OF ADJECTIVES

Re-read Introduction: English Grammar, Section 7.

Using the verb 'to be' there are two ways of saying 'the prophet is good':

(1) ὁ προφήτης ἐστιν ἀγαθος.

(2) ἀγαθος ἐστιν ὁ προφήτης.

Note that in both examples ἀγαθος is not an object (which would be accusative) but a complement. It completes the sense of the verb 'to be' (which is a verb of incomplete predication) and is put in the nominative.

It will be noticed that whereas in the **attributive use** the article always immediately precedes the adjective:

ὁ ἀγαθος προφήτης   or   ὁ προφήτης ὁ ἀγαθος

in the **predicative use** there is no immediately preceding article:

ὁ προφήτης ἐστιν ἀγαθος   or   ἀγαθος ἐστιν ὁ προφήτης.

This means that it is possible in Greek to drop the verb 'to be' altogether without any confusion arising. So that we get the following table:

Attributive position
(with article)
the good prophet

(1) ὁ ἀγαθος προφήτης
(2) ὁ προφήτης ὁ ἀγαθος

Predicative position
(no article)
the prophet is good

(1) ὁ προφήτης ἀγαθος
(2) ἀγαθος ὁ προφήτης

On the whole the New Testament writers prefer to keep the verb 'to be' with predicative adjectives, but it is important to master the differences between the attributive and predicative positions in cases where there is no verb to help distinguish them.

PRESENT INDICATIVE OF THE VERB 'TO BE'

Singular	1	εἰμι	I am
	2	εἶ	you are
	3	ἐστι(ν)	he, she, it is
Plural	1	ἐσμεν	we are
	2	ἐστε	you are
	3	εἰσι(ν)	they are

Note that the second person singular εἶ is printed with a circumflex accent to distinguish it from the common word εἰ, meaning 'if', which is unaccented. (See Vocab. 39.) Cf.

εἰ Υἱος εἶ του Θεου.   (Matt. 4. 3)
If you are the Son of God.

EXERCISE 12

A

1. Ὁ Θεος ἐγειρει τον Ἰησουν ἐκ των νεκρων.   2. μακαριοι οἱ καθαροι ἐν τῃ καρδιᾳ.   3. ὁ Υἱος του ἀνθρωπου οὐ ζητει την δοξαν την ἰδιαν, ἀλλα την δοξαν του Θεου.   4. ὁ πλουσιος φιλει τους πτωχους;   5. οἱ δικαιοι εἰσιν υἱοι του Θεου.   6. οἱ ἁγιοι βλεπουσιν την δοξαν των οὐρανων και μαρτυρουσιν ταις φωναις των ἀγγελων.   7. ὁ Χριστος ἐχει τριτον πειρασμον ἐν τῃ ἐρημῳ.

B

Translate the following in two different ways without using the verb 'to be'.

1. The cloud is small.   2. The evil eye.   3. The laws are old.
4. The holy life.   5. The second hour.   6. The sons are free.
7. The new heavens and the new earth.   8. Are the demons strong?
9. Its own reward.   10. The righteous soul.   11. The generation is rich.   12. The right eye.   13. Is love pure?

C

In these sentences use εἰμι to translate the verb 'to be'.

1. Elijah's servant sees a small cloud in the heavens.   2. Are you worthy?   3. The enemies of Christ are children of the devil. 4. You are the Christ.   5. The evil see the second death, for they do not love the wisdom of God.   6. Few find the way of life. 7. The old wine is good, but the new is bad.   8. The strong man looses the slave from the prison.   9. We are like sheep.   10. Is it a different tomb?   11. The rich are not free from the authority of God. 12. I am the first and the last.   13. Hypocrite, you are the slave of dead works.   14. The tax-collectors have fruits worthy of repentance for Jesus.   15. The Pharisee's prayer is not clean.   16. He has a different authority.   17. The old teaching is not like the parables of the Lord.   18. You are the enemies of the cross of Christ. 19. Blessed are the disciples' hearts.

LESSON 13

The Imperfect Indicative Active
Compound verbs

THE IMPERFECT INDICATIVE ACTIVE

Re-read Introduction: English Grammar, Section 12.

The Imperfect Indicative Active of λυω is as follows:

ἐλυον	I was loosing, I used to loose
ἐλυες	you were loosing, you used to loose
ἐλυε(ν)	he was loosing, he used to loose
ἐλυομεν	we were loosing, we used to loose
ἐλυετε	you were loosing, you used to loose
ἐλυον	they were loosing, they used to loose

It will be noticed that this tense not only has endings after the stem, it also has an ἐ- in front of the stem. This is known as the **augment**. It indicates action in the past.

To get the Imperfect of φιλεω the rules of contraction of Lesson 4 have to be applied. Then (except that there is no movable ν in the third person singular) λυω is followed exactly:

ἐφιλεον → ἐφιλουν		ἐφιλεομεν → ἐφιλουμεν	
ἐφιλεες → ἐφιλεις		ἐφιλεετε → ἐφιλειτε	
ἐφιλεε → ἐφιλει		ἐφιλεον → ἐφιλουν	

Verbs beginning with a vowel

If the verb begins with a vowel, it is not possible to prefix a separate augment. Instead, various vowel changes take place. The basic rule is simple: *the vowel is lengthened*.

e.g.   ε becomes η

       ο   ω[1]

       α, however, does not become ᾱ, but, η.

The following table gives the rules for **initial vowel changes in formation of past tenses**:

α → η	αι → η	αυ → ηυ
ε → η	ει → η	ευ → ηυ (or remains ευ[2])
ο → ω	οι → ῳ	

Examples:

Present	Imperfect
ἀκουω	ἠκουον
ἐγειρω	ἠγειρον
αἰτεω	ᾐτουν
οἰκοδομεω	ᾠκοδομουν (Vocab. 14)
εὑρισκω	ηὑρισκον

---

[1] ι also becomes ῑ. (To all appearances, that is, it remains unchanged.) There are no words of this type to be learnt at this stage. See, however, ἰαομαι, p. 170, n. 1 and the Imperfect of ἱστημι, p. 184.

[2] Because of the symmetry of the table, ηυ will be regarded as the regular form, though ευ is in fact used rather more frequently. Attention will be called to any departure from the ηυ form.

The augmented form of ἔχω is irregular:

ἔχω   εἶχον

As these changes take place at the beginning of the words they must be carefully noticed, otherwise it will not be possible to find the words in a lexicon, where verbs are given under the Present tense.[1]

THE MEANING OF THE IMPERFECT

As we saw in Lesson 3, the Greek Present tense corresponds most closely to the English Present Continuous tense, usually referring to continuous or repeated action in the present. Similarly the Imperfect denotes <u>continuous or repeated action in past time</u>, and is most closely represented by the English Past Continuous. In order to impress this fact on the memory, the Greek Imperfects should be translated by the English Past Continuous forms in Exercise 13, even if they are sometimes rather clumsy. Experience will show in due course that the English Past Simple ('I loosed', 'I loved') may in fact often be a sufficient translation.

The Present and Imperfect are sometimes said to be *linear tenses*. Continuous action can be thought of as a line:

———————————————

and repeated action as a line of dots:

. . . .

We shall later meet another type of tense which can be represented by a single dot. (See Lesson 24.)

COMPOUND VERBS

In English we have two ways of linking together the sense of a verb and a preposition. The preposition can either be immediately prefixed to the verb, forming a compound verb such as 'OVERthrow', 'UNDERstand', 'UPgrade', 'OUTnumber'; or (which is much more common) it can follow the verb as a separate word, e.g. 'go over', 'bring under', 'send up'. In Greek the former method is used a great deal and there are many compound verbs.

[1] See further, p. 97.

They can be divided roughly into three types:

(1) Those in which the <u>original force</u> of both verb and preposition is fully <u>preserved</u>, e.g.

ἀγω	I lead *or* bring	βαλλω	I throw
ἀπαγω	I lead away	ἐκβαλλω	I throw out

φερω   I carry
προσφερω   I bring to, offer

(2) Those in which the preposition serves merely to <u>intensify</u> or complete the meaning of the verb. (This is known as the 'perfective' use of the preposition.) E.g.

λυω	I loose	θνησκω ⎫	I die
ἀπολυω	I release	ἀποθνησκω ⎭	

(There was probably originally a subtle distinction between θνησκω and ἀποθνησκω like the difference between 'die' and 'die off'. This distinction has now disappeared and ἀποθνησκω is the ordinary word for 'die'.)

(3) Those in which the presence of the preposition seems (in appearance at least) <u>completely to have altered</u> the sense of the verb, e.g.

γινωσκω	I know
ἀναγινωσκω	I read (the root meaning of ἀνα is 'up')

With compound verbs the <u>augment comes between the preposition and the verb</u>. Prepositions like ἀπο which end in a vowel, drop the vowel when another vowel immediately follows;[1] ἐκ becomes ἐξ.

Examples:

	Present	Imperfect
	ἀποθνησκω	ἀπεθνησκον
	ἐκβαλλω	ἐξεβαλλον
	ἀπαγω	ἀπηγον
but	περιπατεω	περιεπατουν (Vocab. 14)

---

[1] This applies to ἀνα, δια, ἐπι, κατα, μετα, παρα, ὑπο, but not to περι and προ. For the treatment of such prepositions when they are used as separate words, see Lesson 16.

55

EXERCISE 13

A

1. Ὁ Ἰησους παρελαμβανεν μικρα παιδια, και τα μικρα παιδια ηκουεν του Ἰησου.   2. οἱ ἁμαρτωλοι οὐχ ὑπηκουον τω προφητῃ.
3. Παυλος ἐδιδασκεν το εὐαγγελιον και ἐπιστευετε τοις λογοις.
4. ἀνεγινωσκεν ἐν τω βιβλιω του παλαιου νομου.   5. ὁ δε Χριστος φερει σταυρον και περισσευει ἐν ἀγαπῃ.   6. ὁ ἁγιος ἀγγελος ἠνοιγεν θυραν ἐν τοις οὐρανοις.   7. ὁ οὐν νεανιας ὁ πλουσιος ὑπηγεν εἰς τον ἰδιον οἰκον.   8. χαιρομεν ἐν Κυριω, ἀγει γαρ την ἐκκλησιαν εἰς την ἀληθειαν.   9. ὁ Χριστος ἐξεβαλλεν τους πονηρους ἐκ του ἱερου;   10. οἱ δικαιοι οὐ προσεφερον θυσιας ἐν ἑτερω ἱερω.
11. ἐκλαιομεν και ἐπροφητευομεν την ὀργην ἐξ οὐρανου.   12. το γαρ συνεδριον ἐπεγινωσκεν την σοφιαν της διδαχης της χηρας.
13. ἱματιον δε ὁ ἐργατης ἐνδυει το παιδιον και πειθει τους πρεσβυτερους παραβολῃ.   14. προσεφερομεν το ἀργυριον τω τελωνῃ, ἀλλ' ἐδιωκεν τους πλουσιους και τους πτωχους.   15. οἱ ἐχθροι του λαου ἀπεθνησκον ἐν φυλακῃ, ὁ δε κριτης ἀπελυεν ὀλιγους δουλους.   16. οὐκ ἐδιδασκεν τα τεκνα, οὐδε ἀπηγεν την ἰδιαν γενεαν ἀπο των ὁδων της ἀδικιας.

B

1. They were teaching the gospel to the disciples.   2. The virgins were departing from the house.   3. They were carrying the slave's boat to the sea.   4. The prophets used to teach the children in the houses.   5. You were offering honour to the Lord, O angels.
6. Hypocrite, you were obeying the crowd.   7. They were bringing the sheep together to the trees.   8. The child was reading the scriptures in the temple.   9. We were leading the soldiers away from the sea.   10. John the Baptist was not doing signs.   11. The Lord used to lead the disciples into the desert.   12. Therefore you were persuading the people.   13. The saints were rejoicing, but sin was abounding.   14. Was he throwing out demons?   15. We were receiving the head of James.   16. You were releasing the slaves.   17. They were weeping and dying, for they were not

hearing the Lord nor the promise.   18. Jesus was opening the eyes of the blind, and they were recognising their own friends.   19. He was pursuing the unbelieving widow.

LESSON 14

Demonstratives, ὅλος

For the next two lessons, re-read Introduction: English Grammar, Sections 5; 6 A (3) (6).

DEMONSTRATIVES

In both Greek and English οὗτος 'this' and ἐκεῖνος 'that' can be used as either demonstrative pronouns or demonstrative adjectives. They are used as pronouns in the sentence, 'This is that'; as adjectives in the sentence 'This prophet read that book'.

ἐκεῖνος ('that') is declined as follows:

		M.	F.	N.
Singular	N.	ἐκεῖνος	ἐκείνη	ἐκεῖνο
	A.	ἐκεῖνον	ἐκείνην	ἐκεῖνο
	G.	ἐκείνου	ἐκείνης	ἐκείνου
	D.	ἐκείνῳ	ἐκείνῃ	ἐκείνῳ
Plural	N.	ἐκεῖνοι	ἐκεῖναι	ἐκεῖνα
	A.	ἐκείνους	ἐκείνας	ἐκεῖνα
	G.	ἐκείνων	ἐκείνων	ἐκείνων
	D.	ἐκείνοις	ἐκείναις	ἐκείνοις

The endings, it will be noted, are exactly the same as the endings of ἀγαθός, except in the nominative and accusative singular neuter, where the ending is -o instead of -ον.

57

οὗτος ('this') is declined as follows:

		M.	F.	N.
Singular	N.	οὗτος	αὕτη	τουτο
	A.	τουτον	ταυτην	τουτο
	G.	τουτου	ταυτης	τουτου
	D.	τουτῳ	ταυτῃ	τουτῳ
Plural	N.	οὗτοι	αὗται	ταυτα
	A.	τουτους	ταυτας	ταυτα
	G.	τουτων	τουτων	τουτων
	D.	τουτοις	ταυταις	τουτοις

The irregularities of this declension are covered by three rules:

(1) The **endings** are the same as **the endings of ἐκεινος**.

(2) The **initial sound** (τ or rough breathing) is the same as **the initial sound of the definite article**.

(3) The first syllable can be either ου or αυ. It is not true, as might at first be supposed, that ου is used for masculine and neuter and αυ for feminine. The rule is:

Where there is an o in the ending, there is an o in the stem. Thus the nominative plural neuter is ταυτα, and the genitive plural feminine is τουτων.

In English we do not use the article with a demonstrative adjective. We say, 'This sheep'; not, 'The this sheep' or 'This the sheep'. But in Greek the noun always has the article and **οὗτος and ἐκεινος stand in the predicative position**. Thus:

This sheep: (1) τουτο το προβατον

or (2) το προβατον τουτο

In order to say 'This is the sheep', εἰμι must be used: τουτο ἐστιν το προβατον.

When a demonstrative stands by itself without any word expressed for it to agree with, a noun must be supplied in English. Thus οὗτος means 'this man', ἐκεινη 'that woman', ταυτα 'these things'.

ὅλος

ὅλος means 'whole'. Its use is similar to that of the demonstratives. To say 'the whole', the noun must again have the article and ὅλος be placed in the predicative position. But it is declined regularly, like ἀγαθος -η -ον.

Thus: The whole sheep: (1) ὅλον το προβατον
                              or   (2) το προβατον ὅλον

EXERCISE 14

A

1. Οὗτοι οἱ ἀνθρωποι ἀπεθνησκον ἐν τῃ ἐρημῳ. 2. ἐκεινα δε τα δενδρα ἐβαλλον εἰς την θαλασσαν. 3. αὗται ἐμενον ἐν τῳ πλοιῳ. 4. ὁ γαρ Θεος σωζει ταυτας ἀπο του πονηρου. 5. οὐ γαρ κρινομεν ταυτα. 6. ἐλεγομεν τας ἐπαγγελιας ταυτας ἐν τῃ ἐκκλησιᾳ; 7. ἐκεινοι δε ἐξεβαλλον δαιμονια. 8. ἐν ἐκεινῃ τῃ ἡμερᾳ ηὐλογουν την σοφιαν του Κυριου. 9. ἐν τῃ ὡρᾳ ἐκεινῃ ἐχαιρομεν. 10. τον δε οἰνον ἐλαμβανεν και ηὐχαριστει τῳ Θεῳ. 11. παρεκαλουμεν και ἐφωνουμεν, ἀλλ' οὐκ ἠκολουθουν. 12. ὅλος δε ὁ ὀχλος ἠδικει και οὐ διηκονει οὐδε προσεκυνει τῳ Θεῳ. 13. τα παιδια ἠσθενει, ἀλλ' ὁ πλουσιος περιεπατει ἐν ταις ὁδοις της ἀδικιας. 14. ὁ στρατιωτης ὁ πονηρος κρατει και δει τον ἐργατην τῳ δενδρῳ. 15. οἱ πτωχοι ἐγαμουν και κατῳκουν ἐν τῃ γῃ. 16. ὁ οὖν σοφος κυριος ἐλεει τους δικαιους και οἰκοδομει οἰκιας ταις χηραις. 17. ὅλη γαρ ἡ συναγωγη ἐδοκει ὁμοια προβατοις.

B

1. This woman was following the young man. 2. That evil servant used to bind his own son. 3. These elders seem blind. 4. The happy elder was calling the whole crowd. 5. This second brother therefore used to serve and worship God in a different temple. 6. The paralysed were walking, the rich were encouraging the poor, the strong were building houses for the elders, the whole people was giving thanks. 7. They marry and dwell in the village in peace and honour.[1] 8. He

[1] 'Peace' and 'honour' do not require the article here.

used to have mercy on the saints, for they were ill.   9. The devil takes hold of small children and injures the church.   10. For the Lord saves the souls of men from the evil one.   11. Love and truth are in the eternal kingdom of God.   12. And in that day we were hearing the gospel and casting out demons.

LESSON 15

αὐτος, ἑαυτον, ἀλλος, ἀλληλους
Imperfect of εἰμι

αὐτος

αὐτος, αὐτη, αὐτο is declined like ἐκεινος.

It has three uses:

(1) **Personal pronoun (third person).**

αὐτος	he	αὐτη	she	αὐτο	it
αὐτον	him	αὐτην	her	αὐτο	it
αὐτου	of him, his	αὐτης	of her, her	αὐτου	of it, its
αὐτῳ	to him	αὐτῃ	to her	αὐτῳ	to it

αὐτοι	αὐται	αὐτα	they
αὐτους	αὐτας	αὐτα	them
αὐτων	αὐτων	αὐτων	of them, their
αὐτοις	αὐταις	αὐτοις	to them

Examples:

(a) πεμπει αὐτους ἐκ του ἱερου. He is sending them out of the temple.

(b) οὑτοι εἰσιν οἱ οἰκοι αὐτου. These are his houses (the houses of him).

(c) αὐτος σωζει τον λαον. He saves the people.

In sentence (b) it will be seen that the genitive of the personal pronoun is used as a *possessive pronoun* ('his', 'her', 'its', 'their').[1]

[1] Personal and possessive pronouns of the first and second person are dealt with in Lesson 19.

In sentence (c) σωζει would of course sufficiently translate 'he saves' without the addition of αὐτος. Its inclusion would probably suggest some emphasis. It is to be noted, however, that in this case it is a personal pronoun, not an emphasising pronoun. An emphasising pronoun is linked with a noun.

(2) **Emphasising pronoun.** In this use αὐτος goes in the *predicative position.*

(a) αὐτος ὁ Κυριος
   or   } σωζει τον λαον   The Lord himself[1] saves the
(b) ὁ Κυριος αὐτος   people.

(3) **Identical adjective.** In this use αὐτος goes in the *attributive position.*

(a) ὁ αὐτος Κυριος
   or   } σωζει τον λαον   The same Lord saves the
(b) ὁ Κυριος ὁ αὐτος   people.

ἑαυτον

A **reflexive pronoun** is always in the predicate. It refers back to the subject of the sentence, the pronoun and the subject being the same person (or thing). There is therefore no nominative of the reflexive pronoun. Apart from this, the third person reflexive pronoun, ἑαυτον, is declined just like αὐτος.[2]

Singular	A.	ἑαυτον	ἑαυτην	ἑαυτο
	G.	ἑαυτου	ἑαυτης	ἑαυτου
	D.	ἑαυτῳ	ἑαυτῃ	ἑαυτῳ
Plural	A.	ἑαυτους	ἑαυτας	ἑαυτα
	G.	ἑαυτων	ἑαυτων	ἑαυτων
	D.	ἑαυτοις	ἑαυταις	ἑαυτοις

Examples:

ὁ Ἰησους οὐ σωζει ἑαυτον   Jesus does not save himself.
ὁ Ἰησους ἐπεγινωσκεν τουτο ἐν   Jesus was perceiving this in him-
   ἑαυτῳ   self.

[1] The emphasising pronoun will mean 'himself', 'herself', 'ourselves', etc. according to the context. An emphasising pronoun is occasionally linked with another pronoun, e.g. John 3. 28: 'you yourselves'. It can also be used with a verb whose subject is only expressed in the verb ending, e.g. 1 Cor. 9. 27: 'I myself'; cf. Ex. 15 c 5: 'we ourselves'.

[2] Reflexive pronouns of the first and second person are dealt with in Lesson 19.

ἄλλος

There are two ordinary words for 'other': ἕτερος and ἄλλος.[1] ἄλλος is declined like ἐκεινος:

ἄλλος   ἄλλη   ἄλλο

When it is used with a noun, however, it stands (not in the predicative position, like ἐκεινος, οὑτος and ὁλος but) in the attributive position. Thus:

The other sheep: (1) το ἄλλο προβατον

or   (2) το προβατον το ἄλλο.

ἀλλήλους

From ἄλλος is formed the **reciprocal pronoun** ἀλλήλους, 'one another'. ἀλλήλους of course has no nominative and no singular. The forms found in the New Testament are:

A. ἀλλήλους
G. ἀλλήλων
D. ἀλλήλοις

Examples:

φιλουμεν ἀλλήλους	We love one another.
φιλοι ἐσμεν ἀλλήλων	We are friends of one another.
γραφομεν ἐπιστολας ἀλλήλοις	We write letters to one another.

IMPERFECT OF εἰμι

The Imperfect tense of the verb 'to be' is as follows:

ἤμην	I was
ἠς or ἠσθα	you were
ἠν	he, she, it was
ἠμεν or ἠμεθα	we were
ἠτε	you were
ἠσαν	they were.

[1] In classical Greek ἕτερος is the correct word when speaking of *the other of two*, but in the New Testament this distinction between the two words has almost disappeared.

EXERCISE 15

A

1. Ἐθεωρουμεν τους οἰκους αὐτων.   2. οὑτος ἠν μαθητης Ἰωανου του βαπτιστου.   3. ἠμεν γαρ δουλοι της ἁμαρτιας.
4. ἠτε οὐν διακονοι του λαου.   5. οἱ υἱοι αὐτου ἠσαν κακοι.
6. αὑτη γαρ ἠν ἡ ἐντολη αὐτου.   7. αἱ λοιπαι της κωμης συνηγον τα προβατα αὐτων ἐν μεσῳ του ἀγρου.   8. αὐτος ὁ Ἰησους οὐ προσεκυνει ἀλλ' οἱ μαθηται αὐτου.   9. ἡ ζωη μενει ἐν αὐτοις.
10. ἐκεινοι ἠσαν ἑτεροι ἀρτοι και ἀλλο ποτηριον.   11. ἠς ὑποκριτης και ἠμεθα τυφλοι.   12. ἠμην ἀγαπητος, ἀλλ' ἐμισειτε ἀλληλους.   13. ἠσθα πονηρα.

B

Express in two different ways: 1. This face.   2. The whole face.
3. The face itself.   4. That face.   5. The same face.   6. The other face.   7. His own face.

Express in one way: 8. A different face.   9. The faces of one another.   10. They were persuading themselves.

C

1. In the beginning was the Word.[1]   2. This is the love of God.
3. The same disciples were giving thanks to the rich tax-collector.
4. You used to see her sons in the house.   5. We ourselves were receiving them into the other boat.   6. You were in the temple in those days.   7. This is eternal life.   8. They were holy and beloved.   9. Their children were in the assembly.   10. They were reading the Scriptures to one another in the synagogue.   11. These same Jews used to hear and follow their own prophets.   12. The Baptist himself used to teach his disciples.   13. Another child throws himself into the sea.

[1] Do not express the first article.

63

Cases, time, prepositions
Preparatory use of 'there' and 'it'

Re-read Lesson 10: Further uses of Accusative, Genitive and Dative.

CASES

We saw there how certain prepositions take or (as it is said) 'govern' certain cases. Prepositions do not, strictly speaking, 'govern' the cases of the nouns which they precede. The case is really the governing element in the expression; the preposition only serves to make clear the exact sense in which the case is used. This, at least, was true in the earlier history of the language, but as the language developed the prepositions mastered the cases. As the horse in the fable called in the man to help him against the stag, and allowed him to get on his back, so the cases called in the help of the prepositions, and then found themselves weakened or even destroyed. Nevertheless, it is important and helpful to try to understand as fully as possible the basic idea of the cases, for it at once brings together in an intelligible way uses which at first seem arbitrary.

TIME

Consider, for instance, the ways of expressing time.

(1) The *accusative* represents *extension* in time, just as it does extension in space. Therefore **time how long** is **accusative**,

> e.g. δυο ἡμερας (acc. pl.)   for two days
> μενουσιν την ἡμεραν ἐκεινην   they remain that day.

(2) The *genitive* represents the '*genus*' or *kind* of time. Take the sentence: 'He journeyed by day.' Which 'kind of time' did he have on his journey? He journeyed 'during the day-time'. **Time during which** is therefore **genitive**. So:

> ἡμερας   (gen. sing.).   by day

(3) The *dative* represents a <u>*place* or *point* in time</u> (a *locative* use). Therefore **time at which** is **dative**,

e.g.   τῇ τρίτῃ ἡμέρᾳ   on the third day.

None of these uses requires a preposition, though a preposition may on occasions be added as well, e.g. 'on the third day' could be translated ἐν τῇ τρίτῃ ἡμέρᾳ.

PREPOSITIONS WITH THREE CASES
παρά

Consider also the preposition παρα. παρα means 'beside', and it can take three possible cases: accusative, genitive or dative. When the meaning of παρα is combined with one of the meanings of the cases, we get the following results:

(1) **παρα** with **accusative** is motion **to beside** or **alongside**,
βαλλει αὐτο παρα την ὁδον   he throws it beside the way
περιπατει παρα την θαλασσαν   he walks beside the sea.

(2) **παρα** with **genitive** is motion **from beside**, an *ablative* use,
ἀνθρωπος παρα του Θεου   a man from God.

(3) **παρα** with **dative** is **rest beside**, a <u>*locative* use</u>,
μενουσιν παρ' αὐτῳ   they remain with him.

ἐπι

ἐπι, meaning 'upon', can also take three cases, but in the New Testament the distinctions between the uses of the cases have become blurred. The student, however, should use **accusative** if the idea is **motion-to-upon**, and **dative** (i.e. *locative*) if the idea is **rest upon**,

βαλλει ἀλλα ἐπι την γην
την καλην
μενει ἐπι τῃ πετρᾳ

he throws others on the good earth
he remains upon the rock.

One particular use of ἐπι with **genitive**, meaning **in the time of**, should be noted:

ἐπ' Ἡλειου του προφητου   in the time of Elijah the prophet.

PREPOSITIONS WITH TWO CASES [16]

With many prepositions the connection between the root idea of the case and the meaning of the preposition is no longer clear, and it is probably best simply to learn the meanings as a vocabulary. This applies to most of the words which follow.

PREPOSITIONS WITH TWO CASES

Six prepositions which can take either accusative or genitive are set out below, together with easy phrases which may help to fix their commonest meanings in the memory.

(1) διά

| Acc. | because of | δια τουτο | because of this |
| Gen. | through | δια του ἱερου | through the temple |

(2) μετά

| Acc. | after | μετα ταυτα | after these things |
| Gen. | with | μετ᾽ αὐτων | with them |

(3) ὑπέρ

| Acc. | above | ὑπερ τον διδασκαλον | above the teacher |
| Gen. | on behalf of | ὑπερ των προβατων | for the sheep |

(4) ὑπό

| Acc. | under | ὑπο ἐξουσιαν | under authority |
| Gen. | by | ὑπο του διαβολου | by the devil |

Note. ὑπο meaning *by* is used for an *agent* (i.e. a person), while the *dative* without a preposition is used for an *instrument* (i.e. a thing). See Lesson 10, and see further Lesson 17.

(5) κατα[1]

| Acc. | according to | κατα τον νομον | according to the law |
| Gen. | against | κατα της ψυχης | against the soul |

---

[1] The root meaning of κατα is 'down', but this is seldom found except in compound verbs, such as καταβαινω 'I go down' (Vocab. 25). There are many possible translations of κατα-with-accusative. Two additional common expressions are given in the vocabulary.

(6) περι is used in all the three English senses of 'about':

Acc. approximately περι την τριτην ὡραν about the third hour
round ὀχλος περι αὐτον a crowd round him
Gen. concerning περι των νεκρων concerning the dead

Some further prepositions which take only one case are given in the vocabulary. For revision purposes, Lesson 16 and the vocabulary should be used together.

PREPARATORY USE OF 'THERE' AND 'IT'

In English the word 'there' is sometimes used without any local force, but simply to show that the subject is going to follow the verb. This *preparatory 'there'* is not translated in Greek.

E.g. ἐστιν μισθος ἐν τοις οὐρανοις.
There is a reward in heaven.

Similarly with 'it'. With expressions like 'it is lawful', 'it is necessary', 'it is good', the subject follows the verb. 'It is lawful to heal on the sabbath' is equivalent to 'To-heal-on-the-sabbath is lawful'.

EXERCISE 16

p 64

A

1. Λαλουμεν κατα την ἀληθειαν. 2. ἠγον μετα των στρατιωτων ἡμερας. 3. ὁ διδασκαλος ἐστιν ὑπερ τον μαθητην. 4. ἡ αὐτη χηρα περιεπατει περι την κωμην. 5. ἐδιδασκον καθ' ἡμεραν ἐν τῳ ἱερῳ. 6. ὁ Κυριος ἐλαλει δια του προφητου αὐτου. 7. οὐκ ἐστε ὑπο νομον, ἀλλ' ὑπο την ἀγαπην. 8. ἀπεθνησκεν ἐπι τῳ θρονῳ Ἰσραηλ. 9. ἠν ἀγγελος παρα του Θεου. 10. περιπατουσιν μετ' ἀλληλων παρα την θαλασσαν. 11. ἠμεθα ἁμαρτωλοι ἐνωπιον του Θεου. 12. ἐμπροσθεν του ναου ἐστιν ὁ του κριτου θρονος. 13. προ ἐκεινης της ὡρας οὐκ ἐθεωρουν την δοξαν αὐτου οὐδε ἠκουον την φωνην αὐτου. 14. οἱ τελωναι συν ἀλλοις ἁμαρτωλοις ηὑρισκον σωτηριαν. 15. ἠν περι την τριτην ὡραν. 16. δι' ἀνθρωπον ἐστιν ὁ θανατος, ἀλλ' ὁ Χριστος τηρει τους ἰδιους μαθητας ἑως της παρουσιας αὐτου. 17. χωρις αὐτου ἀσθενουμεν.

B

1. They were departing privately to their own houses.   2. God was leading them through temptation until the last day.   3. God is for (i.e. on behalf of) his people, but the workmen of Satan are against the church.   4. The evil man is dead because of sin.   5. After this we used to speak to one another.   6. They know about clothes apart from the teaching of the book.   7. For I am a man under authority. 8. He is remaining with him this day.   9. He throws stones upon the fields of his enemy.   10. There were poor in Israel in the time of Elijah the prophet.   11. On the third day they were seeking a sign from him out of heaven.   12. The joy of salvation abounds apart from the law.

LESSON 17

The Passive voice of the Present and Imperfect Indicative
Agent and instrument

THE PASSIVE VOICE OF THE PRESENT AND
IMPERFECT INDICATIVE

Re-read Introduction: English Grammar, Section 13.

The Passive voice is formed in Greek by the use of inflections, and not by the use of the auxiliary verb 'to be' as in English.

The Passive of the Present and Imperfect Indicative of λυω is as follows:

Present Indicative Passive

λυομαι	I am being loosed
λυῃ	you are being loosed
λυεται	he is being loosed
λυομεθα	we are being loosed
λυεσθε	you are being loosed
λυονται	they are being loosed

68

Imperfect Indicative Passive

ἐλυομην	I was being loosed
ἐλυου	you were being loosed
ἐλυετο	he was being loosed
ἐλυομεθα	we were being loosed
ἐλυεσθε	you were being loosed
ἐλυοντο	they were being loosed

As in the case of the Active voice, a simple tense 'I am loosed', 'I was loosed', etc., will often be a sufficient translation.

The Present and Imperfect Indicative Passive of -εω verbs are entirely regular. The rules of contraction of Lesson 4 have to be applied, and the following forms of φιλεω result:

Present Indicative Passive

φιλεομαι	→ φιλουμαι	φιλεομεθα	→ φιλουμεθα
φιλεῃ	→ φιλῃ	φιλεεσθε	→ φιλεισθε
φιλεεται	→ φιλειται	φιλεονται	→ φιλουνται

Imperfect Indicative Passive

ἐφιλεομην	→ ἐφιλουμην	ἐφιλεομεθα	→ ἐφιλουμεθα
ἐφιλεου	→ ἐφιλου	ἐφιλεεσθε	→ ἐφιλεισθε
ἐφιλεετο	→ ἐφιλειτο	ἐφιλεοντο	→ ἐφιλουντο

AGENT AND INSTRUMENT

A verb in the Passive will often be followed by an *agent*. Consider the sentences:

ὁ ἀγγελος λυει τον ἀποστολον   The angel is loosing the apostle.

ὁ ἀποστολος λυεται ὑπο του ἀγγελου   The apostle is being loosed by the angel.

Both these sentences express the same idea, but they express it in different ways. It will be noticed that when a sentence with a verb in the active voice is turned into a sentence with a verb in the passive voice, as has been done in the sentences given above, the object of the first sentence, 'the apostle', becomes the subject of the second, while the subject of the first sentence, 'the angel', is introduced in English by the preposition 'by'.

But consider the sentence:

ὁ κοσμος τηρειται τῃ σοφιᾳ του Θεου.
The world is being kept by the wisdom of God.

It will be seen that the *form* of this sentence is the same in English as that of the second sentence given above. In Greek, however, the sentences are not the same in form: the *preposition followed by a genitive* is used in the one sentence, and a simple *dative* in the other. This is because the doer of the action in the first sentence is a living person, i.e. 'the angel'; but the thing that does the action in the second sentence is not a living person, but 'wisdom'. The former is spoken of as the *agent*; the latter as the *instrument*.[1] It is possible to have both agent and instrument with the same verb, e.g.

ὁ ἀποστολος λυεται ὑπο του ἀγγελου λογῳ
The apostle is being loosed by the angel by (*or*, with) a word.

EXERCISE 17

These exercises are designed to give further practice in the use of the Passive and of prepositions. There is no new vocabulary. This is a suitable point for a thorough revision of the vocabularies so far learnt.

A

1. Ἐπεμπεσθε ὑπο των διδασκαλων προς ἑτερον ὀχλον.   2. ἐν τουτῳ τῳ τοπῳ ἐθεωρουμεν τοις ὀφθαλμοις τον Κυριον των οὐρανων. 3. οὑτοι οἱ λογοι ἐλαλουντο ὑπο των ἀποστολων ἐνωπιον των πρεσβυτερων.   4. τα δε προβατα ἐδιωκετο λιθοις ὑπο των παιδιων.   5. ἐπεμπομεθα μετα των προφητων ἐμπροσθεν του ὀχλου.   6. δια τουτο ἐπειθου τοις λογοις των κριτων.   7. προ τουτων οἱ τελωναι ἐδιδασκοντο συν τοις νεανιαις.   8. οἱ υἱοι αὐτοι ἠσθιον τους αὐτους ἀρτους.   9. τυφλε ὑποκριτα, οὐ περιπατεις κατα τας ὁδους του νομου.   10. σταυρος ἐποιειτο ὑπο των ἐργατων ἑκαστῳ ἁγιῳ ἐν Ἱεροσολυμοις.   11. οἱ φιλοι ἐπεμπον

---

[1] As we saw on p. 45, n. 1, what we now call the dative was originally three separate cases: dative, locative and instrumental.

ὀλίγους ἄρτους πρὸς ἀλλήλους, καὶ ὀλίγον οἶνον καὶ ἱκανὸν ἀργύριον
πρὸς τοὺς ἀξίους ἀδελφοὺς¹ ἐν φυλακῇ.   12. ὦ Ἰερουσαλημ, οὐχ
εὑρίσκῃ πιστη, εἶ γὰρ κατὰ τῆς ἀληθειας.   13. παρεκαλουμεθα
τοις λογοις τῆς διαθηκης ἐν ἐκεινῳ τῳ χρονῳ.²   14. ἠγομεν τὰς
καθαρας θυσιας δια του ἱερου ὀπισω των πλουσιων του συνεδριου.
15. μετ᾽ ἐκεινας τὰς ἡμερας οἱ λοιποι στρατιωται ὑπηγον ἐξω τῆς
κωμης.   16. ἐκλαιετε ὑπερ των ἀπιστων καὶ των ἀκαθαρτων.

B

1. The word of God was being read by the apostles.   2. The tomb
was being built under the temple.   3. Because of this the judges were
being persuaded by the faithful teachers.   4. You were leading the
people after the beloved prophet through the desert to Jerusalem.
5. After this they were being sought for by the whole crowd.   6. The
stones were upon the earth above the river.   7. The throne was being
carried by the workmen to another place beside the house.   8. The
world was being made through the Son of God.   9. O hypocrite, you
are not speaking about the commandments of the Lord.   10. The
young men themselves were being taught by their own teachers.
11. Therefore after these things we used to speak the word of God to
the disciples.   12. You were being roused³ by the powerful words of
the prophet's anger.

¹ A more polished Greek would add an article here: τους ἐν φυλακῃ—'the
ones ἐν φυλακῃ' or 'who were ἐν φυλακῃ'. The article can be used with a prepositional phrase as with an attributive adjective. But Koiné Greek is not so
particular. Cf. οἱ ἀγγελοι ἐν οὐρανῳ (Mark 13. 32).
² See Lesson 16, 'Time at which'.
³ Use ἐγειρω.

LESSON 18

The relative pronoun
The Present Imperative
Questions

For the next two lessons, re-read Introduction: English Grammar, Sections 5 (9), 14 (2), 18.

THE RELATIVE PRONOUN

The relative pronoun is the same in form as the endings of ἐκεῖνος with rough breathings added:

		M.	F.	N.	M., F.	N.
Singular	N.	ὅς	ἥ	ὅ[1]	who, that	which, that
	A.	ὅν	ἥν	ὅ	whom, that	which, that
	G.	οὗ	ἧς	οὗ	whose, of whom	of which
	D.	ᾧ	ᾗ	ᾧ	to whom	to which
Plural	N.	οἵ	αἵ	ἅ	who, that	which, that
	A.	οὕς	ἅς	ἅ	whom, that	which, that
	G.	ὧν	ὧν	ὧν	whose, of whom	of which
	D.	οἷς	αἷς	οἷς	to whom	to which

The relative pronoun always refers back to some noun or pronoun, expressed or implied, in another clause. This noun or pronoun is called its _antecedent_.

In Greek the relative pronoun agrees with its antecedent in number and gender, but not necessarily in case. The case of a relative pronoun

---

[1] It will be noticed that the forms ὁ ἡ οἱ αἱ occur in the declension of both relative pronoun and definite article. When a word of this form is found it is usually obvious from the context which part of speech it is. But this is a case where a knowledge of accents will often help one to identify the part of speech more quickly. In an accented text the _relatives_ always _have an accent_ (usually grave, though occasionally acute), whereas the _articles_ almost always _do not have one_. (There are rare occasions when the article has an accent, e.g. Acts 1. 13.) We shall always print the relatives ἥ ὅ (neut.) οἵ αἵ with a grave accent, and the article ὁ (masc.) ἡ οἱ αἱ without.

depends on the function which it performs in the *relative clause* in which it stands.

Examples:

(1) βλεπω τους πρεσβυτερους οἳ ἀκολουθουσιν
I see the elders who are following.

In this example πρεσβυτερους is in the accusative case because it is the object of the clause in which it stands. οἳ is in the nominative case because it is the subject of the clause in which it stands. The student should carefully consider the reason for the cases of the relative pronouns in the examples which follow:

(2) οἱ δουλοι οὓς πεμπετε φωνουσιν
The slaves that you are sending are calling.

(3) αὑτη ἐστιν ἡ γραφη ἣ τηρειται ἐν τη συναγωγη
This is the writing that is kept in the synagogue.

(4) αὑτη ἐστιν ἡ γραφη ἣν εἰχεν ὁ ἀποστολος — ℵB.
This is the writing which the apostle used to have.

(5) τα παιδια ἁ ἐδιδασκον κλαιει
The children whom I was teaching are weeping.

(6) ὁ προφητης οὗ ἀναγινωσκεις τα βιβλια ἁγιος ἐστιν
The prophet whose books you are reading is holy.

(7) οἱ νεανιαι οἷς ποιω τουτο δουλοι εἰσιν
The young men for whom I am doing this are slaves.

The relative clauses in the examples given above are all **adjective clauses**, because they qualify and explain their antecedents just like adjectives.

The antecedent of the relative pronoun is often unexpressed,

e.g. ὁς οὐ λαμβανει τον σταυρον αὑτου, οὐκ ἐστιν ἀξιος (Matt. 10. 38)
He who does not take his cross, is not worthy.

THE PRESENT IMPERATIVE

All the forms of verbs which have been given so far have been in the Indicative mood, the mood which is generally used in making statements or asking questions.

The Imperative mood is used to express commands, exhortations and entreaties.

The forms of the Present Imperative are as follows:

		Present Imperative Active		Present Imperative Passive	
Singular	2	λυε	loose	λυου	be loosed
	3	λυετω	let him loose	λυεσθω	let him be loosed
Plural	2	λυετε	loose	λυεσθε	be loosed
	3	λυετωσαν	let them loose	λυεσθωσαν	let them be loosed

It will be noticed that, apart from the second person singular, the final letters of both conjugations are the same: -ω, -ε, -ωσαν. These terminations are found in *all* Imperative conjugations. Therefore, once the Present Imperative Active has been learnt, it is only necessary to learn the singular of other Imperative tenses. The plural forms follow automatically.

The Present Imperative of -εω verbs is entirely regular:

φιλεε	→ φιλει	φιλεου	→ φιλου
φιλεετω	→ φιλειτω	φιλεεσθω	→ φιλεισθω
φιλεετε	→ φιλειτε	φιλεεσθε	→ φιλεισθε
φιλεετωσαν	→ φιλειτωσαν	φιλεεσθωσαν	→ φιλεισθωσαν

The meaning of the Present Imperative

As we saw in Lesson 13, the Present is a *linear tense*, which can be represented either by a line

_____

or by a line of dots

. . . .

Therefore, as would be expected, the Present Imperative denotes a command or entreaty to *continue* to do an action, or to do it *repeatedly*.

It is not always possible to bring this out in translating a Present Imperative into English, as we have no convenient form of expression which is equivalent to it. An attempt to express in full the force of the Greek Present Imperative is made in the translation of the following examples, though it should be remembered that such translations are usually over-translations.

βαλλετε τους λιθους   Keep on throwing the stones.
τηρειτω τας ἐντολας   Let him continue to keep the commandments.

74

Imperatives in the negative

A verb in the Imperative is negatived by μη instead of οὐ, and by μηδε instead of οὐδε.[1]

Example:

μη περιπατει ἐν ταις ὁδοις της ἀδικιας, μηδε χαιρε συν τοις ἀκαθαρτοις
Do not (continue to) walk in the ways of unrighteousness, nor rejoice with the unclean.

QUESTIONS

μη (or μητι) is also used in hesitant questions, or in questions which expect the answer 'No'.

οὐ (or οὐχι) is used in questions which expect the answer 'Yes'. There are therefore four types of direct question:

(1) **Ordinary questions.** ἐστιν ὁ Χριστος; means 'Is he the Christ?'

(2) **Hesitant questions.** μη (or μητι) ἐστιν ὁ Χριστος; can either mean: 'Is he perhaps (or, Can it be that he is) the Christ?', or it can belong to:

(3) **Questions expecting the answer 'No'.** 'He is not the Christ, is he?', cf. μητι ἐγω Ἰουδαιος; (John 18. 35) 'Am I a Jew?'

(4) **Questions expecting the answer 'Yes'.** οὐκ (or οὐχι) ἐστιν ὁ Χριστος; means 'He is the Christ, isn't he?' This last differs from the ordinary negative *statement* only by the presence of a question-mark (or, in the spoken language, by the tone of voice). οὐκ ἐστιν ὁ Χριστος. means 'He is not the Christ'.

EXERCISE 18

A

1. Λαμβανε το ποτηριον και χαιρε ἐν τουτῳ τῳ δευτερῳ σημειῳ της δικαιοσυνης, της εἰρηνης και της ζωης.   2. ἡ ἀρχη της ἐξουσιας ἐστιν ᾗ δοκει ὁμοια νεῳ οἰνῳ.   3. διο ζητειτε το προσωπον του Κυριου ἐν προσευχη ἐν τοις σαββατοις.   4. ἐν καιρῳ πειρασμου προσφερετε την θυσιαν της μετανοιας και ποιειτε ἐργα της ὑπομονης.   5. βλεπεσθωσαν ὑπο των σοφων.   6. ἐγειρου ἐκ των νεκρων.

---

[1] μη is in fact used regularly with everything except the Indicative, as will be seen when the Infinitive, Participle, Subjunctive and Optative are reached.

7. θεραπευεσθε τη προσευχη.   8. ὦ Κυριε, θεραπευε τον δεξιον ὀφθαλμον του ἐλευθερου διακονου.   9. οὐχι ἡ πρωτη ἠν ἐσχατη; 10. οἱ νεκροι μη εἰσιν μακαριοι;   11. μητι ἐκαλει κακους εἰς τον φοβον του Θεου;   12. ὁ ἁγιος εὐλογεισθω.   13. πειθου ὑπο των πρεσβυτερων· μη ὑπακουε τοις νεανιαις.   14. ἀνοιγετε ἑκαστην θυραν, τουτο γαρ ἐστιν δυνατον παρα τω Θεω.   15. την δικαιοσυνην ἐνδυετε την καρδιαν[1] και θυσιαι προσφερεσθωσαν ἐν μεσω του ναου.   16. μη κρινεσθω μηδε ἀδικεισθω.

B

1. Therefore let it be thrown beside the way.   2. Be loosed from sin daily.   3. Be saved from the authority of evil men.   4. Let the commandments themselves be kept.   5. Let him be led away to the council of Satan.   6. Let not the clean dwell in the midst of sin, nor unclean hearts have joy in the rewards of the rich.   7. There was a beautiful boat upon the sea, but the people did not have money for it. 8. Let the teacher who is worthy of honour believe the book and worship God.   9. There is a new opportunity for the rest who remain. 10. The virgins who were eating the bread were not judging themselves. 11. Hypocrite, repent and hate the sins which you are doing. 12. Young man, hear the promises which I am making with my own tongue.   13. Let them take the teaching of the new covenant and bear witness to the only head of the everlasting kingdom.   14. Can it be that the small are strong?   15. Is not a little wine sufficient for an unbelieving generation?   16. They were following sinners, for they were like sheep.

REVISION TESTS 2

The student should not proceed further until he can get high marks in these tests.

Allow 1 hour each for Tests A and B. The total number of marks for each Test is 80; the marks for each question are shown in square brackets.

[1] ἐνδυω in the active takes a double accusative. The piece of clothing used and the person or thing clothed are both put in the accusative.

A

1. Give the nominative singular, and the ending (only) of the genitive singular, of the Greek words for: beginning, child (2 words), cloud, covenant, desert, eye, face, friend, honour, judge, kingdom, life (2), place, prayer, reward, sacrifice, salvation, sea, servant, sinner, stone, temptation, tomb, tongue, truth, virgin, voice, widow, wine, work, world, young man. [16 marks]

2. Give the nominative singular masculine, and the endings of the nominative singular feminine and neuter, of the Greek words for: beautiful, beloved, clean, different, eternal, evil, faithless, first, free, last, little, new (2), old, only, poor, possible, remaining, second, small, worthy. [10]

3. Give the Greek for the following, writing -εω verbs in their un-contracted forms: I ask, I bring, I build, I call (2), I depart, I find, I hate, I make, I raise, I read, I seek, I take. [6]

4. Decline in the singular (masculine, feminine and neuter): μακαριος, ὁς. [4]

5. (a) List the seven words which have the -o ending in the neuter singular. [4] (b) What word (in addition to the demonstratives) is always put in the predicative position? [1] (c) Parse ὁ and ὁ. [2]

6. Give the Present Indicative of εἰμι. [1]

7. Give the Present Imperative Active and the Imperfect Indicative Passive of λυω. [2]

8. Give the three rules of contraction of -εω verbs. [3]

9. Give the Greek for: I used to have, I was inhabiting, I used to lead away, I used to have mercy on, I was putting on, I used to serve, I used to throw out, I was walking. [8]

10. Describe the three main case ideas now expressed by the dative. [3]

11. Give two uses of δια, ὑπερ and ὑπο and four uses of κατα. [10]

12. Repeat Exercise 15 B. [10]

B

1. Give the nominative singular, and the ending (only) of the genitive singular, of the Greek words for: anger, boat, brother, commandment,

77

cross, crowd, cup, death, door, fear, fruit, garment, glory, guard, head, heart, hour, house (2 words), joy, law, money, people, place, price, promise, righteousness, Scripture, sign, soul, tax-collector, way, workman. [16 marks]

2. Give the nominative singular masculine, and the nominative singular feminine and neuter (endings only), of the Greek words for: alone, believing, blind, dead, each, good (2), happy, holy, just, like, other (2), powerful, rich, right, small, strong, sufficient, third, unclean, young. [10]

3. Give the Greek for the following, writing -εω verbs in their uncontracted forms: I bless, I do, I eat, I go, I heal, I keep, I look at, I obey, I perceive, I receive, I repent, I say. [6]

4. Decline in full in the plural: οὗτος. [3]

5. Give the Imperfect of εἰμι (including alternative forms). [2]

6. Give the Present Imperative Passive and the Imperfect Indicative Active of φιλεω. [2]

7. Give in tabular form the eight rules for initial vowel changes in the formation of past tenses. [4]

8. List the five verbs (with their meanings) which usually take the dative. [2]

9. Describe the two main case ideas now expressed by the genitive. [2]

10. How are the cases used in expressions of time? [3]

11. Give one way of expressing 'in the time of', 'apart from'; two ways of expressing 'until', 'after'; three ways of expressing 'to', 'before'; and four ways of expressing 'with'. [16]

12. How are questions expressed? [4]

13. Repeat Exercise 15B. [10]

LESSON 19

Personal, possessive and reflexive pronouns

Re-read Introduction: English Grammar, Sections 5, 6A (4).
In Lesson 15 we dealt with αὐτος and ἑαυτον, which are pronouns of
the third person. We now come to pronouns of the first and second
person.

PERSONAL PRONOUNS

ἐγω	I		συ	you
ἐμε, με	me		σε	you
ἐμου, μου	of me, my		σου	of you, your
ἐμοι, μοι	to *or* for me		σοι	to *or* for you
ἡμεις	we		ὑμεις	you
ἡμας	us		ὑμας	you
ἡμων	of us, our		ὑμων	of you, your
ἡμιν	to *or* for us		ὑμιν	to *or* for you

In Greek it is not necessary to say: ἐγω λυω because the personal
ending of the verb sufficiently shows the person and number of the
subject without the addition of a pronoun. The nominative of the
personal pronouns therefore often suggests some emphasis:

> οὐχ ὡς ἐγω θελω, ἀλλ' ὡς συ (Matt. 26. 39)
> Not as I will, but as you will.

The longer forms of the first person singular ἐμε, ἐμου, ἐμοι tend to
be used for emphasis and they are normal with prepositions.[1]

Further ways of expressing the third person personal pronoun

We have already seen two ways of expressing 'he', 'she', 'it', etc.:

(1) αὐτος. (See Lesson 15. This is far the commonest use.)

(2) οὗτος and ἐκεινος sometimes have this weakened sense. (See
Vocab. 14.)

---

[1] But with προς and with the adverb-prepositions ἐνωπιον, ἐμπροσθεν, ὀπίσω,
the shorter forms (με, μου) are usual.

Examples:

οὗτος ἦν ἐν ἀρχῃ (John 1. 2)   He was in the beginning (R.S.V.).

λεγουσιν αὐτῃ ἐκεινοι (John 20. 13)   They say to her.

(3) There is a third way: the article followed by δε. This is most commonly used in narrative to begin a sentence which introduces a new subject. Thus Mark 16. 5, 6 reads:

They were amazed. And *he* says to them   ὁ δε λεγει αὐταις.

μεν AND δε

Words are often contrasted by the use of the two particles μεν and δε: 'on the one hand...on the other hand...'. (This is usually a clumsy over-translation. It is often sufficient to leave μεν untranslated and to translate simply 'but'.) The following is an example of μεν and δε used with a personal pronoun:

’Εγω μεν εἰμι Παυλου, ’Εγω δε ’Απολλω (1 Cor. 1. 12)
I (on the one hand) am of Paul, I (on the other hand) am of Apollos.

μεν and δε can also be used to express 'some...others...'. In this case the plural article is followed by μεν in the first clause and by δε in the second:

οἱ μεν ἦσαν συν τοις ’Ιουδαιοις, οἱ δε συν τοις ἀποστολοις (Acts 14. 4)
Some were with the Jews, and others with the apostles.

POSSESSIVE PRONOUNS AND ADJECTIVES

The usual way of expressing the possessive is by use of the genitive of the personal pronoun:

μου	my	σου	your
ἡμων	our	ὑμων	your

There are, however, possessive adjectives, and these often carry some emphasis. In common use are:

ἐμος -η -ον	my	σος -η -ον	your

80

When used attributively they take the article:

παρακαλω σε περι του ἐμου τεκνου (Philemon 10)
I beseech you for (concerning) my child.
ἡ ἐμη διδαχη οὐκ ἐστιν ἐμη (John 7. 16)
My teaching is not mine.

We have already seen (in Lesson 15) that αὐτου 'his', 'its', αὐτης 'her', and αὐτων 'their' do the work of the third person possessive adjective.

REFLEXIVE PRONOUNS

Singular

As we have seen in the case of ἑαυτον, reflexive pronouns can have no nominative forms. The first and second persons also of course have no neuter forms.

In the singular they are made up of a combination of ἐμε and σε with αὐτος, giving:

ἐμαυτον -ην	myself	σεαυτον -ην	yourself
ἐμαυτου -ης		σεαυτου -ης	
ἐμαυτῳ -ῃ		σεαυτῳ -ῃ	

ἐγω ἀπ' ἐμαυτου λαλω (John 7. 17)
I speak from myself.
συ περι σεαυτου μαρτυρεις (John 8. 13)
You bear witness concerning yourself.

Plural

In the plural, ἑαυτους does duty for the first and second persons ('ourselves', 'yourselves') as well as for the third person ('themselves'):

μαρτυρειτε ἑαυτοις (Matt. 23. 31)
You bear witness to yourselves.

EXERCISE 19

A

1. Κρατειτε ἐμε, Λαε 'Ιουδαιας, και σωζετε ἑαυτους ἐκ ταυτης της πονηρας γενεας. 2. διηκονουν σοι και ἐδουν ἑαυτους τῃ αἰωνιῳ διαθηκῃ σου. 3. ᾠκοδομουμεν οἰκιας ὑμιν ἐξω της κωμης παρα

τῳ ποταμῳ.   4. τα προβατα τα ἐμα ἀκουει τον λογον τον ἐμον
και τηρει αὐτον.   5. ὁ λογος ὁ σος ἀληθεια ἐστιν.   6. ἐγω γαρ
οὐ μονον ἀσθενω, ἀλλα καθ' ἡμεραν ἀποθνησκω.   7. ὁ μεν το
βιβλιον ἀναγινωσκει, ἐγω δε ὑπακουω αὐτῳ.   8. ἡμεις μεν
ἐπεγινωσκομεν την ἀληθειαν, οἱ δε ἐδιωκον τους πιστους.   9. κἀγω
προσφερω θυσιας, ἁς παραλαμβανει ὁ Θεος.   10. ὁ δε οἰκος μου
ἠν οἰκος προσευχης.   11. κἀκεινος γαμει την μακαριαν παρθενον.
12. συ περι σεαυτου μαρτυρεις. ἡ μαρτυρια σου ἐστιν ἀκαθαρτος.
13. ἐγω δε οὐκ ἐλαλουν ἐξ ἐμαυτου.   14. κἀγω εἰμι ἐν μεσῳ
ὑμων ὡς διακονος.   15. μη ποιειτε την δικαιοσυνην ὑμων
ἐμπροσθεν των ἀνθρωπων, ὡσπερ οἱ ὑποκριται ποιουσιν ἐν ταις
συναγωγαις.   16. ὑμεις οὐκ ἐστε ἐκ του κοσμου καθως ἐγω οὐκ
εἰμι ἐκ του κοσμου.   17. ὁ διδασκαλος ὁς οὐκ ἐστιν μετ' ἐμου
κατ' ἐμου ἐστιν.   18. οἱ μεν πειθουσιν, οἱ δε παρακαλουσιν μονον.

B

Where words are in italics, express the personal pronoun separately.

1. *We* were calling and weeping, but *you* used not to have mercy upon
us.   2. It used to seem wise to me, but *they* followed a different way.
3. Lord, have mercy upon us day by day until your second coming.
4. My teaching is not mine.   5. They take hold of Jesus and injure
him.   6. But *he* used to say, 'Hypocrite, depart from me'.   7. And
this is the sign of your coming.   8. Prayer is being made by me and
by your people.   9. You love your enemy as yourself.   10. Are
you saying this about yourself?   11. And *I* have soldiers under
myself.   12. I am not as[1] the rest of men.   13. According as I
hear I judge.   14. Love one another as I love you.   15. But *he*
says to us, 'Bring the poor to me'.   16. Some were being released,
others were dying.   17. And your prayers are being heard.   18. Some
were slaves, but others were free.

[1] Use ὡσπερ.

δυναμαι

Present Infinitive

Uses of the infinitive

Re-read Introduction: English Grammar, Section 14 (4), 19; also Lesson 16 for the use of the preparatory 'it'.

δυναμαι

δυναμαι 'I am able' is conjugated as follows:

Present Indicative		Imperfect Indicative		Infinitive	
δυναμαι	I am able	[1] ἐδυναμην	I was able	δυνασθαι	to be able
δυνασαι		ἐδυνασο			
δυναται		ἐδυνατο			
δυναμεθα		ἐδυναμεθα			
δυνασθε		ἐδυνασθε			
δυνανται		ἐδυναντο			

[1] The Imperfect sometimes has a lengthened augment: ἠδυναμην.

The endings of these conjugations are almost the same as those of the Present and the Imperfect Indicative Passive of λυω, though they are in a slightly more primitive form. In δυναμαι the fact that -μαι and -σαι are personal endings related to με and σε becomes obvious. δυνα-μαι, δυνα-σαι is '(am) able I', '(are) able you'. The structure of λυ-ο-μαι and ἐ-λυ-ο-μην is properly: (augment) (ἐ), stem (λυ), variable vowel (ο or ε), personal ending. In the second person singular the σ has dropped out and contractions have taken place:

λυ-ο-μαι	ἐ-λυ-ο-μην
λυ-ε-(σ)αι → ῃ	ἐ-λυ-ε-(σ)ο → ου
λυ-ε-ται	ἐ-λυ-ε-το
λυ-ο-μεθα	ἐ-λυ-ο-μεθα
λυ-ε-σθε	ἐ-λυ-ε-σθε
λυ-ο-νται	ἐ-λυ-ο-ντο

We have seen ε+ο→ ου in Lesson 4. ε+α→η and ε+αι→η are regular contractions. For further examples, see γενη (Lesson 29), ἀληθη (Lesson 30).

THE PRESENT INFINITIVE

The forms of the present infinitives of λυω, φιλεω and εἰμι are as follows:

Active		Passive	
λυειν	to loose	λυεσθαι	to be loosed
φιλειν	to love	φιλεισθαι	to be loved
	εἰναι	to be	

USES OF THE INFINITIVE

Infinitive used as subject or object

The infinitive is a **neuter verbal noun**.

As a noun it may stand as the subject or object of another verb:

Subject   ἐξεστιν θεραπευειν ἐν τῳ σαββατῳ
It is lawful to heal on the Sabbath.

Object   παραγγελλει (Vocab. 26) τον Παυλον ἀγεσθαι καθ᾽ ἡμεραν
He commands Paul to be brought daily.

As a verb it has <u>tense and voice</u> and it may have an object. It is often said to have a subject. The so-called 'subject' of the infinitive does not conform to the rule in Lesson 5 that the subject of the verb is put in the nominative. **The 'subject' of the infinitive is put in the accusative**. In the sentence above, τον Παυλον (accusative) is used with ἀγεσθαι. Similarly, we have:

δει ἀνθρωπον ἐσθιειν
A man must eat (it is necessary for a man to eat),

where ἀνθρωπον (accusative) is used with ἐσθιειν.

καλον ἐστιν ἡμας εἰναι μετ᾽ αὐτου
It is good (for) us to be with him,

where ἡμας (accusative) is used with εἰναι.

Though it is usual to describe this accusative as the subject of the infinitive, it is not strictly correct. It is really what is known as an *adverbial accusative* or an *accusative of general reference* or an *accusative of respect*.

He commands *in respect to Paul* a being brought ('to be brought').

In respect to a man eating ('to eat') is necessary.

In respect to us it is good to be with him.

Nonetheless it is convenient to call it loosely the 'subject'.

ἐξεστιν, 'it is lawful', and παραγγελλω, 'I command' are apparent exceptions to this rule, since they take a dative, even with an infinitive. Thus:

ἐξεστιν αὐτοις θεραπευειν ἐν τῳ σαββατῳ

It is lawful *for them* to heal on the Sabbath.

παραγγελλει αὐτοις τον Παυλον ἀγειν

He commands *them* to bring Paul.

But in these cases the αὐτοις belongs to the main verb, and no accusative of respect is called for.

Infinitives with the negative

Infinitives (like Imperatives) are negatived by μη.

Consequence clauses

The accusative and infinitive introduced by ὡστε is often used to express the result of the action of the main verb,

e.g. ὡστε μη χρειαν ἐχειν ἡμας λαλειν (1 Thess. 1. 8)

So that we have no need to speak.

The articular infinitive

The infinitive's character as a noun is seen particularly clearly when a (neuter) article is placed in front of it. ὁ ἡ το

This 'articular infinitive' is frequently used in connection with a preposition, the preposition and infinitive together making a phrase which can generally best be translated by an adverbial clause in English. As this form of expression is quite unlike English, the examples below and in Exercises 20 and 21 should be studied with particular care, because it is a very common usage in Greek.

Examples:

(1) **ἐν** *followed by the dative* of the articular infinitive can express the **time at which** something occurs. It will usually be translated 'while' or 'when'.

ἐν δε τῷ ὑπαγειν αὐτον οἱ ὀχλοι συνεπνιγον αὐτον (Luke 8. 42)
And while he was departing the crowds thronged him.

(2) **προ** *followed by the genitive*, meaning **before**:
εἰχον προ του τον κοσμον εἰναι παρα σοι (John 17. 5)
(The glory which) I had with you before the world was.

(3) **μετα** *followed by the accusative*, meaning **after**:
μετα το παραδοθηναι[1] τον Ἰωανην (Mark 1. 14)
After John was arrested.

(4) **δια** *followed by the accusative*, meaning **because**:
δια το εἰναι φιλον (Luke 11. 8)
Because he is a friend.

Purpose clauses

The infinitive can be used in three ways to express purpose. (The first introduces us to new meanings of εἰς and προς.)

(1) **εἰς** or **προς** *followed by the accusative* of the articular infinitive:

ἐζητουν κατα του Ἰησου μαρτυριαν εἰς το θανατωσαι[2] αὐτον (Mark 14. 55)
They were seeking witness against Jesus, in order to kill him.

εἰς το δυνασθαι ἡμας παρακαλειν (2 Cor. 1. 4)
(Who encourages us) so that we may be able to encourage.

προς το δυνασθαι ὑμας (Eph. 6. 11)
(Put on the whole armour of God) that you may be able (to stand).

(2) **Purpose can also be expressed by the infinitive alone.** (The following examples contain words and constructions which have not yet been dealt with, but the force of the infinitive is just the same in the Greek as in the English):

[1] First Aorist Infinitive Passive of παραδιδωμι, see Lesson 42.
[2] Aorist Infinitive, see Lessons 24, 40. This could be expressed more literally: 'with a view to the killing him'.

ἤλθομεν προσκυνησαι αὐτῳ (Matt. 2. 2)
We have come *to worship* him.
μη νομισητε ὁτι ἠλθον καταλυσαι τον νομον (Matt. 5. 17)
Do not think that I have come *to destroy* the law.
ὑπαγω ἁλιευειν (John 21. 3)
I am going off *to fish*.

✓ (3) Quite commonly του (the genitive of the definite article) is inserted before the infinitive, without in any way affecting the sense.

μελλει γαρ Ἡρῳδης ζητειν το παιδιον του ἀπολεσαι αὐτο (Matt. 2. 13)
For Herod is about to seek the child *to destroy* him.

EXERCISE 20

A

1. Ἠθελον διωκειν ἡμας ἑως (ἀχρι) της ἐσχατης ὡρας.   2. αἱ νεφελαι ὑπαγουσιν και αἱ ψυχαι των ἀνθρωπων θελουσιν εὐχαριστειν. 3. μελλω πειθειν τους ἀξιους πρεσβυτερους κατοικειν χωρις των ἁμαρτωλων.   4. ἐδυνασθε σοφους φιλους ἐχειν;   5. διδασκαλε, δει ἡμας πιστευειν.   6. ἠθελομεν οὐν θεραπευειν τους υἱους αὐτων.   7. ἐξεστιν ἡμιν παραλαμβανειν την βασιλειαν των οὐρανων;   8. ἐπεμπεν τους δουλους αὐτου καλειν τους πτωχους και τους τυφλους.   9. ὁ γαρ Θεος πεμπει τον υἱον αὐτου σωζειν τον κοσμον.   10. παρεκαλουμεν τον λαον ὑπακουειν τοις προφηταις.   11. οἱ δε ὀχλοι ἐχαιρον ἐν τῳ αὐτους ἀκουειν και βλεπειν τα σημεια ἁ ἐποιει.   12. προ του αὐτους ὑπαγειν ὁ Πετρος ἠσθιεν μετ᾽ αὐτων.   13. και δια το περισσευειν την ἀδικιαν ἡ ἀγαπη ἀποθνησκει;   14. ὁ ἀνεμος ἠν ἰσχυρος ὡστε βαλλειν το πλοιον ἐπι τας πετρας.   15. το δε περιπατειν ἐν ταις ὁδοις αὐτου ἀγαθον ἐστιν τοις υἱοις των ἀνθρωπων.   16. οἱ δε νεανιαι ἐμενον ἐμπροσθεν της θυρας του ἱερου δια το τον πρεσβυτερον ἀποθνησκειν.   17. οὐ μισω τον ἐχθρον μου ὡστε με δυνασθαι τον Θεον φιλειν.   18. ἐγραφον εἰς το ὑμας ἐπιγινωσκειν την ἀγαπην μου.   19. παραλαμβανω το εὐαγγελιον προς το σωζεσθαι.   20. χρειαν γαρ ἐχετε του ἡμας διδασκειν ὑμας[1] την ἀληθειαν.

[1] Note the double accusative. With διδασκω the person taught is put in the accusative.

B

1. But are bad men able to find wisdom?   2. Did he not wish to be released from sin?   3. They were not willing to obey the elders. 4. It is not lawful for them to take the money from the tax-collectors, is it?   5. I am a man, but you are children.   6. We wish to look at the temple of the God of Israel.   7. We are sending the slaves to call the blind and the poor.   8. It was necessary for Jesus to lead the disciples away from Galilee.   9. I wished him to heal my child, but he would not.   10. Jesus is about to ask them to send sufficient bread.   11. I am not able to exhort them to give thanks for[1] the coming of the Sun of Righteousness.   12. Are we able to do this? 13. I was sending the messenger to you, but he was not willing to depart.   14. They wish to read the books which you have.   15. But the people believed John to be a prophet.   16. And while the elders were being gathered together we remained in the fields.   17. And Jesus was healing the poor, so that the crowd rejoiced.   18. But they encouraged Peter because he taught the commandments.   19. And she used to have the clothes in order to be beautiful.

LESSON 21

The Future Active

The Future Active is formed by inserting the letter σ between the stem and the endings of the Present:

λυσω   I shall loose
λυσεις
λυσει
λυσομεν
λυσετε
λυσουσι(ν)

[1] ὑπερ.

88

If the stem ends in a mute (the term used for the nine consonants listed below), the σ will combine with it in the following manner:

(Gutturals)　κ,　γ,　χ + σ → ξ

(Labials)　π,　β,　φ + σ → ψ

(Dentals)　τ,　δ,　θ + σ → σ

So:

ἀνοιγω　　ἀνοιξω

ἐχω　　　ἐξω　　　(but observe the change of breathing)

βλεπω　　βλειψω

γραψω　　γραψω

πειθω　　πεισω

-εω verbs lengthen ε to η before the σ:

φιλεω　　φιλησω

καλεω, however, is an exception, giving:

καλεω　　καλεσω

With the so-called contracted verbs like φιλεω, contractions only take place when the ε is immediately followed by a vowel. In the case of φιλησω, where a consonant (σ) has been inserted between the stem and the endings, the endings behave just like those of λυω.

EXERCISE 21

A

1. Οὐκ ἀδικησουσίν τα τεκνα;　　2. καλεσεις δε το παιδιον Πετρον;
3. και ἀνοιξει τους ὀφθαλμους των τυφλων οἱ συναγονται ἐν τη συναγωγη.　　4. πεμψω προς αὐτους σοφους και προφητας, ἀλλ' οὐκ ἀκουσουσιν αὐτων οἱ υἱοι Ἰσραηλ.　　5. προφητευσεις τω λαω τουτω και ὑπακουσουσιν σοι.　　6. οἱ διακονοι της συναγωγης οὐ διωξουσιν τους νεανιας ἐν τω σαββατω.　　7. οἱ λεπροι ἑξουσιν τα προβατα ἃ σωζεται ἀπο των ἀνεμων και της θαλασσης.　　8. οἱ δε τα ἱματια ἐνδυσουσιν τας χηρας.　　9. ἐν δε τω τον ὀχλον ἀκουειν τον λογον τα δαιμονια ἠγεν θυσιας του προσφερειν αὐτας τω Σατανα.　　10. θελω γαρ μενειν μεθ' ὑμων ταυτην την ἡμεραν προ του με ἀκολουθειν τω Ἰησου ἐν τη ὁδω του σταυρου.　　11. ἠσθενει δε το δενδρον δια το μη ἐχειν γην.　　12. πεμπουσιν οὐν αὐτον εἰς τους

89

φίλους αὐτου εἰς τὸ αὐτὸν εὐλογειν τὸν Θεον μετ᾽ αὐτων. 13. οὐχί
ἐστιν ὁ καιρος του πιστευειν; 14. διο φωνει ἡμιν καθ᾽ ἡμεραν προς
τὸ παρακαλειν ἡμας. 15. και ἐχεις την ἐξουσιαν του περιπατειν
ἐν τῃ Γαλιλαιᾳ.

B

1. I will open the books which are in the synagogue. 2. We shall
behold the face of the Lord in the temple which is being built in
Jerusalem. 3. We will send the slaves to pursue them as far as
Judaea. 4. He will speak these things to the crowds in parables.
5. Do not bless evil men, for the evil will not see the sun. 6. Are
you about to believe one another? 7. Shall we then persuade our
own brothers to throw out their right eyes? 8. And they will call the
child Jesus, for he is saving his people from their sins. 9. And he
will have a voice like the voice of an angel. 10. And before the
world was, I am. 11. Do not do your righteousness for men to see.

LESSON 22

Verb-stems and tense-stems

So far we have been concerned with two tense-stems: the **present stem**
from which the Present and Imperfect are formed; and the **future
stem** from which the Future is formed. These are secondary stems
formed from a more fundamental **verb-stem**. It so happens that in λυω
the verb- and present stems are both λυ, but in most verbs they differ.

The fact that the meanings of verbs are given in lexicons under the
form of the Present Indicative tends to fix attention upon it, and to
produce the impression that it is the original and most important form
of the verb. This, however, is not the case. The Present stem is really
derived from the verb-stem, and is generally a lengthened form of the
verb-stem. *The verb-stem is the most important part of the verb.*

Below are given examples of three types of verb in which (*a*) the verb-stem is modified to form the Present; and (*b*) the σ of the Future is added to the verb-, not the Present, stem.

(1) Verbs which add τ to the verb-stem to form the Present stem.

Examples:

Stem	Present	Future	
καλυπ	ἀποκαλυπτω	ἀποκαλυψω	I reveal
κρυπ	κρυπτω	κρυψω	I hide

(2) Verbs in which the verb-stem ends in a guttural which is softened to σσ to form the Present stem.

κηρυκ	κηρυσσω	κηρυξω	I proclaim
πραγ	πρασσω	πραξω	I do

(3) Verbs ending in ζω in the Present. These are mostly formed from stems ending in δ and they make their futures in -σω.

βαπτιδ	βαπτιζω	βαπτισω	I baptise
δοξαδ	δοξαζω	δοξασω	I glorify

κραζω, however, is formed from a stem ending in a guttural (γ), and therefore makes its Future in -ξω.

κραγ	κραζω	κραξω	I cry out

EXERCISE 22

A

1. Ἐγγισω δε εἰς ἑκαστον ἀγαπητον ἀδελφον.   2. Ἐλπιζετε ἐν τῳ Θεῳ, ἀνοιξει γαρ θυραν ὑμιν ἐν τῃ χρειᾳ ὑμων.   3. καθαριζετε τας ἰδιας καρδιας και περιπατησετε ἐνωπιον μου ἐν ὁδοις της χαρας.   4. κρυπτε το προσωπον σου ἀπο των ἁμαρτιων μου. 5. ὁ δε πτωχος κραξει ἐν μεσῳ του ἱερου.   6. βαστασομεν τον παραλυτικον προς την θυραν, και ἑτοιμασουσιν παραλαμβανειν αὐτον.   7. οἱ λοιποι, οἳ θαυμαζουσιν την ἐξουσιαν αὐτου, κηρυξ-ουσιν την ἀγαπην αὐτου.   8. ἐγγισω δε ἀχρι του πρωτου μνημειου.   9. καθιζει ἐπι τῳ θρονῳ του οὐρανου, ἀλλ’ οἱ ἁγιοι ἐλπισουσιν θεωρειν την παρουσιαν αὐτου ἐπι ταις νεφελαις. 10. κηρυσσετε τας ἐπαγγελιας και φυλασσετε τας ἐντολας ἐν τῳ ὑμας ἑτοιμαζειν την ὁδον της δοξης.

B

1. The faithful widow will sit in prayer and her witness will not cause the other women[1] to stumble.   2. He will have mercy upon me, and I shall have eternal salvation.   3. Buy your sacrifices and sanctify the Sabbath.   4. The disciples whom John was baptising remained with Jesus.   5. Will he not reveal his face to the unbelieving soul? 6. The lepers will cry out in their need.   7. The devil will tempt you, but *I* will guard you.   8. Do righteousness to one another and you will glorify the only God.   9. O Peter, I will test you and evil men will wonder at your steadfastness.   10. Will you then buy the clothes and carry them to the brothers?   11. And I will reveal the sin of the men who practise unrighteousness, and they will hide their eyes from me.

LESSON 23

The Middle voice
The Future of εἰμι

THE MIDDLE VOICE: MEANING

In addition to the Active and Passive voices with which we are familiar in English, Greek has also a Middle voice. No attempt will be made to give any generalised explanation of the meaning of the Middle, which must be left to more advanced text-books. The meaning in fact varies from verb to verb. It will be sufficient if the student simply learns the meanings given in the vocabularies.

It may, however, be said that:

(1) Though some *forms* of the Middle are the same as the Passive, **the Middle is in meaning much closer to the Active than to the Passive.** In fact the meaning of Active and Middle are often in-

---

[1] No separate word for 'women' is required. Cf. ἐκείνη, 'that woman', Lesson 14.

distinguishable. It is better to think of the Middle as a sort-of-Active, than as a sort-of-Passive.

ἐνδύω, 'I put on' is a good example of a verb which in both Active and Middle must be translated by the Active voice in English. But in this case the two voices are clearly distinguished in meaning:

    ἐνδύω (Active)   *means* I put (clothes) on (someone else)
    ἐνδύομαι (Middle)   I put (clothes) on (myself)

(2) Verbs in the Middle are usually **Deponent.**

A deponent verb is one which is Middle or Passive in form, but Active in meaning.

All the Middle and Passive verbs in Vocabulary 23 are deponent.

(3) Some verbs are always Active in some tenses and Middle in others. The Future in particular is often Middle in form. For instance, the following have (irregular) deponent Futures:

    Present Active   Future Middle
    γινώσκω   γνώσομαι   I know
    λαμβάνω   λήμψομαι   I take[1]

(4) A few Middles are, however, so different in meaning from their Actives that they must be translated by a quite different English word,

    e.g.   ἄρχω (Active)   I rule
            ἄρχομαι (Middle)   I begin

But our concern now is not with meaning, but with form.

THE MIDDLE VOICE: FORMS

(1) The forms of the **Present and Imperfect Middle** are exactly the same as those of the Passive:

Present:	λύομαι	Imperfect:	ἐλυόμην
	λύῃ		
	λύεται	Imperative:	λύου
	λυόμεθα		
	λύεσθε	Infinitive:	λύεσθαι
	λύονται		

[1] Other examples may be seen in the list of verbs, pp. 227–8, e.g. -βαίνω, ἐσθίω, -θνῃσκω, ὁράω, πίνω, πίπτω.

ἔσομαι [23]

Whether these forms are in fact Middle or Passive can only be determined from the context.

(2) The **Future Middle**, like the Future Active, inserts σ after the stem, and then it adds the same endings as the Present Passive:

λυσομαι	λυσομεθα
λυσῃ	λυσεσθε
λυσεται	λυσονται

THE FUTURE OF εἰμι

The Future of εἰμι, formed from the stem ἐσ-, has endings like the Future Middle of λυω, except that the ε is omitted from the ending of the third person singular:

ἔσομαι	ἔσομεθα
ἔσῃ	ἔσεσθε
ἔσται	ἔσονται

EXERCISE 23

A

1. Ἐπορευομεθα δε προς την θαλασσαν μετα των μαθητων.
2. ἠρνουντο ἀρα τον Κυριον ὁς τηρει αὐτους ἀπο του πονηρου;
3. μη ἀποκρινου τῃ φωνῃ.   4. ἀπηρχοντο γαρ προς την ἐρημον ἐν ᾗ αὐτος ὁ Ἰωανης ἐβαπτιζεν.   5. και ἀπεκρινομην τοις ἀγγελοις οἱ ἠρχοντο ἀπο των πρεσβυτερων.   6. μη ἐργαζεσθε την ἀδικιαν.   7. κἀκεινος δεχεται τους ἁμαρτωλους οἱ ἐρχονται προς αὐτον και ἐσθιει μετ' αὐτων.   8. ἁπτου των κεφαλων των παιδιων ἁ πεμπω.   9. οὐδε οἱ ἰσχυροι δουλοι οὑς ἐδεχετο ἐργαζονται μονον.   10. δεχεσθω πρωτον το βιβλιον ὁ γραφει ὁ ἀποστολος.   11. διηρχομεθα οὖν τους ἀγρους αὐτων και ἠκολουθουμεν ὀπισω του δευτερου τελωνου.   12. ἁπτεσθωσαν των νεων λιθων του ἱερου του τριτου ὁ οἰκοδομειται τῳ Κυριῳ.   13. ἐβουλοντο δε ἀκουειν τους ἐσχατους λογους οὑς ἐλαλει ὁ Ἰησους.
14. οὑτος ἀρχεται οἰκοδομειν, ἀλλ' οὐ δυναται ποιειν το ἐργον.
15. δει ὑμας ἀποκρινεσθαι ταυτῃ τῃ γενεᾳ.   16. παραγγελλω[1] σοι

[1] This word is used in Lesson 20.

94

ἐξερχεσθαι ἐκ της οἰκιας.   17. οὐ γαρ μελλετε ἐρχεσθαι προς με;
18. ὁ δε οὐκ ἠθελεν πορευεσθαι ἐν ταις ὁδοις της ἀληθειας.   19. οὗτος
ἀρχων[1] της συναγωγης ὑπῆρχεν.   20. ἀργυριον οὐχ ὑπαρχει μοι·
ὁ δε ἐχω, τουτο προσφερω.   21. αὐτος ὁ Χριστος ἀρξει της
ἐκκλησιας, και ὁ λαος αὐτου προσευξεται και εὐαγγελισεται.
22. ἀσπαζεσθε ἀλληλους μετα χαρας.   23. ὁ Θεος λογισεται
δικαιοσυνην αὐτῳ χωρις ἐργων.   24. και παρεγινοντο και ἐβαπτιζ-
οντο ὑπο του Ἰωανου.   25. παραγινεται δε ὁ πρωτος προς τον
κυριον αὐτου.   26. μη φοβου τους λοιπους ἐχθρους, μονον
πιστευε.   27. οὐδε γενησεσθε ἀνθρωποι της ὀργης.   28. δυνατη
γαρ ἐσται ἐνωπιον ὁλου του λαου.   29. δει γαρ ἐνδυεσθαι τον
καινον ἀνθρωπον.

B

1. Reckon yourselves to be dead.   2. Shall I become a powerful
friend like the rich man?   3. The evil ruler feared John.   4. The
church becomes like a beautiful virgin, whom God is preparing for[2]
eternal life.   5. And you shall be holy to the Lord.   6. Therefore
we shall take the cup of salvation with joy.   7. And *I* shall know as
he knows.   8. We wished to go and greet you, but he wishes you to
come and pray with us.   9. But I will become wise and will come to
him in the fear of the Lord.   10. He will not injure his own right eye,
will he?   11. And keep the holy commandments which you receive
from the teachers.   12. Do not deny the Lord of glory who will save
you from the evil world.   13. But we were going through the fields
in which the slaves were working.   14. Let him receive the messengers who proclaim the kingdom of heaven.   15. Brothers, do not
answer the teacher.   16. Some were going to their houses and others
to the temple.   17. Jesus is being led into the same desert to be
tempted by the devil.   18. But we were going to John to be baptised
by him.   19. Jesus therefore was beginning to send the apostles to
preach the gospel to the whole house of Israel.   20. *I* shall be first,
but *you* will be last.

[1] See note on ἀρχω in Vocab. 23.
[2] εἰς.

The First Aorist Active

FIRST AND SECOND AORIST

In this and the following lesson we deal with the two types of Aorist.

The First (or Weak) Aorist is so called to distinguish it from the Second (or Strong) Aorist, a tense which is formed in a different way. Very few verbs have both Aorists. When they do, they almost always have the same meaning.[1]

THE GENERAL IDEA OF THE AORIST TENSE

In the Aorist the action is thought of in its simplest form. In contrast with the linear tenses (Present and Imperfect), which can be thought of as a line or line of dots:

——————————————— or ••••••••••••••••••

the Aorist is a *punctiliar* (or point) tense, which can be thought of as a single dot:

•

The action of the verb is thought of as simply happening, without any regard to its continuance or frequency.

THE MEANING OF THE AORIST INDICATIVE

This means that in the Indicative the sense of the Imperfect approximates to that of the English Past Continuous: 'I was loosing', while that of the Aorist approximates to that of the English Past simple: 'I loosed.'

---

[1] The two Aorists may be compared, in this respect, with the weak and strong forms of the Past tense in English. Very few verbs in English have both weak and strong Past tense forms; if they have, the meaning of the forms is identical.

Example.   Present: crow   Weak Past: crowed   Strong Past: crew.

FORMS OF THE FIRST AORIST ACTIVE

Indicative		Imperative	
ἔλυσα	I loosed		
ἔλυσας	you loosed	λυσον	loose
ἔλυσε(ν)	he loosed	λυσατω	let him loose
ἐλύσαμεν	we loosed		
ἐλύσατε	you loosed	λυσατε	loose
ἔλυσαν	they loosed	λυσατωσαν	let them loose

Infinitive: λυσαι   to loose

It will be noticed (*a*) that the Indicative has an augment, because (like the Imperfect, cf. Lesson 13) it represents action in the past. Since the Imperative never relates to the past and the Infinitive does not necessarily do so, they have no augment;

(*b*) that the characteristic of the First Aorist Active is the σα after the stem. (Note the two exceptions: ἔλυσε(ν) and λυσον.) This σ inserted between the stem and the endings produces the same consonantal changes as in the Future:

	Present	Future	First Aorist
	διωκω	διωξω	ἐδιωξα
	γραφω	γραψω	ἐγραψα
	πειθω	πεισω	ἐπεισα
	κρυπτω	κρυψω	ἐκρυψα
	κηρυσσω	κηρυξω	ἐκηρυξα
	βαπτιζω	βαπτισω	ἐβαπτισα
	κραζω	κραξω	ἐκραξα
	φιλεω	φιλησω	ἐφιλησα
but	καλεω	καλεσω	ἐκαλεσα

θελω is also irregular:

	θελω	θελησω	ἠθελησα

THE MEANING OF THE AORIST IMPERATIVE

It is not possible, without resorting to over-translation, to give any general rendering of the Aorist Imperative which will differentiate it from the Present Imperative.[1] But it will be obvious at once from the difference in idea between a linear and a punctiliar tense, that the Present Imperative will be used to denote a command to continue to do an action or to do it habitually, and the Aorist Imperative to denote a command simply to do an action without regard to its continuance or frequency.

The difference of meaning is well seen in the parallel versions of a petition in the Lord's Prayer given in two of the gospels. The verb used in Luke is the Present Imperative of διδωμι 'I give',[2] whereas Matthew uses the Aorist Imperative:

τον ἀρτον ἡμων τον ἐπιουσιον διδου ἡμιν το καθ᾽ ἡμεραν (Luke 11. 3)
Our daily bread give to us (keep on giving us) day by day.

τον ἀρτον ἡμων τον ἐπιουσιον δος ἡμιν σημερον (Matt. 6. 11)
Our daily bread give to us today.

The Present Imperative is linear; it denotes a continuous act of giving, day after day. The Aorist Imperative is punctiliar; it denotes a single act of giving: 'for today'.

THE MEANING OF THE AORIST INFINITIVE

The Aorist Infinitive differs in meaning from the Present Infinitive just in the same way as the Aorist Imperative differs in meaning from the Present Imperative. The one is punctiliar, the other is linear. The Aorist has no thought of continuance or frequency, whereas the Present Infinitive denotes that the action is to be regarded as continuous or repeated.

The Aorist Infinitive is consequently used more frequently than the Present, and the student should always use it unless there is good reason to the contrary.

Examples:

γραφειν τα αὐτα καλον ἐστιν ὑμιν (Present)
To keep on writing the same things is good for you.

ἐλπιζω γραψαι ἐπιστολην ὑμιν (Aorist)
I hope to write a letter to you.

---

[1] See the discussion on p. 74.
[2] This verb is explained in Lesson 42.

EXERCISE 24

A

1. Οὐδὲ ἐδίωξαν τους τελωνας οἳ ἀπηγον τα προβατα.   2. οἱ δε
λεπροι ἐπιστευσαν τω λογῳ του Ἰησου;   3. ἐπεμψας γαρ τας
χηρας ἀγορασαι τα ἱματια.   4. σωσον το ἀργυριον ἀπ᾽ αὐτης.
5. σωζε τον λαον σου ἀπο του πονηρου.   6. μετα ταυτα ἐπεισα-
μεν αὐτους κρυψαι τα παιδια.   7. ἐκαθαρισαμεν οὐν ἑαυτους ἐν τω
ποταμῳ.   8. ὁ δε διδασκαλος αὐτος ἐθαυμασεν την σοφιαν των
ἰδιων μαθητων.   9. βουλονται δε ἀδικησαι την τιμην των λοιπων;
10. βαστασον το ἑτερον πλοιον ἀπο της θαλασσης.   11. ἁγιασατε
ἑαυτους, ἐγγιζει γαρ ἡ ἡμερα του Κυριου.   12. ἡ γαρ φωνη του
Ἰωανου ἐκραξεν ἐν τῃ ἐρημῳ, Ἑτοιμασατε την ὁδον τω Κυριω.
13. και ἐτηρησαμεν τας ἐντολας ἃς ἠκουσαμεν ἀπο των πιστων
στρατιωτων.   14. καλον ἐστιν ἡμας πρασσειν την δικαιοσυνην.
15. μετα τουτο ἑκαστος ἠνοιξεν τους ὀφθαλμους τυφλου.   16. ταυτα
γαρ ἠθελησαν βλεψαι οἱ ἀγγελοι.   17. και ἐνεδυσαν αὐτον τα
ἱματια αὐτου.

B

1. And they baptised the tax-collectors in the river.   2. You were
going through the beautiful land to prepare the free people.   3. Strong
workman, hide the stones which abound in the field.   4. Do not
continue to cause[1] the brethren who were ill to stumble.   5. But
they followed one another.   6. For you revealed the commandments
and promises to the church.   7. Shall we begin to read the books?
8. Cleanse and sanctify your hearts.   9. Is it lawful for them to heal
on the Sabbath?   10. Save your people, O Lord, from the unrighteousness of this world.   11. Therefore hide yourselves and your
children in Jerusalem.   12. Let love and peace and righteousness
dwell in your hearts.   13. And her enemy wondered at her steadfastness.   14. It is good for them to keep on reading the same things.
15. After this I will reveal my authority and my needs to them.
16. He wished to call the tax-collectors to the sacrifice.   17. And his
tongue injured others.   18. Apart from me you seem to be weak.

[1] Use Present Imperative.

LESSON 25

The Second Aorist Active
Principal parts

THE SECOND AORIST ACTIVE

The endings of the Second (or Strong) Aorist Indicative Active are the same as those of the Imperfect. The endings of the Second Aorist Imperative Active are the same as those of the Present Imperative. The ending of the Second Aorist Infinitive Active is the same as that of the Present Infinitive.

The Second Aorist can be distinguished from the Imperfect and the Present Imperative and Infinitive only by the stem. The Imperfect and Present Imperative and Infinitive are formed from the present stem. The Second Aorist Indicative, Imperative and Infinitive are usually formed from the verbal stem.

Take for example βαλλω I throw:

Verbal stem βαλ		Present stem βαλλ	
Second Aorist Indicative	Second Aorist Imperative	Imperfect Indicative	Present Imperative
ἐβαλον		ἐβαλλον	
ἐβαλες	βαλε	ἐβαλλες	βαλλε
ἐβαλε(ν)	βαλετω	ἐβαλλε(ν)	βαλλετω
ἐβαλομεν		ἐβαλλομεν	
ἐβαλετε	βαλετε	ἐβαλλετε	βαλλετε
ἐβαλον	βαλετωσαν	ἐβαλλον	βαλλετωσαν

Second Aorist Infinitive: βαλειν   Present Infinitive: βαλλειν

The following are the common verbs with Second Aorists:

ἀγω	ἠγαγον	I lead	βαλλω	ἐβαλον	I throw
ἁμαρτανω	ἡμαρτον	I sin	εὑρισκω	εὑρον	I find
ἀποθνησκω	ἀπεθανον	I die	ἐχω	ἐσχον	I have

100

καταλειπω	κατελιπον	I leave	πινω	ἐπιον	I drink
λαμβανω	ἐλαβον	I take	πιπτω	ἐπεσον	I fall
μανθανω	ἐμαθον	I learn	φευγω	ἐφυγον	I flee
πασχω	ἐπαθον	I suffer			

Some verbs have no Present stem formed from the verbal stem. Instead the Present of a quite different verb is used. In consequence we get this strange link-up of Presents and Second Aorists in the following five very common verbs:

ἐρχομαι	ἠλθον	I come	ὁραω	εἰδον	I see
ἐσθιω	ἐφαγον	I eat	φερω	ἠνεγκον[1]	I carry
λεγω	εἰπον	I say			

As the meanings of these Aorists are sometimes given in lexicons under the totally different word in the Present tense, it is specially important that they be carefully learnt.

Second Aorist stems with First Aorist endings

In the case of ἠλθον, εἰπον, εἰδον and ἠνεγκον First Aorist endings are often added to Second Aorist stems,

e.g. ἐν φυλακῃ ἡμην και ἠλθατε προς με (Matt. 25. 36)
I was in prison and you came to me.

οἱ δε εἰπαν, Πιστευσον ἐπι τον Κυριον Ἰησουν (Acts 16. 31)
And they said, Believe on the Lord Jesus.

ἐλθατω ἡ βασιλεια σου (Luke 11. 2)
Thy kingdom come.

Διδασκαλε, ἠνεγκα τον υἱον μου προς σε (Mark 9. 17)
Teacher, I brought my son to you.

εἰπον τῃ ἐκκλησιᾳ[2] (Matt. 18. 17)
Tell the church.

These forms should be regarded as 'Second Aorist with First Aorist endings', since they are not true First Aorists.

[1] γ before κ is pronounced n: Lesson 1, p. 19 n. (1).
[2] εἰπ-ον has the second person singular First Aorist Imperative ending like λυσα-ον and like πιστευσα-ον above. With Second Aorist ending, it would be εἰπ-ε.

γινωσκω and -βαινω

γινωσκω and -βαινω (meaning 'I go', but only found in compounds) have slightly different Second Aorist forms. The endings contain a long vowel throughout, and the third person plural has -σαν instead of -ν:

ἔγνων	-εβην
ἔγνως	-εβης
ἔγνω	-εβη
ἔγνωμεν	-εβημεν
ἔγνωτε	-εβητε
ἔγνωσαν	-εβησαν

PRINCIPAL PARTS

So far we have met examples of Present, Future and Aorist tense-stems all derived from the verb-stem. It is possible for one verb to have as many as six stem variations. This sounds alarming. But fortunately, although *stems* are sometimes apparently arbitrary, the *endings* of verbs are almost always perfectly regular. So a complete knowledge of a verb can be obtained if the initial words of six tenses are known. It is then simply a matter of adding the appropriate endings of λυω to the stems of these tenses.

The six tenses are:

(1) Present Active (or Middle)

(2) Future Active (or Middle)

(3) Aorist Active (or Middle)

(4) Perfect Active

(5) Perfect Passive

(6) Aorist Passive

The first person singular of each is used and together they make up the so-called principal parts of a verb.

Thus the first three principal parts of λυω are:

$$\underline{λυω} \quad \underline{λυσω} \quad \underline{ἐλυσα}$$

If the principal parts of about forty verbs are learnt (and they are not all very irregular), all the common verb forms of the New Testament will be known.

The list of the Second Aorists given above is repeated in Vocabulary 25, and, in some cases, the Future has also been added, so completing the verb's first three principal parts. It is important to learn these principal parts in their proper order as they arise. In some cases it will not be necessary to learn all the principal parts. New parts will be added only if they are useful, and they will be added at the stage when they can best be understood.

EXERCISE 25

A

1. Μετα ταυτα ἀπεθανεν ὁ πτωχος.   2. ἀνεβημεν εἰς το ἱερον ἐν ἐκεινῃ τῃ ὡρᾳ.   3. ὦ Κυριε, ἡμαρτον ἐνωπιον σου.   4. ἰδου ἠνεγκομεν τους λιθους ἀπο της θαλασσης.   5. τα δενδρα οὐδε ἐπεσεν εἰς τον ἀγρον.   6. οἱ ἰσχυροι ἐφευγον ἀπο των νεανιων. 7. οἱ δε προφηται ἐφυγον εἰς την ἐρημον.   8. πορευου ἐξω της κωμης και λαβε τον καρπον ἀπο των ἐργατων.   9. ἐλθετω τα παιδια προς με.   10. ἐσχεν τα βιβλια του ἀδελφου μου.   11. εὑρον δε το ἀργυριον και αὐτο ἠνεγκον αὐτοις ὡστε αὐτους παραλαβειν τον μισθον αὐτων.   12. οἰσει δε τον σταυρον και πιεται το ποτηριον. 13. λημψομεθα την δυνατην σωτηριαν αὐτου και γνωσομεθα την εἰρηνην αὐτου.   14. καταβησονται παρα τον ποταμον και προσοισουσιν θυσιαν.   15. ὑπηγεν[1] δε και ἐβαλεν αὐτο εἰς την θαλασσαν. 16. και ἐν τῳ ἀγαγειν αὐτους το παιδιον του προσενεγκειν αὐτο τῳ Κυριῳ, ὁ λαος ηὐλογησεν τον Θεον.

---

[1] ὑπαγω when used intransitively never uses the Aorist. It always expresses the past tense by the Imperfect. Imperatives and infinitives are always Present. Cf. 26 A 12.

103

B

1. Therefore we cast ourselves into the river.   2. But you took the clothes which the elders sent for the poor.   3. Did they then flee from the face of the judges?   4. This is the stone that fell from heaven.   5. The virgin had a son, and they called him Jesus. 6. For the Son of man must suffer.   7. After these days we went to Galilee.   8. On this account they left the sheep in the fields and departed.   9. It is necessary for the crowd to eat the bread and drink the wine which the same young men carried to them.   10. The other prophet who had the first book died alone.   11. Lo! He knew our hearts.   12. For they learnt to suffer and they will see his face. 13. She left the house and will come into the temple.   14. And we saw the sun and said words of joy and repentance.   15. We ate and drank with him on the earth and we shall eat and drink with him in heaven.

LESSON 26

The Future and Aorist of liquid verbs

ὅτι

THE FUTURE AND AORIST OF LIQUID VERBS

The Future and Aorist of verbs whose stems end in a so-called liquid letter,

$$\lambda \quad \mu \quad \nu \quad \text{or} \quad \rho$$

present some peculiarities:

(1) They have no σ before the endings.

(2) The Future has the endings of the Present tense of φιλεω.[1] (These endings are added to the verbal stem. As the table below shows, there is usually a lengthening of this stem both in the Present and in the Aorist. ἀποστελλω provides an example of three different stems in the first three principal parts.)

---

[1] The explanation of this is that these futures originally ended in -εσω, but the σ has dropped out. So for ἀρε(σ)ω we have ἀρω.

MB You must know the Vocabulary ⟵

LIQUID VERBS

First (or Second)

Present	Future	Aorist	
αἱρω	ἀρω	ἠρα	I lift up
σπειρω	σπερω	ἐσπειρα	I sow
ἐγειρω	ἐγερω	ἠγειρα	I raise
ἀπο-κτεινω	ἀπο-κτενω	ἀπ-εκτεινα	I kill
ἀπο-στελλω	ἀπο-στελω	ἀπ-εστειλα	I send
ἀγγελλω	ἀγγελω	ἠγγειλα	I announce
μενω	μενῶ	ἐμεινα	I remain
κρινω	κρινῶ	ἐκρινα	I judge
βαλλω	βαλω	(ἐβαλον)	I throw

ἀποθνησκω has a deponent Middle Future:

ἀπο-θνησκω	ἀπο-θανουμαι	(ἀπ-εθανον)	I die

The **First Aorist Imperative** of αἱρω (by analogy with λυσον) is: ἀρον.
The **First Aorist Infinitive** of αἱρω (by analogy with λυσαι) is: ἀραι.
The **Present** and **Future** of αἱρω are conjugated as follows:

αἱρω	ἀρω
αἱρεις	ἀρεις
αἱρει	ἀρει
αἱρομεν	ἀρουμεν
αἱρετε	ἀρειτε
αἱρουσι(ν)	ἀρουσι(ν)

As the verbal stem (used in the Future) and the Present stem generally differ, the fact that the endings of the singular and of the third person plural are the same causes no difficulty. In the case of μενω and κρινω, however, both stems and endings are the same, and the meaning must be inferred from the context. In an accented text the Present is accented μένω μένεις μένει μένουσιν and the future μενῶ μενεῖς μενεῖ μενοῦσιν. This is an accentual distinction worth noting. We shall add the circumflex accent when using the four Future forms of these two verbs which would otherwise be ambiguous, but we shall add no accent when using the Present tense or the first and second person Future plural.[1]

[1] I.e., Present: κρινω κρινεις κρινει κρινομεν κρινετε κρινουσιν.
Future: κρινῶ κρινεῖς κρινεῖ κρινουμεν κρινειτε κρινοῦσιν.

ὅτι

There are three common uses of ὅτι:

(1) ὅτι can be used causally, i.e. meaning **because.**

(2) It is very frequently used to introduce **dependent** (or **indirect**) **statements.** See Introduction: English Grammar, Section 17.

(3) There is the use known as **ὅτι recitative.**

(1) ὅτι *used causally*

This calls for no special comment. It is used just like the English 'because'.

(2) ὅτι *introducing dependent statements*

There is a whole class of verbs meaning 'to say', 'believe', 'feel', 'know', 'learn', etc., which are for convenience known as *verbs of saying or thinking*. These are frequently followed by object clauses (beginning with the word 'that') which express dependent statements. 'That' is usually translated by ὅτι and the object clause is put in the Indicative, e.g.

θεωρω ὅτι προφητης εἶ συ (John 4. 19)

I see that you are a prophet.

Dependent statements in the past

When, however, the words or thoughts were in the past, the Greek idiom differs from the English. In Greek *the tense of the verb which was used by the original speaker or thinker when he uttered the words or framed the thought is always retained,* and the verb in the object clause is not put into the past tense as it is in English.

In English we say, 'He heard that he *was* ill'. The words that the man actually heard were, 'He *is* ill'. In Greek the present tense is retained, and we have:

ἠκουσεν ὅτι ἀσθενει (John 11. 6)

Similarly,   ἠκουσεν ὅτι 'Ιησους ἐρχεται (John 11. 20)

She heard that Jesus *was* coming.

Sometimes English uses a Pluperfect. But the same rule applies: the tense used by the original speaker or thinker must be recalled. Thus:

> οὐκ ἐπίστευσαν οἱ Ἰουδαῖοι ὅτι ἦν τυφλός (John 9. 18)
> The Jews did not believe that he *had been* blind,

i.e. in thought they denied the statement in the Imperfect, 'He used to be blind'.

Luke 2. 20 records how the shepherds praised God for all the things which

> ἤκουσαν καὶ εἶδον
> they had heard and seen.

In their direct speech they praised God 'for all the things which we heard and saw (just now)'. The Greek tense is therefore Aorist, but the English tense is Pluperfect. (See also John 9. 35.)

Thus we may say that in English, after a past main verb, the tense of the verb in the object clause is put one stage further into the past: the Past is used instead of the Present, and the Pluperfect instead of the Past. But in Greek the tense used by the original speaker or thinker is retained.

The student should always ask himself what were the original words uttered, or the original thought framed, before trying to translate such sentences as these.

(3) ὅτι recitative

ὅτι can also be used to introduce a *direct statement*, in which case it is not translated. This so-called ὅτι recitative is simply equivalent to inverted commas.

An indirect statement after ὅτι will normally begin with a small letter, and a direct statement with a capital letter.

Examples of the three uses are:

(1) ὑμεῖς οὐ πιστεύετε, ὅτι οὐκ ἐστε ἐκ τῶν προβατων τῶν ἐμῶν (John 10. 26)
You do not believe, because you are not of my sheep.

(2) εἶπον οὖν ὑμῖν ὅτι ἀποθανεῖσθε ἐν ταῖς ἁμαρτιαις ὑμῶν (John 8. 24)
I said to you therefore that you will die in your sins.

(3) and (1) ὑμεις λεγετε ὁτι Βλασφημεις, ὁτι εἰπον Ὑιος του Θεου
εἰμι (John 10. 36)

You say, 'You are blaspheming', because I said, 'I am the Son
of God'.

It will be seen from the last example that a direct statement can be
made with or without an introductory ὁτι. Βλασφημεις has the ὁτι
recitative, whereas Ὑιος του Θεου εἰμι is without it.

EXERCISE 26

A

1. Ὁτε δε οἱ στρατιωται ἠλθον εἰς την οἰκιαν ἀπηγγειλαν ὁτι
ἀπεστειλεν αὐτους.   2. οὑτοι κρινουσιν τας χηρας και ἀποκτεν-
ουσιν τα τεκνα αὐτων;   3. οὐ μενειτε ἐν τω τοπω τουτω ἀλλ'
ἀποθανεισθε ἐν τη γη των ἐχθρων ὑμων.   4. οἱ δε ἀποστολοι
ἐσπειραν τον λογον ἐν ταις καρδιαις των ὀλιγων οἱ ἠθελον ὑπακουειν
αὐτω.   5. ἠρεν οὐν τον σταυρον και ἠλθεν ὀπισω του Ἰησου.
6. ἐν ἐκεινω τω καιρω οἱ κριται ἐκριναν τας ἀπιστους.   7. ἐμεινα
δε ἐν τω ἰδιω τοπω ἑως ἀνεγνω το βιβλιον.   8. δυνασθε πιειν το
ποτηριον ὁ δει με πιειν;   9. ἐμειναμεν δε ἐν τω ἱερω ἑως οἱ
ἐργαται ᾠκοδομουν τον θρονον.   10. ὁτε δε ἠκουσαν ταυτα παρα
της χηρας ἐμειναν παρ' αὐτη.   11. οὐδε ὠφειλες ἀργυριον τοις
τελωναις.   12. ὁ δε Ἰησους εἰπεν τω παραλυτικω, Ἀρον αὐτο
και ὑπαγε εἰς τον οἰκον σου· ὁτε δε ἠκουσεν ταυτα ἠρεν αὐτο και
ὑπηγεν. /13. ἀπεστειλαμεν οὐν τους ἀγγελους ἑτοιμασαι την
ὁδον.   14. ὁ προφητης εἰπεν ὁτι Δυνατον ἐστιν. εἰπεν ὁτι
δυνατον ἐστιν. εἰπεν, Δυνατον ἐστιν.   15. παρηγγειλατε αὐτοις
μη ἀδικησαι ὀλον τον λαον.   16. και τουτο ἠκουσαμεν παρ' αὐτου
ὁτι δει ἡμας φιλειν τους ἀδελφους ἡμων.   17. ἀλλ' οἱ Φαρισαιοι
ἐλεγον ὁτι ἐσθιει παρα ἁμαρτωλω.   18. οἰσεις δε τον σταυρον ὀπισω
μου.   19. και ἐρει ταυτα αὐτη ὁτι φιλουσιν ἀλληλους.   20. ἐμαθες
ὁτι ἐρχεται ὁ ἰσχυρος κριτης.   21. εἰπαν ὁτι ἱκανον οἰνον πινουσιν.
22. ἐγνων ὁτι ὁ Κυριος ἐπεμψεν τον ἀγγελον εἰς το σωζειν με.
23. εἰδον ὁτι ἠγαγομεν τον ὀχλον εἰς την αὐτην συναγωγην.

B

1. Send the young men to rouse the soldiers.   2. But he took the child and departed.   3. They will not die in the desert, for the soldiers will save them.   4. Therefore I will judge my people at that time. 5. And the Pharisees went to eat bread with[1] the prophet.   6. And when he heard these words he sent them to kill his enemy.   7. They will remain in the house while the paralysed man is dying.   8. We announced therefore that the apostle had fallen.   9. But you ought not to judge these widows.   10. And he will cast out[2] his right eye, because you are weak.   11. When the disciples came to the village they sowed the word in the hearts of the people.   12. Will you not kill the evil men, O Lord?   13. You will throw the stones beside the temple.   14. But the Pharisees said that the disciples of John did not eat with[1] tax-collectors and sinners.   15. I shall fall but not die, because you will raise me.   16. And they will say, 'He died on the first day while we were working'.

LESSON 27

The First and Second Aorist Middle

γίνομαι

THE FORMATION OF THE AORIST MIDDLE

The conjugation of the two Aorist Middle Indicative tenses follows closely the Imperfect Middle ἐλυόμην. The First Aorist, however (as might be expected), inserts the characteristic σα, and the Second Aorist uses its own Second Aorist stem.

[1] Use παρα.
[2] Use ἐκβαλλω.

First Aorist		Second Aorist	
Indicative		Indicative	
ἐλυσαμην	I loosed	ἐγενομην	I became
ἐλυσω[1]		ἐγενου	
ἐλυσατο		ἐγενετο	
ἐλυσαμεθα		ἐγενομεθα	
ἐλυσασθε		ἐγενεσθε	
ἐλυσαντο		ἐγενοντο	

The Imperative and Infinitive follow the Present Middle in a similar way:[2]

Imperative		Imperative	
λυσαι	loose	γενου	become
λυσασθω		γενεσθω	
λυσασθε		γενεσθε	
λυσασθωσαν		γενεσθωσαν	
Infinitive		Infinitive	
λυσασθαι	to loose	γενεσθαι	to become

THE USE OF THE FIRST AORIST MIDDLE

The **First Aorist Middle** is found mainly in deponent verbs such as those already learnt in Voc. 23. They are regularly formed. It is necessary merely to recall the ordinary rules for initial vowel changes in the formation of past tenses and for the combination of mutes with σ to obtain the following forms:

Present Middle	Aorist Middle
ἁπτομαι	ἡψαμην
ἀρχομαι	ἠρξαμην
δεχομαι	ἐδεξαμην
ἐργαζομαι	ἠργασαμην
εὐαγγελιζομαι	εὐηγγελισαμην

---

[1] ἐλυσω is a contraction of ἐ-λυ-σα-(σ)ο as ἐγενου is a contraction of ἐ-γεν-ε-(σ)ο. When this is realised, the correspondence between the Imperfect and First Aorist Middles is seen to be exact.

[2] Except for λυσαι, which has no similarity to the Present form. *Note:* λυσαι is also the form of the First Aorist Infinitive Active.

(ἀποκρινομαι has mainly Passive forms, but ἀπεκρινατο, 'he answered', is sometimes found.)

The first three principal parts of a typical deponent verb are thus:

δεχομαι   δεξομαι   ἐδεξαμην

THE USE OF THE SECOND AORIST MIDDLE; γινομαι

The **Second Aorist Middle** is found in ἀπολλυμι, whose form is explained in Lesson 44:

ἀπολλυμι   I destroy   ἀπωλομην   I perished

and in the extremely common

γινομαι   I become, etc.   ἐγενομην   I became, etc.

The first three principal parts of γινομαι are thus:

γινομαι   γενησομαι   ἐγενομην

γινομαι has a wide range of possible translations besides 'become'. It can mean 'come into being', 'happen', 'appear', 'arise', 'be made', 'be', or even 'come'. For the last, cf.

ἐγενετο φωνη ἐκ της νεφελης (Mark 9. 7)
There came a voice out of the cloud.

γινομαι is not a verb of motion, but in English 'came' is a somewhat more idiomatic translation than 'was'.

The Imperative of εἰμι is very rare. γινομαι is generally used to express the Imperative of the verb 'to be', e.g.

μη γινεσθε ὡς οἱ ὑποκριται (Matt. 6. 16)
Do not be as (like) the hypocrites.

The common expressions και ἐγενετο and ἐγενετο δε are usually translated in the Authorised Version 'and it came to pass'. They are literal translations of a Hebrew idiom, which gives a certain vividness to a narrative, but which in reality adds nothing to the sense. It has come into Christian use through the Septuagint. Sometimes we find a very literal imitation of the Hebrew, such as:

και ἐγενετο και αὐτος διηρχετο (Luke 17. 11)
lit. and it came to pass and he was going through.

The New English Bible considers it unnecessary to translate και ἐγενετο και and renders it simply: 'he was travelling through'.

EXERCISE 27

A

1. Ὑμεις μεν ἠρνησασθε τον ἁγιον και δικαιον κατ' ἰδιαν, ὁ δε ἠρνησατο αὐτον ἐμπροσθεν ὁλου του λαου.   2. ἡ χηρα ἡψατο μονον του ἱματιου αὐτου, ἀλλ' εἰπεν Μη μου ἁπτου.   3. ἠσπασατο αὐτους ἀλλ' ἠρξαντο παρακαλειν αὐτον ἀπελθειν.   4. αὐτον δει τον οὐρανον δεξασθαι, ἀλλ' ὀψομεθα αὐτον ἐν τῃ ἡμερᾳ της δευτερας παρουσιας αὐτου.   5. ὁ δε ἀπεκρινατο Εὐαγγελισαι αὐτῳ.
6. αὐτον δε λογιζομαι φιλον, ἐργον γαρ καλον ἠργασατο ὑπερ ἐμου.
7. οἱ οὐν μαθηται αὐτου ἠρξαντο ὁδον ποιειν.   8. ὁ δε πρωτος παρεγενετο και εἰπεν, Κυριε, βουλομεθα μαθειν προσευξασθαι.
9. ὁ πρεσβυτερος γενεσθω ὡς ὁ διακονος.   10. και ἐγενετο ἐν τῳ εἰναι αὐτους ἐν τῃ οἰκιᾳ οἱ σοφοι παρεγενοντο εἰς Ἱεροσολυμα.
11. κἀκεινος ἀπωλετο, ἀλλ' οἱ υἱοι αὐτου οὐκ ἀπωλοντο.   12. ἠρξω ἀπο των ἐσχατων ἑως των πρωτων.   13. διο γινεσθε σοφοι προς ἀλληλους.   14. οὐκ ἐνεδυσατο ἱματιον και ἐν τῃ οἰκιᾳ οὐκ ἐμενεν.   15. και ἐγενετο ἐν τῳ σπειρειν ἀλλα[1] ἐπεσεν παρα την ὁδον.

B

1. And Jesus began to say to the crowds concerning John, 'He prepared my way'.   2. Let a man deny himself and come after me.   3. Peter, go into the house of the unbelieving woman and greet her.   4. And on that day the remaining saints preached the gospel and worked righteousness.   5. But he went up into the temple to pray. 6. Sinner, receive the word with fear.   7. Do not be like the hypocrites, but be faithful to one another.   8. And it came to pass, as he sowed, the seeds[1] fell beside the way.   9. He was in the world, and the world came into being through him, and the world did not know him.   10. It is not lawful for a prophet to perish outside Jerusalem. 11. Peter, do not be faithless.

[1] This refers back to the neuter plural word σπερματα, 'seeds'; see Vocab. 29. σπερματα is required again in 27 B 8.

REVISION TESTS 3

The Verb

Allow 50 minutes each for Tests A and B. Total number of marks: 60 for each test.

When writing out conjugations, give the first word in full, then only the endings.

A

1. Give the following tenses of λνω:
   Active: Present Indicative, First Aorist Indicative, Present Imperative, First Aorist Infinitive.
   Middle: Imperfect Indicative, Future Indicative, Present Imperative, First Aorist Imperative.
   Passive: Present Indicative. [9 marks]
2. Give the rules of contraction of -εω verbs. [3]
3. Give the Future and Aorist Indicative of βαλλω. [2]
4. Give the Imperfect and Infinitive of εἰμι. [2]
5. Give the Present Indicative and Infinitive of δυναμαι. [2]
6. Tabulate the contractions of mutes with σ. [3]
7. Give the Second Aorist Indicative Active of -βαινω. [1]
8. Give the Greek for: I am beside, I bind, I build, I buy, I cleanse, I draw near, I exhort, I follow, I heal, I am ill, I injure, I keep, I have mercy on, it is necessary, I obey, I persecute, I practise, I reckon, I recognise, I rejoice, I repent, I rule, I seek, I seem, I cause to stumble, I tempt. [13]
9. Give the Greek for: I shall begin, I shall deny, I shall pray, I shall receive (two words), I shall prepare. I fled, I hid, I learnt, I perished, I sinned, I was throwing out. [6]
10. Give the first three principal parts of the verbs meaning: I loose, I become, I command, I cry out, I depart, I die, I eat, I fall, I have, I know, I lift up, I look at, I raise, I remain, I say. [15]
11. Give simple Greek sentences illustrating four uses of the infinitive. [4]

B

1. Give the following tenses of φιλεω:

Active: Imperfect Indicative, Future Indicative, First Aorist Imperative, Present Infinitive.

Middle: Present Indicative, First Aorist Indicative, First Aorist Infinitive.

Passive: Imperfect Indicative, Present Imperative. [9 marks]

2. Give the rules for initial vowel changes in the formation of past tenses [3]

3. Give the Aorist Indicative, Imperative and Infinitive Middle of γινομαι. [3]

4. Give the Present and Future of εἰμι. [2]

5. Give the Imperfect Indicative of δυναμαι, mentioning the alternative forms. [1]

6. Give the Second Aorist Indicative Active of γινωσκω. [1]

7. Give the First Aorist Imperative and Infinitive of αἰρω. [2]

8. Give the Greek for: I am about, I bless, I call (two words), I fear, I guard, I hate, I hope, I inhabit, it is lawful, I marry, I open, I proclaim, I put on, I release, I reveal, I sanctify, I serve, I sit, I take hold of (two words), I am weak, I weep, I wonder at, I worship, I do wrong. [13]

9. Give the Greek for: I shall glorify, I shall go down, I shall greet, I shall read, I shall touch. I left, I was owing, I was preaching the gospel, I suffered, I was walking, I was wishing (two words). [6]

10. Give the first three principal parts of the verbs meaning: I loose, I announce, I bring, I carry (2 words), I come, I drink, I find, I go up, I judge, I kill, I see, I send (with a commission), I sow, I take. [15]

11. Give ten verbs which usually take the dative and three which usually take the genitive. [2]

12. Explain the use of tenses in object clauses after verbs of saying or thinking in a past tense. [3]

LESSON 28

Third Declension masculine and feminine nouns with consonant stems

THE THIRD DECLENSION

The Third Declension contains all nouns which do not belong to the First or Second Declension.

The basic classification of the Third Declension is into:
(1) nouns whose stems end in a consonant:
    (*a*) masculine and feminine nouns (Lesson 28);
    (*b*) neuter nouns (Lesson 29); together with
    (*c*) certain adjectives and pronouns (Lesson 30).
(2) nouns whose stems end in a vowel (Lesson 31).

MASCULINE AND FEMININE NOUNS WITH CONSONANT STEMS

The endings of these nouns are as follows:

	Singular	Plural
N.	Various	ες
A.	α	ας
G.	ος	ων
D.	ι	σι(ν)

The vocative will not be included in this declension. It is usually the same as the nominative. The occasional exceptions will be noted in the vocabularies.

Since the nominative singular takes various forms and since there are no general rules for determining the gender, it is necessary to learn nominative singular, stem and gender all at once in order to have a full knowledge of a Third Declension word. It is most convenient to learn the words in the form in which they are set out in the vocabularies: nominative singular, genitive singular, article, meaning. Thus:

ἀστηρ	ἀστερος	ὁ	star
ἐλπις	ἐλπιδος	ἡ	hope

The stem can be found by taking away the -ος from the genitive singular. Thus the stem of ἀστηρ is ἀστερ and is declined as follows:

ἀστηρ	ἀστερες
ἀστερα	ἀστερας
ἀστερος	ἀστερων
ἀστερι	ἀστερσι(ν)[1]

Formation of the dative plural

When σιν is added to the stem to form the dative plural, the same consonantal changes take place as in the forming of the future of verbs (Lesson 21):

(gutturals)	κ, γ, χ	+ σιν → ξιν
(labials)	π, β, φ	+ σιν → ψιν
(dentals *and also* ν)	τ, δ, θ, ν	+ σιν → σιν

Examples:

Nominative	Genitive	Dative plural	
σαρξ	σαρκ-ος	σαρξιν	flesh
αἰων	αἰων-ος	αἰωσιν	age
νυξ	νυκ-τ-ος	νυξιν	night

Stems ending in αντ, εντ, οντ take the following forms:[2]

$$αντ + σιν → ασιν$$
$$εντ + σιν → εισιν$$
$$οντ + σιν → ουσιν$$

Example:

ἀρχων	ἀρχοντος	ἀρχουσιν	ruler

Irregular nouns

The following words are somewhat irregular:

πατηρ πατρος ὁ	father
μητηρ μητρος ἡ	mother
θυγατηρ θυγατρος ἡ	daughter

---

[1] ἀστερσιν is not in fact found, but it is given here to illustrate the general form. In Greek literature the dative plural of ἀστηρ appears in a variety of forms, of which ἀστρασιν is the commonest.

[2] These forms will be found of great importance when the participle is reached in Lesson 36.

They are all declined like πατηρ, as follows:

πατηρ	πατερες
πατερα	πατερας
πατρος	πατερων
πατρι	πατρασι(ν)

The stem is in fact πατερ, but it contracts in the genitive singular and in the dative singular and plural. In addition the dative plural has an irregular ending -ασιν.

EXERCISE 28

A

1. Σωζομεθα γαρ τη ἐλπιδι και τη χαριτι του Θεου.   2. και ἐγειρευθε ταις χερσιν της γυναικος.   3. φυλασσεσθωσαν οἱ παιδες ὑπο των Ἑλληνων.   4. ἀπεστειλαν δε οἱ ἀρχοντες τους στρατιωτας νυκτος.   5. οἱ αὐτοι οὐν ἠραν την εἰκονα Σιμωνος.   6. οὐ μενουσιν ἐν τη γη αὐτων εἰς τον αἰωνα;   7. ἐν τω πρωτω μηνι ἐλαβες τον καρπον του ἀμπελωνος ταις γυναιξιν των ἀλλων μαρτυρων. 8. ὁ τυφλος πατηρ ἐφιλει την θυγατερα αὐτου.   9. ἰδε, ὠ γυναι, οἱ των οὐρανων ἀστερες μαρτυρουσιν τω Σωτηρι.   10. φαγη γαρ την σαρκα του υἱου του ἀνθρωπου.   11. και αὐτην ἀπεκτεινεν τοις ποσιν της εἰκονος ἡ ἐπεσεν ἐν μεσω του ναου.   12. ὁ δε μισθος οὐ λογιζεται[1] κατα χαριν.   13. δει οὐν ἀνδρα καταλιπειν τον πατερα και την μητερα αὐτου.   14. μετα το ἀποθανειν τον πατερα αὐτου κατῳκησεν ἐν τη γη ταυτη.

B

1. Woman, you did not find sufficient money for the rulers, did you?
2. And the teacher himself sent his own children into the vineyard.
3. But the night and the day will not remain for ever and ever.
4. After these things we looked at the star with them.   5. And we announced that he was a Saviour for women.   6. Their flesh is weak, but the witnesses are being saved by grace.   7. But they worked with the hands and the feet.   8. The saviour is above the teacher, because he died on behalf of the sheep.   9. But beautiful daughters will become like their mothers.   10. In the last month hope will abound.   11. Because of this they will carry the image through the temple.   12. Apart from the flesh of the Son we shall not have

---

[1] In form λογιζεται can be either deponent middle or (as here) passive.

eternal life in ourselves.   13. Because the girl is under authority, she is not tempted by the devil.   14. Because we are not under law, but under grace.   15. The husband and the wife are the same flesh.

LESSON 29

Third Declension neuter nouns

Neuter nouns of the Third Declension all have consonant stems, but they are of two distinct types.

NEUTER NOUNS: FIRST TYPE

The first is like ἀστηρ, except that

(1) the accusatives are the same as the nominatives (as always in neuter nouns);

(2) there is an -α ending in the nominative and accusative plural.

The endings are therefore:

	Singular	Plural
N.A.	Various	-α
G.	-ος	-ων
D.	-ι	-σι(ν)

σωμα σωματος το, 'body' (stem σωματ), is declined as follows:

N.A.	σωμα	σωματα
G.	σωματος	σωματων
D.	σωματι	σωμασι(ν)

NEUTER NOUNS: SECOND TYPE
With stems ending in -ες

The second type is at first sight quite different.

γενος γενους το, 'race', is declined as follows:

N.A.	γενος	γενη
G.	γενους	γενων
D.	γενει	γενεσι(ν)

It will be seen that the nominative singular ending is the same as that of λογος, but that the declension as a whole is quite different from that of Second Declension masculine words. Thus words of the -ος -ους το type need to be carefully noted and learnt.

These forms are not in fact as arbitrary as they look. Apart from the nominative singular, they are all due to the dropping of the final ς of the stem γενες. Contractions have taken place thus:

—	γενε(σ)α → γενη (see p. 83 footnote)
γενε(σ)ος → γενους	γενε(σ)ων → γενων (see -εω contractions,
	Lesson 4)
γενε(σ)ι → γενει	γενε(σ)σιν → γενεσιν

EXERCISE 29

A

1. Ἐλεος δε θελω και οὐ θυσιαν.   2. και οἱ ἐχθροι Ἰουδα ἀπεκτειναν μερος του ἐθνους πυρι.   3. ἑξομεν ἀρα βαπτισμα μετανοιας δια του αἱματος αὐτου;   4. ποιησει δε σημεια και τερατα τῳ γενει ἡμων.   5. οἱ δε παιδες ἐλαβον τα σκευη ἐκ του ὑδατος.   6. ἰσχυρα δε ῥηματα κριματος ἐξηλθεν ἐκ του στοματος σου.   7. ἐγω γαρ οὐκ ἠλθον ποιησαι το θελημα μου, ἀλλα το θελημα του Κυριου ὁς ἀπεστειλεν με.   8. διο ἐρχεται ἐν ἐλεει εἰς τα μελη του σωματος αὐτου.   9. και τα ἐθνη γνωσεται το ὀνομα αὐτου.   10. μετα ταυτα ἡψατο του ὠτος τῃ χειρι αὐτου.   11. το ὑδωρ περισσευει ἐν τοις σκευεσιν.   12. τα ῥηματα του στοματος αὐτου ἠν τοις ὠσιν των ἐθνων.   13. κατα το αὐτου ἐλεος ἐσωσεν ἡμας.

B

1. But God is rich in mercy.   2. He said therefore that he was not the light, but was coming to bear witness concerning the light. 3. And we went through fire and water, for the spirit of compassion dwelt in us.   4. And he will open the ears of the multitudes who cannot hear.   5. Not even the years of the mountains will be for ever; for the end will be the darkness of the judgement.   6. But we ourselves are members of his body.   7. For the seed of Abraham

must eat the Passover.   8. See my hands and my feet.   9. He is the way of light for the multitudes.   10. And they will say to the mountains, 'Fall on us'.   11. And there will be wonders in the darkness of the night, blood and fire and fear.   12. But the end of the way will be the light of the Spirit.   13. But, unbelieving woman, you said that you knew the will of God.   14. And they will do wonders in his name.   15. But he put[1] the seed into a vessel on the day of the Passover.   16. The Jews therefore became a part of the whole race.   17. Can the feet say to the hands, 'We have no need of you, because you are not members of the body'?   18. And the Holy Spirit will remain with them for ever and ever.   19. And the world perished by water.

LESSON 30

Third Declension adjectives
Interrogative and indefinite pronouns

THIRD DECLENSION ADJECTIVES: FIRST TYPE

There are also two types of Third Declension Adjective. In certain respects these correspond closely to the two neuter noun declensions. The common words of the first group are comparative adjectives, e.g.

πλειων   πλειον   more   got voc 30

Masculine Feminine	Neuter	Masculine Feminine	Neuter
πλειων	πλειον	πλειονες	πλειονα
πλειονα	πλειον	πλειονας	πλειονα
πλειονος	πλειονος	πλειονων	πλειονων
πλειονι	πλειονι	πλειοσι(ν)	πλειοσι(ν)

---

[1] Use βαλλω. βαλλω and its compounds are often used in a weakened sense, cf. 13A 9, 32A 11.

It will be seen that the masculine and feminine endings are of the ἀστηρ type and the neuter forms are of the σωμα type.

When $\dfrac{\pi\lambda\epsilon\iota\omega\nu\ \pi\lambda\epsilon\iota o\nu}{\pi\lambda\epsilon\iota o\nu a}$ has been learnt the whole declension follows automatically.

INTERROGATIVE AND INDEFINITE PRONOUNS

τις

The interrogative and indefinite pronouns (Introduction: English Grammar, Section 5) belong to this same group. The interrogative 'who?' 'what?' differs from the indefinite pronoun 'someone', 'anyone', 'a certain one', 'something', etc., only in accent. The unaccented form of both is:

τις	τι	τινες	τινα
τινα	τι	τινας	τινα
τινος	τινος	τινων	τινων
τινι	τινι	τισι(ν)	τισι(ν)

When $\dfrac{\tau\iota\varsigma\ \tau\iota}{\tau\iota\nu a}$ has been learnt, the rest of the declension follows automatically.

We shall always print the interrogative with an acute accent on the first syllable: τίς τί τίνα, and the indefinite without any accent.[1]

---

[1] (Not important at this stage.) All forms of the indefinite pronoun belong to a small class of words (called *enclitics*) which are closely joined to the word that precedes. (Others are: τε; με, μου, μοι; σε, σου, σοι (when not emphatic); and the Present Indicative of εἰμι, except second singular εἶ.) They, therefore, never stand first in the sentence.

In a fully accented text these words sometimes have an accent (which may be either acute or grave), but more usually they have no accent at all. The interrogative and indefinite pronouns are normally easy to distinguish. In its two-syllable forms the interrogative carries an acute accent on the *first* syllable, e.g. τίνες; whereas the corresponding indefinite can only have an accent on the *second* syllable. It can be τινες, τινές or τινὲς. In the single syllable forms, the interrogative always has an acute accent (τίς, τί), whereas the indefinite is nearly always without an accent (τις, τι). (There are, however, rare cases where the single syllable indefinite also has an acute accent, which might cause it to be confused with the interrogative, e.g. John 12. 47; 16. 30.)

ὅστις

The indefinite relative pronoun, ὅστις 'whoever', is a combination of
ὅς and τις, both parts of which decline. Thus we get the nominative
forms:

$$\text{ὅστις} \quad \text{ἥτις} \quad \text{ὅτι (or ὅ τι)}^1 \quad \text{οἵτινες} \quad \text{αἵτινες} \quad \text{ἅτινα}$$

In the New Testament the nominative is the only case in common use,
and the distinction in meaning between ὅς and ὅστις has almost
disappeared. Therefore it is usually correct to translate it like an
ordinary relative: 'who', 'which', etc.[2]

Examples of the use of τίς τις and ὅστις are:

ἀλλα τί ἐξηλθατε ἰδειν; (Matt. 11. 8)
But what did you go out to see?

εἰ τις ἔχει ὦτα ἀκουειν ἀκουετω (Mark 4. 23)
If anyone has ears to hear, let him hear.

Both τίς and τις may be used adjectivally:

τίνα μισθον ἔχετε; (Matt. 5. 46)
What reward do you have?

γυναικες τινες...αἵτινες διηκονουν αὐτοις (Luke 8. 2, 3)
Certain women...who used to wait upon them.

τί often means 'why?'

τί δε με καλειτε, Κυριε Κυριε; (Luke 6. 46)
Why do you keep calling me 'Lord, Lord'?

ADJECTIVES OF THE THIRD DECLENSION: SECOND TYPE

The second type of Third Declension Adjective has a stem ending in -ες
and undergoes contractions similar to those of γενος:

$$\text{ἀληθης} \quad \text{ἀληθες} \quad \text{true}$$

---

[1] ὅτι the pronoun needs to be distinguished from ὅτι the conjunction.
Modern editors therefore usually write the pronoun as two words: ὅ τι.

[2] It seems likely that there was a tendency to substitute ὅστις for ὅς in the
nominative to avoid confusion between the relatives ἥ, ὅ, οἵ, αἵ and the article
ὁ, ἥ, οἱ, αἱ. See p. 72 n. 1 and C. F. D. Moule, *An Idiom Book of N.T. Greek*,
pp. 123 f.

Masculine Feminine	Neuter	Masculine Feminine	Neuter
ἀληθης	ἀληθες	ἀληθεις	ἀληθη
ἀληθη	ἀληθες	ἀληθεις	ἀληθη
ἀληθους	ἀληθους	ἀληθων	ἀληθων
ἀληθει	ἀληθει	ἀληθεσι(ν)	ἀληθεσι(ν)[1]

EXERCISE 30

A

1. Διαθηκην κρεισσονα ἐπεμψεν ἡτις ἐστιν ἐν τῳ αἱματι του Σωτηρος.   2. κἀγω οὐκ εἰμι μειζων αὐτου;   3. ὁ δε Ἰησους ὑπηγεν πληρης του Ἁγιου Πνευματος.   4. Ἀβρααμ, ἡ δικαιοσυνη σου περισσευει, ὁτι ἐστιν πλειων της δικαιοσυνης του γενους σου. 5. τί οὐκ ἠν ἡ μαρτυρια αὐτου ἀληθης; ἡ σαρξ ἀσθενης ἐστιν. 6. εἰπατε Τίς ἐστιν ἀξιος ἐν αὐτῃ τῃ κωμῃ;   7. ὁ δε ἀδελφος σου ἐχει τι κατα σου.   8. και τινες των Φαρισαιων εἰπαν ἐν ἑαυτοις, Τί βλασφημει;   9. ὁστις γαρ ἐχει παραλημψεται πλειον.   10. τί σοι δοκει, Σιμων; συ τίνα με λεγεις εἰναι; 11. δυναται τις εἰσελθειν εἰς την οἰκιαν του ἰσχυρου;   12. ὁτι ἐστιν ὁ σοφος ὁστις ᾠκοδομησεν την ἰδιαν οἰκιαν ἐπι την αὐτην πετραν.   13. γινεται τα ἐσχατα του ἀνθρωπου χειρονα των πρωτων.

B

1. But they will receive[2] a reward which is better than life.   2. The Christ then is greater than the temple.   3. For he was a man full of grace and truth.   4. The first workmen said, 'We shall receive[2] more honour'.   5. But the true elders in compassion encourage their weak children.   6. Whoever wishes to come after me, let him deny himself. 7. A certain saint died and did not leave children.   8. For when we were in the flesh we were slaves of sin.   9. These are the men who

---

[1] Apart from the nominative singular and the masculine and feminine accusative plural (which follows the nominative), the contractions are quite regular:

ἀληθε(σ)α → η	ἀληθε(σ)ες → εις
ἀληθε(σ)ος → ους	ἀληθε(σ)ων → ων
ἀληθε(σ)ι → ει	ἀληθε(σ)σιν → εσιν

[2] Use λαμβανω or παραλαμβανω. λαμβανω often means 'receive'.

123

hear the words of the multitude.   10. Can this man be worse than
Judas?   11. Why do you tempt me, hypocrite? Whose is this image?
12. Some speak according to (the) flesh, but the Spirit is against the
flesh.

LESSON 31

Third Declension nouns with vowel stems

υ STEMS

There are nine nouns in the New Testament (none of them very
common) with stems ending in υ. Some of these are masculine and some
feminine. They are declined exactly like ἀστήρ, except for the accusative
singular, which ends in ν. Thus:

ἰχθυς ἰχθυος ὁ fish

ἰχθυς	ἰχθυες
ἰχθυν	ἰχθυας
ἰχθυος	ἰχθυων
ἰχθυϊ	ἰχθυσι(ν)

ι AND ευ STEMS

Much more important are those with stems in ι and in ευ, which are
declined as follows:

πολις πολεως ἡ city   βασιλευς βασιλεως ὁ king

πολις	βασιλευς
πολιν	βασιλεα
πολεως	βασιλεως
πολει	βασιλει
πολεις	βασιλεις
πολεις	βασιλεις
πολεων	βασιλεων
πολεσι(ν)	βασιλευσι(ν)

Labials.
ΠΕΜΠΩ
ΓΡΑΦΩ

palatal
ΔΙΔΑΣΚΩ
ΕΧΩ

Dental
εδςαζω
σπιθω

—OUR LADY OF THE SNOWS

This painting has hung in the student chapel of the Gregorian University in Rome since the time of St. Francis Borgia, the third Superior General of the Society of Jesus. It is also known as OUR LADY, PROTECTORESS OF THE PEOPLE OF ROME.

Compliments of:
The Gregorian University Foundation
106 West 56th Street
New York, NY 10019

Note. (1) Though strictly speaking the stems end in ι and in ευ (and the nominative ending is simply *s*), it is better for practical purposes to think of the endings as -ις -εως and -ευς -εως.

(2) All these nouns with ι stems have nominative singular in -ις and genitive singular in -εως, and all are feminine. And all nouns with ευ stems have nominative singular in -ευς and genitive singular in -εως, and all are masculine. They are always, therefore, of the form: -ις -εως ἡ and -ευς -εως ὁ.

(3) In each case (as with ἀληθεις) the nominative and accusative plurals are the same.

(4) βασιλευς follows πολις exactly, except in the accusative singular and dative plural.

(5) Nouns like πολις -εως ἡ with vowel stems need to be carefully distinguished from those with consonant stems like ἐλπις ἐλπιδος ἡ and χαρις χαριτος ἡ.

EXERCISE 31

A

1. Ἰδου, ζητῃ ὑπο της μητρος και των ἀδελφων σου.   2. και οἱ ἀνδρες περιεπατουν ἐν ταις πολεσιν συν ταις γυναιξιν αὐτων. 3. παρηγγειλεν οὐν ταις ἰδιαις θυγατρασιν ἑτοιμασαι τον ἰχθυν τῳ βασιλει.   4. ἐγω μεν βαπτιζω ὑμας ὑδατι, ἐκεινος δε βαπτισει ἡμας δυναμει.   5. οὑτοι εἰσιν οἱ ἀνθρωποι οἱτινες λεγουσιν ἀναστασιν μη εἰναι.   6. ἐγω γαρ παρα ἀνθρωπου οὐ παρελαβον αὐτο, ἀλλα δι᾽ ἀποκαλυψεως.   7. θελεις πιστιν και ἀγαθην συνειδησιν;   8. και ἐσται χειρων χρονος κρισεως και θλιψεως.   9. ὁ γαρ μαθητης οὐ φιλει πατερα και μητερα ὑπερ ἐμε.   10. δια τί οὐ περιπατουσιν κατα τας παραδοσεις των ἱερεων;   11. ἐκεινος δε οὐκ ἐχει ἀφεσιν εἰς τον αἰωνα.   12. θλιψις δε γενησεται δια τον λογον.

B

1. And the scribes must take the fishes out of the water for the priests. 2. But by his faith he will open the ears of her father.   3. And they marvelled (wondered) that he had been talking with the high-priest. 4. For the men said that they had seen the daughter of the king.

5. In the resurrection whose wife will she be?   6. And my knowledge of the mystery came by (according to) revelation.   7. But the traditions of men will not bring the forgiveness of sins.   8. Did you not know the power and the grace of God?   9. For our fathers abounded in faith and knowledge.   10. And they will persecute you from city to city.   11. But their consciences were weak.   12. But the faithful man does not come into judgement.

LESSON 32

Adjectives and pronouns of the First and Third Declensions:
πας, εἰς, οὐδεις, μηδεις, πολυς, μεγας

Some adjectives have the masculine and neuter of the Third Declension and the feminine of the First Declension.

πας

πας πασα παν, 'every', 'all' is declined as follows:

πας	πασα	παν	παντες	πασαι	παντα
παντα	πασαν	παν	παντας	πασας	παντα
παντος	πασης	παντος	παντων	πασων	παντων
παντι	παση	παντι	πασι(ν)	πασαις	πασι(ν)

All that need be learnt is $\frac{\pi\alpha\varsigma \ \pi\alpha\sigma\alpha \ \pi\alpha\nu}{\pi\alpha\nu\tau\alpha}$. The rest follows automatically. The First Declension feminine πασα has a consonant stem and so follows δοξα. The Third Declension παντα shows that the masculine (and neuter) stem is παντ. Then πας παντος follows ἀστηρ ἀστερος and παν παντος follows σωμα σωματος. For the dative plural we utilise the contraction rule of Lesson 28:

$$αντ + σιν \rightarrow ασιν$$

126

πας can be used in the following ways:

(1) It can stand alone:

πας οὖν ὅστις ἀκουει μου τους λογους τουτους (Matt. 7. 24)
Therefore everyone who hears these words of mine.

παντα δι' αὐτου ἐγενετο (John 1. 3)
All things came into existence through him.

(2) It can stand with a noun without an article:

παν δενδρον ἀγαθον καρπους καλους ποιει (Matt. 7. 17)
Every good tree yields good fruit.

(3) It can stand with a noun with an article, usually in the *predicative* position:

πας ὁ ὀχλος ἐζητουν¹ ἁπτεσθαι αὐτου (Luke 6. 19)
All the crowd (the whole crowd) were seeking to touch him.

εἷς

εἷς μια ἑν, 'one', is declined as follows:

εἷς	μια	ἑν
ἑνα	μιαν	ἑν
ἑνος	μιας	ἑνος
ἑνι	μιᾳ	ἑνι

Again, all that need be learnt is εἷς μια ἑν / ἑνα .

(μια has a vowel stem and follows ἡμερα).

εἷς and ἑν, 'one', must be carefully distinguished from εἰς, 'to', and ἐν, 'in'.

οὐδείς AND μηδείς

'No one', 'nothing' is expressed by οὐδείς, when used with the Indicative, and by μηδείς, when used with other moods. These are declined exactly like εἷς except that the prefix οὐδ- or μηδ- is added in

---

¹ Note the singular (collective) subject and the plural verb. It is technically a breach of concord, but this *construction according to sense* is common both in Greek and English. In English we could translate either 'were seeking' or 'was seeking'.

127

the masculine and neuter and the prefix οὐδε- or μηδε- in the feminine, giving:

οὐδ|εις	οὐδε|μια	οὐδ|εν	μηδ|εις	μηδε|μια	μηδ|εν
οὐδ|ενα	οὐδε|μιαν	οὐδ|εν	μηδ|ενα	μηδε|μιαν	μηδ|εν
οὐδ|ενος	οὐδε|μιας	οὐδ|ενος	μηδ|ενος	μηδε|μιας	μηδ|ενος
οὐδ|ενι	οὐδε|μιᾳ	οὐδ|ενι	μηδ|ενι	μηδε|μιᾳ	μηδ|ενι

Examples:

Indicative: πειραζει δε αὐτος οὐδενα (James 1. 13)

     And he himself tempts no one.

Infinitive: παρηγγειλεν αὐτῳ μηδενι εἰπειν (Luke 5. 14)

     He commanded him to tell (it to) no one.

In Greek two negatives do not cancel one another out, so that οὐδεις and μηδεις may be used even when the verb already has a negative:

    οὐκ ἐφαγεν οὐδεν ἐν ταις ἡμεραις ἐκειναις (Luke 4. 2)

    He ate nothing in those days.

    οὐδενι οὐδεν εἰπαν (Mark 16. 8)

    They said nothing to anybody.

πολυς AND μεγας

These adjectives are declined like ἀγαθος, except for the forms in heavy type:

πολυς   πολλη   πολυ   much; *pl.* many

πολυς	πολλη	**πολυ**
πολυν	πολλην	**πολυ**
πολλου	πολλης	πολλου
πολλῳ	πολλῃ	πολλῳ
πολλοι	πολλαι	πολλα
etc.		

μεγας   μεγαλη   μεγα   great

μεγας	μεγαλη	**μεγα**
μεγαν	μεγαλην	**μεγα**
μεγαλου	μεγαλης	μεγαλου
μεγαλῳ	μεγαλῃ	μεγαλῳ
μεγαλοι	μεγαλαι	μεγαλα
etc.		

It will be seen that the regular forms have stems πολλ and μεγαλ, while the irregular forms have the shorter stems πολ and μεγ. Simply learn:

πολυς πολλη πολυ |μεγας μεγαλη μεγα
πολυν   μεγαν

and the rest follows automatically.

EXERCISE 32

A

1. Παραλημψῃ δε την ἐξουσιαν ταυτην ἁπασαν και την δοξαν των βασιλειων. 2. οἱ τεσσαρες λῃσται ἐφυγον εἰς τα ὁρη. 3. το ὀνομα μου μεγα ἐσται ἐν πασιν τοις ἐθνεσιν. 4. οὐδεις θελει πιειν τον οἰνον τουτον; 5. οἱ ἐξ ἱερεις ἠλθον νυκτος και ἠραν τα σωματα των τριων προφητων. 6. και πασα πολις εἰχεν πυλωνας δωδεκα[1] και παν το πληθος ἐχαιρεν. 7. ὠ γυναι, μεγαλη σου ἡ πιστις. 8. και γινωσκομεν ὁτι τα δεκα ῥηματα ταυτα ἀληθη ἐστιν, ὁτι ἐλαλησεν αὐτα ὁ Κυριος δια στοματος Μωϋσεως. 9. και οὐκ ἐγνωσαν ἑως ἠλθεν ὁ μεγας κατακλυσμος και ἠρεν ἁπαντας. 10. πεμπεσθω εἰς των δουλων σπειρειν το σπερμα ἐν τοις τρισιν ἀγροις. 11. συνηρχοντο δε πολλοι ἐκ των ἑπτα κωμων και ἐφερον τους ἀσθενεις και ἐβαλλον αὐτους παρα τους ποδας αὐτου. 12. μηδεις σκανδαλιζετω ἑνα των παιδων τουτων. 13. οἱ δε δυο γονεις αὐτου οὐκ ἐγνωσαν ὁτι μενει ἐν τῃ πολει. 14. οὐχ ἡ γραφη εἰπεν ὁτι ἐκ του σπερματος Δαυειδ ἐρχεται ὁ Χριστος; 15. ἐν δε ἐκεινῃ τῃ ὡρᾳ συναγονται προς αὐτον πολλοι των ἀρχιερεων οἱ λεγουσιν ὁτι οὐκ ἐσται ἀναστασις. 16. μια ἡμερα παρα Κυριῳ ὡς χιλια ἐτη. 17. ὁ δε ἑκατονταρχης ἀπεκρινατο, Ἐγω εἰμι ἀνθρωπος ὑπο ἐξουσιαν και ἐχω ἑκατον στρατιωτας ὑπ᾽ ἐμε. 18. και ὁ ἀριθμος των ἀνδρων ἠν ὡς χιλιαδες πεντε. 19. και ἐλαλησεν δυσιν ἐξ αὐτων.

B

1. Therefore no one can have two masters. 2. And you will open our mouths, O Lord, and every tongue will bless your great name.

[1] It will be noticed that the numeral is sometimes written after the noun.

3. Did you not sow good seed in the three fields?   4. Do not carry anyone to the synagogue on the Sabbath.   5. But you can heal the colonel.   6. But I came into this world for[1] a great judgement.   7. And one of the lepers, when he saw that he was being healed, threw himself at his feet.   8. For the chief priests knew that this word was true.   9. And all the disciples were full of faith and of the Holy Spirit, and they healed those who were ill (i.e. the ill), and cast out many demons.   10. None of the priests believes that there is a resurrection.   11. My friends built a great house in this city.   12. My judgement is true; let no one love the darkness.   13. When they came to the six villages they proclaimed the gospel to all the Gentiles who dwelt in them.   14. When the disciples of John heard that he had died on that day, they came and took away his body.   15. But we have only two loaves and five fish.   16. And he went out by night to the house of Judas, one of the twelve.   17. And a hundred men, with their wives, will remain in the great desert forty days and forty nights.   18. The tribune and a thousand men used to dwell in the three cities.   19. No one can follow two masters.

LESSON 33

Comparison of adjectives
Formation and comparison of adverbs

Re-read Introduction: English Grammar, Sections 6B, 8B.

COMPARISON OF ADJECTIVES

The comparative and superlative degrees of comparison of adjectives in -ος are formed by substituting -τερος and -τατος for the final ς:

$$δικαιος \quad δικαιοτερος \text{ -α -ον} \quad δικαιοτατος \text{ -η -ον}$$

[1] εἰς.

When the last syllable but one of an adjective in -ος is short, the final o is usually[1] lengthened to ω before the addition of the comparative and superlative endings:

σοφος   σοφωτερος   σοφωτατος

The superlatives are declined like ἀγαθος, and the comparatives (with a ρ stem) are declined like ἀγιος.

The irregular comparatives (none of which has a common superlative) have been met in Vocabulary 30:

ἀγαθος	good	κρεισσων	better
κακος	bad	χειρων	worse
μεγας	great	μειζων	greater
πολυς	much, many	πλειων	more

To these should be added one very common irregular superlative:

μικρος small, little   μικροτερος smaller, less
ἐλαχιστος smallest, least

FORMATION AND COMPARISON OF ADVERBS   ως

Adverbs (in the positive) are formed from adjectives by changing the ν of the genitive plural masculine to ς:

καλος	good	gives	καλως	well
ὁμοιος	like		ὁμοιως	in like manner, similarly
ἀληθης	true		ἀληθως	truly
οὑτος	this	gives	οὑτως	in this manner, thus, so

The *comparative* and *superlative* of adverbs are formed by taking the neuter singular of the comparative adjective as the comparative of the adverb and the neuter plural of the superlative adjective as the superlative adverb:[2]

δικαιως		δικαιοτερον		δικαιοτατα	
σοφως		σοφωτερον		σοφωτατα	
εὐ	well	κρεισσον	better		

Also note: μαλλον   more   μαλιστα   most

---

[1] There are exceptions. Cf. ἀνεκτοτερον in Matt. 11. 24, quoted at the end of this lesson.

[2] These forms are in fact neuter accusatives used adverbially. Adverbial accusatives are very common in Greek. Cf. μονον, πρωτον (Vocab. 11), and the 'subject' of the infinitive (Lesson 20).

131

μαλλον (which has no positive) is the word most frequently used for the adverb 'more'. Thus:

παντων ὑμων μαλλον γλωσσαις λαλω (1 Cor. 14. 18)
I speak with tongues more than you all.

The adjective meaning 'more', as we have already seen, is πλειων. We have an example of the use of the adjective in:

ἀπεστειλεν ἀλλους δουλους πλειονας των πρωτων (Matt. 21. 36)
He sent other slaves more than the first.

The adverb 'more' qualifies its verb, i.e. 'I speak more'. The adjective 'more' qualifies its noun, i.e. 'more slaves'.

The comparative is not much used in the New Testament, and the superlative is used even less. The superlative is generally replaced by the comparative, e.g.

μικροτερον παντων των σπερματων (Mark 4. 31)
Least of all the seeds.

μειζων δε τουτων ἡ ἀγαπη (1 Cor. 13. 13)
And the greatest of these is love.

When the superlative is used it is generally elative:

εἰ οὐν οὐδε ἐλαχιστον δυνασθε (Luke 12. 26)
If then you cannot do even a very little thing.

Although (as noted in Vocab. 30) comparatives are usually followed by a *genitive of comparison*, ἡ, 'than', is sometimes used. The two things compared are then put in the same case:

γη Σοδομων ἀνεκτοτερον ἐσται ἐν ἡμερα κρισεως ἡ σοι (Matt. 11.24)
It will be more tolerable on the day of judgement for the land of Sodom than for you.

EXERCISE 33

A

1. Οὐαι, οὐχι ἡ ψυχη πλειον ἐστιν της τροφης; 2. ὁ μειζων ἐν ὑμιν γενεσθω ὡς ὁ νεωτερος. 3. νυν γαρ ἐγγυτερον ἐστιν ἡ σωτηρια ἡμων ἡ ὁτε ἐπιστευσαμεν. 4. ἀληθως οὑτος ὁ ἀνθρωπος

υἱὸς Θεου ἦν.   5. ὁ δε μικροτερος ἐν τῃ βασιλειᾳ των ουρανων μειζων αὐτου ἐστιν.   6. νυνι δε μενει πιστις, ἐλπις, ἀγαπη. τα τρια ταυτα· μειζων δε τουτων ἡ ἀγαπη.   7. ναι, ἐρχεται ὁ ἰσχυροτερος μου ὀπισω μου.   8. μειζονα τουτων ὀψῃ.   9. οἱ δε μειζον ἐκραξαν Κυριε, ἐλεησον ἡμας.   10. ὁμοιως και παντες οἱ μαθηται εἰπαν.   11. αἰρει γαρ το πληρωμα αὐτου ἀπο του ἱματιου και χειρον σχισμα γινεται.   12. ἀμην λεγω ὑμιν Ὁτε ἐποιησατε ἑνι τουτων των ἀδελφων μου των ἐλαχιστων, ἐμοι ἐποιησατε.   13. ἐρει το Ἀμην ἐπι τῃ σῃ εὐχαριστιᾳ;   14. ὑπακουειν δει Θεῳ μαλλον ἠ ἀνθρωποις.   15. λεγω ὑμιν Μειζων ἐν γεννητοις γυναικων Ἰωανου οὐδεις ἐστιν· ὁ δε μικροτερος ἐν τῃ βασιλειᾳ του Θεου μειζων αὐτου ἐστιν.   16. ἐγω γαρ εἰμι ὁ ἐλαχιστος των ἀποστολων.   17. το μωρον του Θεου σοφωτερον των ἀνθρωπων ἐστιν και το ἀσθενες του Θεου ἰσχυροτερον των ἀνθρωπων.   18. ὁ Θεος, ὁς ἐστιν σωτηρ παντων ἀνθρωπων, μαλιστα πιστων.

B

1. The younger of the sons did not wish to work for (on behalf of) his father.   2. Woe to you, hypocrite. You go and do similarly.   3. Their enemies were more than they.   4. For he is stronger than all the kings of the earth.   5. Why are you going to Jerusalem? Surely Jesus is not greater than Abraham?   6. Behold, hope and love are greater than faith, especially love.   7. This good man did all things well.   8. We must obey the king rather than[1] the priest.   9. They say that these days are worse than the days of the fathers.   10. Yes, you killed the wisest of men.   11. He that is least (smaller) will become the greatest.   12. But he cried out more, 'Behold, I am suffering at the hands of my enemies'.   13. Truly I perceive that there is a worse darkness than this.   14. We cannot do the least of these things.   15. Truly I say to you, 'Many prophets wished to see these things'.   16. But he answered them more wisely than his father.

[1] Use ἠ, because the genitive of comparison would be ambiguous.

REVISION TESTS 4

Nouns, pronouns, adjectives and adverbs

Allow 1¼ hours each for Tests A and B. Total number of marks: 100 for each test.

A

1. Express in two different ways: This face; the whole face; the face itself; that face; the same face; the other face; his own face. Express in one way: A different face; the faces of one another; they were persuading themselves. [10 marks]

2. Decline (in all genders) in singular and plural: πολυς, πολις, πλειων, πατηρ, ἐτος, ἐγω, πας. (Only repeat the stem where it is necessary.) [14]

3. Decline in the singular: 'Ηλειας; and all genders of μηδεις, ὁς. [3]

4. Give the comparative of: κακος, μεγας, νεος, εὐ. [4]

5. Give the superlative of: μικρος, δικαιως, σοφος. [3]

6. Give the nominative singular, genitive singular, article and dative plural of the words meaning: city, colonel, darkness, death, ear, enemy, foot, forgiveness, high-priest, hope, husband, image, joy, judgement (two forms), light, mother, mouth, multitude, nation, need, part, passover, power, price, repentance, resurrection, righteousness, ruler, saviour, scribe, sin, spirit, sun, time (2 words), tomb, tongue, truth, vineyard, will, woman, wonder, year. [44]

7. Give the following numerals: 1 (nominative: all genders), 3 (all forms of nominative, genitive and dative), 5, 7, 40, 1000 (both forms). [4]

8. Give the Greek for: whoever (nominative singular all genders), why?, O woman. [3]

9. Give all genders of the nominative singular of the Greek for: better, blind, dead, evil, few, full, possible, remaining, second, strong, sufficient, true. [6]

10. Give five uses of the dative. [5]

11. Give five adjectives which usually stand in the predicative position. [2]

12. Give seven words which have an -o ending in the neuter accusative singular. [2]

B

1. Express in two different ways: This face; the whole face; the face itself; that face; the same face; the other face; his own face. Express in one way: A different face; the faces of one another; they were persuading themselves. [10 marks]

2. Decline (in all genders) in singular and plural: μεγας, βασιλευς, ἀληθης, ἰχθυς, συ, τις. (Only repeat the stem where it is necessary.) [12]

3. Decline in the singular: Ἰουδας, πυρ; and all genders of εἰς, οὑτος. [6]

4. Give the comparative of: ἀγαθος, πολυς, μικρος, δικαιως, σοφως. [5]

5. Give the superlative of: δικαιος, νεος, μαλλον. [3]

6. Give the nominative singular, genitive singular, article and dative plural of the words meaning: age, authority, blood, body, centurion, conscience, cup, daughter, end, father, fish, flesh, grace, hand, judge, kind, king, knowledge, member, mercy, mountain, name, night, peace, priest, revelation, reward, sacrifice, seed, steadfastness, tradition, trouble, vessel, water, witness (abstract, 2 words), word (Third Declension), widow, wind. [39]

7. Give the following numerals: 2 (nominative and dative), 4, 6, 10, 12, 100. [3]

8. Give the Greek for: what?, anyone, a witness, O father, grace (accusative singular). [5]

9. Give all genders of the nominative singular of the Greek for: blessed, clean, eternal, faithless, free, last, like, new, only, poor, right, weak. [6]

10. Give five uses of the accusative and six uses of the genitive. [11]

LESSON 34

Perfect and Pluperfect

Re-read Introduction: English Grammar, Section 12.

As we saw in Lesson 25, a complete knowledge of a verb requires the knowledge of six principal parts. We now come to the fourth and fifth of the principal parts of λυω:

(1) Present Active λυω

(2) Future Active λυσω

(3) Aorist Active ἐλυσα

(4) Perfect Active λελυκα

(5) Perfect Passive λελυμαι

(6) Aorist Passive ἐλυθην (This will be dealt with in the next lesson.)

From λελυκα and λελυμαι are derived all parts of the Perfect and Pluperfect.

The full conjugation is as follows:

Active

Perfect Indicative	Pluperfect Indicative	Perfect Infinitive
λελυκα	(ἐ)λελυκειν	
λελυκας	(ἐ)λελυκεις	
λελυκε(ν)	(ἐ)λελυκει	λελυκεναι
λελυκαμεν	(ἐ)λελυκειμεν	
λελυκατε	(ἐ)λελυκειτε	
λελυκασι(ν)	(ἐ)λελυκεισαν	

Middle and Passive

λελυμαι	(ἐ)λελυμην	
λελυσαι	(ἐ)λελυσο	
λελυται	(ἐ)λελυτο	
λελυμεθα	(ἐ)λελυμεθα	λελυσθαι
λελυσθε	(ἐ)λελυσθε	
λελυνται	(ἐ)λελυντο	

-εω verbs

As in the Future and First Aorist, φιλε lengthens ε to η in the Perfect, giving:

$$\phi\iota\lambda\epsilon\omega \quad \phi\iota\lambda\eta\sigma\omega \quad \dot{\epsilon}\phi\iota\lambda\eta\sigma\alpha \quad \pi\epsilon\phi\iota\lambda\eta\kappa\alpha \quad \pi\epsilon\phi\iota\lambda\eta\mu\alpha\iota$$

NOTES ON THE PERFECT ACTIVE

λε-λυ-κ-α is made up of:

(1) a reduplication: λε
(2) the stem: λυ
(3) κ which *is the characteristic of the First Perfect Active*.

(There are also Second Perfects, see below.)

(4) a personal ending. These endings are the same as those of the First Aorist, except for the third person plural, which is not -αν, but -ασιν.

Reduplication

Reduplication is the placing in front of the verb of the first consonant of the stem followed by ε:

Present	Perfect
λυω	λελυκα
πιστευω	πεπιστευκα

Verbs beginning with χ, φ, θ reduplicate κεχ-, πεφ-, τεθ-:

φιλεω	πεφιληκα
θεραπευω	τεθεραπευκα

Verbs beginning with σ, ζ or ξ (which tend to make clumsy reduplications) usually[1] simply prefix an ἐ. When a verb has an initial vowel, this lengthens in the same way as in the formation of the Imperfect. The ἐ in the one case and the lengthening of vowel in the other are retained in the infinitive:[2]

ζητεω	ἐζητηκα	ἐζητηκεναι
ἀκολουθεω	ἠκολουθηκα	ἠκολουθηκεναι
αἰτεω	ᾐτηκα	ᾐτηκεναι

[1] There are exceptions. The Perfect Active of σωζω, for instance, is σεσωκα. (See the quotation from Mark 5. 34 on p. 139.)
[2] And also in the participle, see p. 150. E.g. ἐζητηκως.

NOTES ON THE PLUPERFECT ACTIVE

(1) The Pluperfect has an augment in addition to the reduplication, hence:

$$\dot{\epsilon}\text{-}\lambda\epsilon\text{-}\lambda\upsilon\text{-}\kappa\text{-}\epsilon\iota\nu$$

This form is cumbersome, and in practice the augment is usually dropped.

(2) The personal endings -ειν, -εις, -ει are identical with the endings of -εβην (Lesson 25), except that ει replaces η.

NOTE ON THE MIDDLE AND PASSIVE

These endings are identical with those of δυναμαι (Lesson 20).[1]

THE SECOND PERFECT

Some perfects are formed by adding the endings direct to the stem without inserting κ. These are Second (or Strong) Perfects.

e.g.   γραφω   γεγραφα

         κραζω   κεκραγα

Many stems of both First and Second Perfect are irregularly formed. The more important ones are to be found in the list of principal parts on pp. 227 f.

THE MEANING OF THE PERFECT

We have so far met three kinds of Greek tense:

(1) The Future, which is in the full sense a time-tense, referring to future time.

[1] *Note on the conjugation of Perfect Passives.* The addition of -μαι, -σαι, -ται to certain consonant stems causes modifications to take place. *It is not necessary for the student at this stage to learn them.* Once the principal parts are known, the forms are usually easy to recognise. The following are given for illustration and reference:

Guttural stem	Labial stem	Dental stem
ἀγω, perf. stem: ἠγ-	γραφω, perf. stem: γεγραφ-	ἁγιαζω, perf. stem: ἡγιασ-
ἠγμαι	γεγραμμαι	ἡγιασμαι
ἠξαι	γεγραψαι	ἡγιασαι
ἠκται	γεγραπται	ἡγιασται
Infinitive: ἠχθαι	Infinitive: γεγραφθαι	Infinitive: ἡγιασθαι

(2) The linear tenses: the Imperfect and (usually) the Present, which are concerned with continuous or repeated action:

——————— or ·········

(3) The punctiliar tenses: the two Aorists, which are concerned with an action simply regarded as an event:

·

With the Perfect we have a fourth kind of tense:

(4) The Perfect represents *a present state resulting from a past action,*

e.g. γεγραπται   it stands written.

That is to say, the Scripture, written in the past, bears its witness now, in the present.

This can be represented by:

·———————————————

Or, if the past action was itself of extended duration before completion, by: ——————— · ———————

This use of the Greek Perfect is not altogether the same as the use of the English Perfect. Usually the English Perfect will accurately translate the Greek Perfect, and the English Past Simple will accurately translate the Greek Aorist, but by no means always. The Greek Aorist is wider in meaning than the English Past Simple, and the Greek Perfect is narrower in meaning than the English Perfect.

Consider the three sentences:

A. Your faith has saved you.
B. Have you not read?
C. He called them.

A speaks of a present state of salvation resulting from an act of faith in the past. It is therefore Perfect in Greek as it is in English:

ἡ πιστις σου σεσωκεν σε. (Mark 5. 34)

B speaks of an action at some indefinite time in the past, without emphasis on the reader's present state. Though Perfect in English it will be Aorist in Greek:

οὐκ ἀνεγνωτε; (Mark 12. 26)

139

C speaks of a simple action in past time. It is therefore Past Simple in English and Aorist in Greek:

$$\dot{\epsilon}\kappa\alpha\lambda\epsilon\sigma\epsilon\nu\ \alpha\dot{v}\tau o v s.\ \text{(Mark 1. 20)}$$

This overlap of Past Simple, Perfect and Aorist can be represented diagrammatically like this:

English Perfect

> A
> present state resulting
> from past action } Greek Perfect

> B
> action in
> indefinite past

English Past Simple

> C
> action in
> definite past

} Greek Aorist

This diagram may be further illustrated by three sentences more closely related to one another:

> A. He has killed her.
> B. He has killed a number of women in his time.
> C. He killed her.

There are occasions when even the Greek Perfect has to be translated by the Past Simple. But such a Perfect may still retain its proper force, e.g.

$$X\rho\iota\sigma\tau o s\ \dot{\alpha}\pi\epsilon\theta\alpha\nu\epsilon\nu\ \kappa\alpha\iota\ \dot{\epsilon}\gamma\eta\gamma\epsilon\rho\tau\alpha\iota\ \tau\eta\ \dot{\eta}\mu\epsilon\rho\alpha\ \tau\eta\ \tau\rho\iota\tau\eta\ \text{(1 Cor. 15. 3, 4)}$$

Christ died (Aorist) and was raised (Perfect) on the third day.

So it must be translated, but $\dot{\epsilon}\gamma\eta\gamma\epsilon\rho\tau\alpha\iota$ suggests the further thought: 'and is a risen Saviour still today!'

In every case the idea of the Greek tense must be discovered and then the nearest equivalent English idiom found.

THE MEANING OF THE PLUPERFECT

The meaning of the Pluperfect corresponds precisely to that of the Perfect, except that the action in past time is thought of as also completed in past time,

e.g. Λαζαρος ἐβέβλητο προς τον πυλωνα αὐτου (Luke 16. 20)
Lazarus had been put[1] at his gate (and, as a result, lay there).

The action was done in the past, its results lasted some time, but at the time of narration the whole completed action lay in the past.

EXERCISE 34

A

1. Παιδια, ἐσχατη ὡρα ἐστιν, και καθως ἠκουσατε ὁτι ἀντιχριστος ἐρχεται, και νυν ἀντιχριστοι πολλοι γεγονασιν.   2. εἰ οὐν ἀξιον θανατου πεπραχα τι.   3. οὐ γεγραπται Ὁ οἰκος μου οἰκος προσευχης;   4. και το εὐαγγελιον ἀπηγγελται ἐν παντι τω κοσμω.   5. ὁτι ἠξαι εἰς ἁμαρτιαν.   6. αἱ δε ἀσθενεις ἠρκασιν τας φωνας αὐτων.   7. και καινη ἀποκαλυψις δεδεκται ὑπο παντων ἡμων.   8. τα γαρ ἐθνη ἀναβεβηκεν εἰς τα Ἱεροσολυμα.   9. ὁλος δε ὁ λαος οὑτος ἐγνωσται ὑπο του Θεου ἀπ᾽ ἀρχης.   10. ὁ Χριστος συν πασιν τοις μελεσιν του σωματος αὐτου ἐγηγερται ἐκ νεκρων.   11. οἱ δε τεσσαρες γραμματεις εὑρηκασιν παντα τα μεγαλα σκευη.   12. ἡ ἀγαπητη θυγατηρ μου τεθνηκεν. τη τριτη ὡρα της νυκτος ἀπεθανεν.   13. ἀχρι του ὀρους ἐφ᾽ ᾡ αὐτων ἡ πολις ᾠκοδομητο.   14. εἰ ἐγνωκειτε το ῥημα ὁ γεγραπται, Ἐλεος θελω και οὐ θυσιαν.   15. αὐτοι μεν ἀπηγγειλαν την παρουσιαν μου, ὑμεις δε οὐκ ἠκουσατε.   16. τα δε ὠτα μου ἀνεῳκται τω ῥηματι αὐτου.   17. Μαρια, παρ᾽ ἡς ἐκβεβληκει ἑπτα δαιμονια.   18. και ἠσαν ἀνθρωποι οἰτινες φονον πεποιηκεισαν.   19. ὁ ἀνθρωπος ἐφ᾽ ὁν γεγονει το σημειον τουτο.   20. ὁ Κυριος εἰς ὁν πεπιστευκεισαν.[2]   21. ὁ Ἰωανης ὁ βαπτιστης

---

[1] For βαλλω in this weakened sense, cf. p. 120 n. 1.

[2] εἰς is the usual preposition after πιστευω, ἐπι occurs sometimes, and ἐν rarely, with virtually no distinction in meaning between them. In the New Testament εἰς is frequently equivalent to ἐν, from which in fact it was originally derived.

κεκραγεν ἐν τῇ ἐρημῳ.   22. περι δε των νεκρων ὁτι ἐγειρονται,
οὐκ ἀνεγνωτε ἐν τῳ βιβλιῳ Μωϋσεως πως εἰπεν αὐτῳ ὁ Θεος...;
23. περι δε τῆς ἡμερας ἐκεινης οὐδεις οἰδεν.   24. ὁτι ᾐδεισαν τον
Χριστον αὐτον εἰναι.   25. θελω δε ὑμας εἰδεναι ὁτι παντος
ἀνδρος ἡ κεφαλη ὁ Χριστος ἐστιν.   26. και γινεται κατακεισθαι
αὐτον ἐν τῇ οἰκιᾳ αὐτου, και πολλοι τελωναι και ἁμαρτωλοι συνα-
νεκεινто τῳ Ἰησου.   27. ἀνεκειτο δε μετα των δωδεκα μαθητων.
28. και συναγεται προς αὐτον ὀχλος πλειστος, ὡστε αὐτον καθησθαι
ἐν πλοιῳ ἐν τῇ θαλασσῃ.   29. και ἐκαθητο ὁ Πετρος μεσος¹
αὐτων.   30. ᾐδεισαν γαρ ἁπαντες ὁτι Ἑλλην ὁ πατηρ αὐτου
ὑπηρχεν.   31. οἰδασιν γαρ ὁτι τεθνηκεν.   32. ὁ δε Θεος
λελαληκεν ταυτα τα ῥηματα εἰς το εἰδεναι ὑμας τίς ἐστιν ἡ ἐλπις της
κλησεως αὐτου.   33. ἀπολελυσθαι ἐδυνατο ὁ ἀνθρωπος οὑτος εἰ
μη ἐπεκεκλητο Καισαρα.²   34. οὐδεις ἐδυνατο αὐτον δησαι, δια το
αὐτον πολλακις δεδεσθαι.²   35. πτωχος δε τις ὀνοματι Λαζαρος
ἐβεβλητο προς τον πυλωνα αὐτου.   36. ἰδετε τον τοπον ὁπου
ἐκειτο το σωμα.

B

1. He has not injured you or your friends.   2. Jude, you must
proclaim the things which you have heard.   3. The slaves of the
ruler have done the work.   4. And he answered, 'What I have
written, I have written'.   5. But because I have become king I will
walk in the ways of my fathers.   6. The poor and the blind have
been thrown into prison.   7. O Lord, in Thee have we trusted.
8. For I reckon that he has done³ nothing worthy of death.   9. But
the Son of Man departs as it is written of him.   10. For we have
announced his second coming.   11. The king of glory has been
lifted up.   12. But he has thrown the books into the river.   13. And
I have known your evil ways.   14. And God raised Jesus on the
third day.   15. I have kept the faith.   16. We know⁴ that you are
true.   17. For he knew the sign that he was about to do.   18. The
whole world lies in the Evil One.   19. But Peter was sitting outside.
20. They heard that he had done³ this wonder.

¹ An alternative to ἐν μεσῳ.   ² Note the slightly irregular form of δεδεσθαι.
³ Use Perfect Infinitive.   ⁴ Use οἰδα in this and the next sentence.

LESSON 35

The Aorist and Future Passives

As we saw in the last lesson, the sixth of the principal parts is the Aorist Passive. There are again both First and Second Aorists in the Passive, as in the Active. From the Aorist Passive can usually be derived corresponding Future Passive tenses.

THE AORIST PASSIVES

The First Aorist Indicative Passive is made up of:

augment + verbal stem + θ + the endings of -$\epsilon\beta\eta\nu$ (Lesson 25).

The Second Aorist Indicative Passive is made up of:

augment + Second Aorist Passive stem + endings of -$\epsilon\beta\eta\nu$.

(The θ, which is characteristic of the First Aorist and First Future Passives, is not found in the Second Aorist and Second Future.)

So we get:

First Aorist Passive		Second Aorist Passive	
Indicative			
ἐλυθην	I was loosed	ἐγραφην	I was written
ἐλυθης		ἐγραφης	
ἐλυθη		ἐγραφη	
ἐλυθημεν		ἐγραφημεν	
ἐλυθητε		ἐγραφητε	
ἐλυθησαν		ἐγραφησαν	

The Imperative and Infinitive are:

Imperative			
λυθητι	be loosed	σπαρηθι[1]	be sown
λυθητω		σπαρητω	
λυθητε		σπαρητε	
λυθητωσαν		σπαρητωσαν	
Infinitive			
λυθηναι	to be loosed	γραφηναι	to be written

[1] σπειρω has been chosen for this conjugation, because γραφω is slightly irregular.

143

Notice that, apart from the θ in the First Aorist, the forms of the endings of the two Aorists differ only in the second person singular Imperative.

THE FUTURE PASSIVES

There are two corresponding Future Passives.

The First Future is made up of:

verb stem + $\underline{\theta\eta\sigma}$ + the endings of the <u>Present Passive</u> of $\lambda\upsilon\omega$.

The Second Future is made up of:

the Second Aorist Passive stem + $\eta\sigma$ + the endings of the Present Passive of $\lambda\upsilon\omega$.

So we get:

First Future Passive		Second Future Passive	
$\lambda\upsilon\theta\eta\sigma\omega\mu\alpha\iota$	I shall be loosed	$\gamma\rho\alpha\phi\eta\sigma\omega\mu\alpha\iota$	I shall be written
$\lambda\upsilon\theta\eta\sigma\eta$		$\gamma\rho\alpha\phi\eta\sigma\eta$	
$\lambda\upsilon\theta\eta\sigma\epsilon\tau\alpha\iota$		$\gamma\rho\alpha\phi\eta\sigma\epsilon\tau\alpha\iota$	
$\lambda\upsilon\theta\eta\sigma\omega\mu\epsilon\theta\alpha$		$\gamma\rho\alpha\phi\eta\sigma\omega\mu\epsilon\theta\alpha$	
$\lambda\upsilon\theta\eta\sigma\epsilon\sigma\theta\epsilon$		$\gamma\rho\alpha\phi\eta\sigma\epsilon\sigma\theta\epsilon$	
$\lambda\upsilon\theta\eta\sigma\omega\nu\tau\alpha\iota$		$\gamma\rho\alpha\phi\eta\sigma\omega\nu\tau\alpha\iota$	

In contracted verbs the short vowel is lengthened before θ, giving for $\phi\iota\lambda\epsilon\omega$: $\qquad \epsilon\phi\iota\lambda\eta\theta\eta\nu \qquad \phi\iota\lambda\eta\theta\eta\sigma\omega\mu\alpha\iota.$

We <u>now have the full principal parts</u> of $\lambda\upsilon\omega$, $\phi\iota\lambda\epsilon\omega$ and $\gamma\rho\alpha\phi\omega$:

$\lambda\upsilon\omega$	$\lambda\upsilon\sigma\omega$	$\epsilon\lambda\upsilon\sigma\alpha$	$\lambda\epsilon\lambda\upsilon\kappa\alpha$	$\lambda\epsilon\lambda\upsilon\mu\alpha\iota$	$\epsilon\lambda\upsilon\theta\eta\nu$
$\phi\iota\lambda\epsilon\omega$	$\phi\iota\lambda\eta\sigma\omega$	$\epsilon\phi\iota\lambda\eta\sigma\alpha$	$\pi\epsilon\phi\iota\lambda\eta\kappa\alpha$	$\pi\epsilon\phi\iota\lambda\eta\mu\alpha\iota$	$\epsilon\phi\iota\lambda\eta\theta\eta\nu$
$\gamma\rho\alpha\phi\omega$	$\gamma\rho\alpha\psi\omega$	$\epsilon\gamma\rho\alpha\psi\alpha$	$\gamma\epsilon\gamma\rho\alpha\phi\alpha$	$\gamma\epsilon\gamma\rho\alpha\mu\mu\alpha\iota$	$\epsilon\gamma\rho\alpha\phi\eta\nu$

MUTE STEMS

In the Future and the First Aorist the placing of the letter θ immediately after the stem again causes certain consonantal changes when the stem ends in a mute (cf. Lesson 21).

$$\kappa, \quad \gamma, \quad \chi + \theta \rightarrow \chi\theta$$
$$\pi, \quad \beta, \quad \phi + \theta \rightarrow \phi\theta$$
$$\tau, \quad \delta, \quad \theta + \theta \rightarrow \sigma\theta$$

Examples:

Verbal Stem	Present	First Aorist Passive	Future Passive
ἀγ	ἀγω	ἠχθην	ἀχθησομαι
πραγ	πρασσω	ἐπραχθην	πραχθησομαι
πεμπ	πεμπω	ἐπεμφθην	πεμφθησομαι
βαπτιδ	βαπτιζω	ἐβαπτισθην	βαπτισθησομαι
πειθ	πειθω	ἐπεισθην	πεισθησομαι

IRREGULAR FORMS

The following important verbs have irregular First Aorist forms:

ἀκουω	ἠκουσθην	σωζω	ἐσωθην
βαλλω	ἐβληθην	λεγω	{ ἐρρηθην / ἐρρεθην
ἐγειρω	ἠγερθην		
καλεω	ἐκληθην	ὁραω	ὠφθην
λαμβανω	ἐλημφθην	φερω	ἠνεχθην

The Aorist Passives given for λεγω, ὁραω and φερω are really from different verbs, as explained in Lesson 25.

The following verbs which we have already met have Second Aorist Passives:

γραφω	ἐγραφην	ἀποστελλω	ἀπεσταλην
σπειρω	ἐσπαρην	κρυπτω	ἐκρυβην

To these should be added:

στρεφω	ἐστραφην	I turn
φαινω	ἐφανην	I shine; *pass.* appear

These irregular Aorists have corresponding Future forms,

e.g.   First Futures: ἀκουσθησομαι, βληθησομαι;
Second Futures: στραφησομαι, φανησομαι.

With the exception of κρυπτω, στρεφω and φαινω, all the above irregular First and Second Aorists belong to verbs whose complete principal parts have to be learnt. ἐκρυβην, ἐστραφην and ἐφανην should therefore be specially noted at this point.

EXERCISE 35

A

1. Ἤχθη δε ὁ Ἰησους ὑπο του πνευματος εἰς τα ὀρη πειρασθηναι ὑπο του διαβολου. 2. αἱ δε γυναικες παρεκληθησαν ὑπο των ἀνδρων αὐτων. 3. το οὐν ὀνομα μου κηρυχθησεται ἐν πασιν τοις ἐθνεσιν. 4. τῃ γαρ χαριτι ἐσωθημεν δια πιστεως. 5. οἱ νεκροι ἐγερθησονται ἐν τῃ ἡμερᾳ της κρισεως τῃ φωνῃ του ἀγγελου. 6. και ὁτε ἐξεβληθη το δαιμονιον ἐθαυμαζεν ὁ ὀχλος, ἐλεγον δε πολλοι ὁτι Ταυτα τα τερατα οὐκ ἐπραχθη ἐν ταις ἡμεραις των πατερων ἡμων. 7. μετα ταυτα ὠφθη¹ πασιν τοις ἀποστολοις. 8. παρηγγειλεν τον ἀνδρα ἐνεχθηναι δια της πολεως. 9. ἐν ἐκεινῃ τῃ ἡμερᾳ πας ὁ λαος κληθησεται ἁγιος τῳ Κυριῳ. 10. και ὁ ἀρχιερευς ἐκρυβη ἐν τοις ὀρεσιν πολλα ἐτη. 11. ποιησω γαρ τα ῥηματα μου ἀκουσθηναι τοις ὠσιν αὐτων. 12. οὐδεις των ἀγγελων ἀκουσθησεται. 13. παντες οἱ ἰχθυες ἐβληθησαν εἰς το ὑδωρ. 14. ταυτα ἐρρηθη δια στοματος Δαυειδ. 15. πεμφθητω εἰς των ἱερεων πεισθηναι ὑπο του βασιλεως. 16. ὁτε καρπον ἐποιησεν το καλον σπερμα ἐφανη και τα ζιζανια. 17. διδασκαλε, φιληθησῃ ὑπο παντος του ἐθνους. 18. τα σωματα των ἁγιων ἐσπαρη ἐν ἀτιμιᾳ, ἐγερθησεται δε ἐν δοξῃ. 19. κληθητωσαν ἀφρονες ὑπο των σοφων του αἰωνος τουτου. 20. πειρασμος ὑμας οὐκ εἰληφεν. 21. ὁ γαρ Θεος εἰρηκεν τουτο δια στοματος παντων των προφητων. 22. δια το ὀνομα μου ἀχθησεσθε εἰς βασιλεις και ἀρχοντας. 23. και σκοτος ἠδη ἐγεγονει και οὐπω ἐληλυθει προς αὐτους ὁ Ἰησους. 24. οἰδας ὁτι οἱ Φαρισαιοι ἐσκανδαλισθησαν; 25. οὐαι, ἐσχηκασιν θλιψιν ἡμερας και νυκτος. 26. πεπεισται γαρ πονηραις γλωσσαις και πεπτωκεν εἰς ἁμαρτιαν. 27. ὁτι οὐ κεκριμεθα ὑπ᾽ αὐτων, ἡμεις οὐ κεκρικαμεν αὐτους. 28. οὑτοι οἱ λογοι γραφητωσαν και ὁ λαος πινετω ἐκ των γραφων.

B

1. All this race was called righteous. 2. Many of these words were written in a book by the high priest. 3. The fish were taken by these boys. 4. We were sown in tribulation, we shall be raised in power.

¹ ὠφθην in the sense of 'appeared to' takes dative.

5. The demon will be cast out and the crowd will wonder.   6. The good seed was carried to the six vessels.   7. And I was sent by the king's servants to seek you.   8. We know that this gospel will be preached to all the Gentiles, and that many will hear.   9. In that day many bodies of the saints were raised, and came into the city, and appeared to many.   10. We wish the sheep to be led to the mountains. 11. But you will be saved by faith and hope.   12. You commanded the stones to be thrown into the water.   13. All these things will be done in the darkness.   14. You have heard that it was said by our fathers, 'You shall not make an image'.   15. We were called weak by many, but we know that our consciences are true.   16. We have seen and borne witness that this man is a prophet.   17. And the young men turned[1] from their sins because great fear had taken them. 18. The Lord therefore has said bad things concerning you.   19. I have found the words of the kingdom for you, but you have not believed me.   20. And they commanded the sacrifice to be brought to the sanctuary.   21. O house of Israel, do not be judged by the unbelieving.   22. Is it not said in the law, 'Nothing shall be saved?' 23. He has saved you; we have been saved similarly.   24. And we have drunk the cup of joy which God has sent.   25. Behold, I have called him.   26. O woman, be sown in anger, but be raised in love. 27. And I have carried a part of the price into the widow's tomb.

LESSON 36

Participles

Re-read Introduction: English Grammar, Sections 15, 16, 18, 19.

THE NATURE OF PARTICIPLES

Being *verbal adjectives*, participles share the characteristics of both verbs and adjectives.

---

[1] Use Aorist Passive.

As a verb a participle has tense and voice and may have an object.

As an adjective it agrees with a noun or pronoun which it qualifies in number, gender and case.

Participles may be divided into two groups:

I. Those with First and Third Declension endings (cf. Lesson 32).

II. Those with First and Second Declension endings.

The latter cause no difficulty; they are all alike and are declined like ἀγαθος.

The former are of four types, according to their endings:

I. Participles with First and Third Declension endings

	Masculine	Feminine	Neuter
Type 1	-ων	-ουσα	-ον
Type 2	-ας	-ασα	-αν
Type 3	-εις	-εισα	-εν
Type 4	-ως	-υια	-ος

Type 1: -ων -ουσα -ον

This covers: (*a*) the Present Active of verbs like λυω; (*b*) the Present Active of verbs like φιλεω; and two other tenses of similar form: (*c*) the Second Aorist Active (e.g. of βαλλω); (*d*) the Present of εἰμι.

(*a*) *Present Participle Active of* λυω: loosing

λυων	λυουσα	λυον	λυοντες	λυουσαι	λυοντα
λυοντα	λυουσαν	λυον	λυοντας	λυουσας	λυοντα
λυοντος	λυουσης	λυοντος	λυοντων	λυουσων	λυοντων
λυοντι	λυουσῃ	λυοντι	λυουσι(ν)	λυουσαις	λυουσι(ν)

When λυων λυουσα λυον λυοντα has been learnt, the rest of the declension follows automatically. It is only necessary to remember (i) that the feminine, since it has a stem ending in σ, is declined like δοξα; (ii) that the rules of Lesson 28 are to be followed in the formation of the dative plurals:

Type 1 οντ + σιν → ουσιν

Type 2 αντ + σιν → ασιν

Type 3 $\epsilon\nu\tau + \sigma\iota\nu \to \epsilon\iota\sigma\iota\nu$

Type 4 $\tau + \sigma\iota\nu \to \sigma\iota\nu$

(b) Present Participle Active of φιλεω: loving

With -εω verbs the rules of contraction are strictly applied (i.e. $\epsilon + o \to ov$; ε before a long vowel or diphthong drops out):

φιλων   φιλουσα   φιλουν

φιλουντα,   etc.

The other tenses which have the same endings as λυων are:

(c) Second Aorist Active   βαλων   βαλουσα   βαλον   having thrown

(d) Present of εἰμι   ὠν   οὐσα   ὀν   being

Type 2: -ας -ασα -αν

First Aorist Participle Active of λυω: having loosed

λυσας	λυσασα	λυσαν	λυσαντες	λυσασαι	λυσαντα
λυσαντα	λυσασαν	λυσαν	λυσαντας	λυσασας	λυσαντα
λυσαντος	λυσασης	λυσαντος	λυσαντων	λυσασων	λυσαντων
λυσαντι	λυσαση	λυσαντι	λυσασι(ν)	λυσασαις	λυσασι(ν)

These endings are the same as those of πας πασα παν.

Type 3: -εις -εισα -εν

This covers two tenses: (*a*) the First Aorist Passive of verbs like λυω; and (*b*) the closely related Second Aorist Passive (e.g. of γραφω):

(a) First Aorist Participle Passive of λυω: having been loosed

λυθεις	λυθεισα	λυθεν	λυθεντες	λυθεισαι	λυθεντα
λυθεντα	λυθεισαν	λυθεν	λυθεντας	λυθεισας	λυθεντα
λυθεντος	λυθεισης	λυθεντος	λυθεντων	λυθεισων	λυθεντων
λυθεντι	λυθειση	λυθεντι	λυθεισι(ν)	λυθεισαις	λυθεισι(ν)

(b) Second Aorist Participle Passive of γραφω: having been written

γραφεις   γραφεισα   γραφεν

149

Type 4: -ως -υια -ος

Perfect Participle Active of λυω: having loosed

λελυκως	λελυκυια	λελυκος
λελυκοτα	λελυκυιαν	λελυκος
λελυκοτος	λελυκυιας	λελυκοτος
λελυκοτι	λελυκυιᾳ	λελυκοτι
λελυκοτες	λελυκυιαι	λελυκοτα
λελυκοτας	λελυκυιας	λελυκοτα
λελυκοτων	λελυκυιων	λελυκοτων
λελυκοσι(ν)	λελυκυιαις	λελυκοσι(ν)

(Note that the feminine, since it has a stem ending in -ι, is declined like ἡμερα.)

II. Participles with First and Second Declension endings. There are seven tenses in this group, and all have the endings:

-μενος   -μενη   -μενον

There are five tenses of verbs like λυω: (a) Present Middle and Passive; (b) First Aorist Middle; (c) Perfect Middle and Passive. In addition, there belong to this group: (d) the Second Aorist Middle (e.g. of γινομαι); and (e) the participle of δυναμαι. They are all declined like ἀγαθος.

(a) *Present Participle Middle and Passive of* λυω: loosing, being loosed

λυομενος	λυομενη	λυομενον	λυομενοι	λυομεναι	λυομενα
λυομενον	λυομενην	λυομενον	λυομενους	λυομενας	λυομενα
λυομενου	λυομενης	λυομενου	λυομενων	λυομενων	λυομενων
λυομενῳ	λυομενῃ	λυομενῳ	λυομενοις	λυομεναις	λυομενοις

(b) *First Aorist Middle:*

λυσαμενος -η -ον having loosed

(c) *Perfect Middle and Passive:*

λελυμενος -η -ον having loosed, having been loosed

(d) *Second Aorist Middle:*

γενομενος -η -ον having become

(e) δυναμαι:

δυναμενος -η -ον being able

All this at first sight seems rather complicated, but in fact the relation between the indicative tenses and the participles is very close. It will be helpful at this stage to study the λυω table on pp. 232 f. Notice the close relation between the principal parts and the corresponding participles:

Principal parts: λυω ἐλυσα (ἐλυσαμην) λελυκα λελυμαι ἐλυθην
Participles: λυων λυσας (λυσαμενος) λελυκως λελυμενος λυθεις

THE USE OF PARTICIPLES

The meanings of the various participles given above are the nearest general English equivalents. Sometimes they will give a perfectly satisfactory translation, but usually some other English idiom is more appropriate.

There are two uses: the adjectival participle and the adverbial participle.

(1) **The adjectival participle.** In this use the adjectival side of the participle is most prominent. The adjectival participle is generally preceded by an article (with which it agrees). This so-called *articular participle* is occasionally used in English in expressions like 'the living', 'the missing'. In the New Testament it is very common. The examples below mean literally 'the believing (ones)', 'the sowing (man)', 'the having-been-sown-by-the-wayside (man)'. The articular participle will usually be best translated by a clause introduced by a relative pronoun, but it may sometimes be translated by a noun:

οἱ πιστευοντες   those who believe, the believers.
ὁ σπειρων   the one who sows, the sower.

οὗτος ἐστιν ὁ παρα την ὁδον σπαρεις (Matt. 13. 19)
This is he that was sown by the wayside.

Notice that any number of qualifying words may be inserted between the article and the participle.

(2) **The adverbial participle.** In this use the verbal side of the participle is most prominent. The adverbial participle is not preceded by the article. When a participle is used adverbially it is equivalent to an adverbial clause modifying some other verb in the sentence. Such participles are best translated into English by a suitable adverbial

clause. The context must decide what kind of adverbial clause the participle in question is equivalent to. Commonest are:

(a) *Temporal clauses.*

(1) καὶ ἐξελθὼν εἶδεν πολυν ὄχλον (Matt. 14. 14)
And when he came (*or,* had come) out, he saw a great crowd.

(2) καὶ ἀκουσαντες οἱ ἀρχιερεις καὶ οἱ Φαρισαιοι τας παρα-βολας αὐτου ἐγνωσαν ὅτι περι αὐτων λεγει (Matt. 21. 45)
And when the chief priests and Pharisees had heard his parables, they knew that he was speaking about them.

(b) *Causal clauses.*

(1) καὶ παντες ἐφοβουντο αὐτον, μη πιστευοντες ὅτι ἐστιν μαθητης (Acts 9. 26)
And they were all afraid of him, because they did not believe that he was a disciple.

(2) ἡ δε εὐσεβεια προς παντα ὠφελιμος ἐστιν, ἐπαγγελιαν ἐχουσα ζωης της νυν καὶ της μελλουσης (1 Tim. 4. 8)
But godliness is profitable for everything, because it has a promise for the life that is now, as well as for that which is to come.

Examples of *concessive clauses* will be found in Exercise 37 B 7, 11; a *conditional clause* in 38 A 23.

In some cases however it is better to translate the Greek participle by an English participle:

ἐν δε ταις ἡμεραις ἐκειναις παραγινεται Ἰωανης ὁ Βαπτιστης κηρυσσων ἐν τῃ ἐρημῳ της Ἰουδαιας, λεγων, Μετανοειτε (Matt. 3. 1)

And in those days appears John the Baptist proclaiming in the desert of Judea, saying, 'Repent'.

The translation which sounds best in English must be chosen.

The meaning of the tense in participles

Generally speaking, the Present Participle denotes action taking place at the same time as the action of the main verb, and the Aorist Participle denotes action which took place before the action of the main verb. See the examples already quoted: (a) (1) (2) are Aorist; (b) (1) (2) are Present.

The Aorist Participle is however sometimes used to describe *attendant circumstances*, i.e. an action taking place at the same time as the action of the main verb, notably in the common expression:

    ἀποκριθεὶς εἶπεν   he answered and said.

The distinction between Aorist and Perfect is the same in the case of participles as in the case of the Indicative. The Aorist speaks simply of an event in the past, the Perfect of an event in the past the results of which are still felt in the present. A good example of the latter is:

    εὖρεν τὸ παιδιον βεβλημενον ἐπι την κλινην και το δαιμονιον ἐξεληλυθος (Mark 7. 30)

She found the child lying in bed, and the demon gone.

The negative with participles

As will have been observed in Sentence (*b*) (1) above, participles (like Imperatives and Infinitives) are negatived with μη.

EXERCISE 36

A

1. Και παραγων παρα την θαλασσαν της Γαλιλαιας εἰδεν Σιμωνα.
2. και ἠλθεν κηρυσσων εἰς τας συναγωγας αὐτων και δαιμονια ἐκβαλλων.   3. πως δυσκολως οἱ τα χρηματα ἐχοντες εἰς την βασιλειαν του Θεου εἰσελευσονται.   4. και ἠσαν οἱ φαγοντες τους ἀρτους πεντακισχιλιοι ἀνδρες.   5. και οἱ διασπαρεντες διηλθον εὐαγγελιζομενοι τον λογον.   6. λεγει αὐτῳ ὁ Ἰησους, Ὁτι ἑωρακας με πεπιστευκας; μακαριοι οἱ μη ἰδοντες και πιστευσαντες. 7. ἀκουων δε Ἀνανιας τους λογους τουτους πεσων ἀπεθανεν, και ἐγενετο φοβος μεγας ἐπι παντας τους ἀκουοντας.   8. και το πνευμα το ἀκαθαρτον φωνησαν φωνη μεγαλη ἐξηλθεν ἐξ αὐτου. 9. και ἠν ἐν τη ἐρημῳ τεσσαρακοντα ἡμερας και τεσσαρακοντα νυκτας πειραζομενος ὑπο του Σατανα.   10. ἀκουσατε οὐν την παραβολην του σπειραντος.   11. και ὠφθη αὐτοις Μωϋσης και Ἡλειας συνλαλουντες μετ' αὐτου.   12. ἐρχεται προς αὐτον Μαρια ἡ καλουμενη Μαγδαληνη, ἀφ' ἡς δαιμονια ἑπτα ἐξεληλυθει. 13. τη ἐκκλησιᾳ του Θεου τη οὐση ἐν Κορινθῳ.   14. ἀρξαμενος ἀπο του βαπτισματος Ἰωανου ἑως ταυτης της ἡμερας.   15. οὑτος

ὁ Ἰησους ὁ ἀναλημφθεις ἀφ᾽ ὑμων εἰς τον οὐρανον παλιν ἐλευσεται.
16. και μη φοβεισθε ἀπο των ἀποκτεινοντων το σωμα, την δε
ψυχην μη δυναμενων ἀποκτειναι· φοβεισθε μαλλον τον δυναμενον και
ψυχην και σωμα ἀπολεσαι ἐν γεεννῃ. 17. πορευθεντες δε
ἀπηγγειλαν τοις ἀρχιερευσιν ἁπαντα τα γενομενα. 18. ταυτην
δε θυγατερα Ἀβρααμ οὐσαν, ἡν ἐδησεν ὁ Σατανας δεκα και ὀκτω
ἐτη, οὐκ ἐδει λυθηναι τῃ ἡμερᾳ του σαββατου; 19. ὁ δε Κορνη-
λιος συνκαλεσαμενος τους συγγενεις αὐτου ἠσπασατο αὐτον. 20. ὁ
δε εἰδως αὐτων την ὑποκρισιν εἰπεν αὐτοις, Τί με πειραζετε;
21. ἡ δε γυνη, εἰδυια ὃ γεγονεν αὐτῃ, ἠλθεν και προσεπεσεν αὐτῳ.
22. φοβηθητε τον μετα το ἀποκτειναι ἐχοντα ἐξουσιαν ἐμβαλειν εἰς
την γεενναν.

B

Participles should be used to translate all the words marked *
and also all the English participles.

1. And those that had preached* the word were sent by the Spirit.
2. And having come to the sea of Galilee the disciples taught many
people.   3. Blessed are those that hear* and those that believe* the
words of this book.   4. Many of the publicans therefore were
baptised repenting of¹ their sins.   5. But he answered* and said, 'You
will not enter the kingdom of heaven'.   6. The sower* sows the
seeds.   7. And when he had come out* he saw a great cross.
8. But we were afraid because we did not believe* that his compassion
was true.   9. And all those that heard* kept the promise in their
hearts.   10. For this is he that was sent* by the king.   11. But
while they were teaching* the people they remained in the temple.
12. And having come out of the city he went to another place.   13. But
the prophet cried, saying, 'Behold the man who comes* after me; him you
will hear'.   14. When the ruler therefore heard* this he was afraid
and all that were* with him.   15. But her husband being a righteous
man wished to divorce (release) her.   16. And when they had come*
to the city those that guarded* it threw them out.   17. But as I was
walking* through the fields I saw a great light from heaven and heard a
voice speaking to me.   18. The scribe remained in the mountain

¹ Use ἀπο.

154

forty days and forty nights writing all the commandments of the law.
19. He who is not* with me is against me.　20. For he feared John,
knowing him (to be) a righteous man.

LESSON 37

The genitive absolute
Periphrastic tenses

THE GENITIVE ABSOLUTE

Sometimes a participle and noun or pronoun are both put in the genitive.
Consider the sentences:

καὶ πορευομένων αὐτῶν ἐν τῇ ὁδῷ εἶπεν τις πρὸς αὐτον (Luke 9. 57)
And as they were going in the way, a certain man said to him.

καὶ ἐκβληθέντος τοῦ δαιμονίου ἐλάλησεν ὁ κωφός (Matt. 9. 33)
And when the demon had been cast out, the dumb man spoke.

It will be noticed that in each case the noun that goes with the
participle is neither subject, object nor indirect object of the main verb.
The clause containing the participle is 'loosed off' from the rest of the
sentence, and the construction is called the *genitive absolute*. (*Absolutus*
is Latin for 'loosed'.) In English we have a *nominative absolute*, e.g.
'This done, he went home'.

This genitive use of the participle is not suitable when the noun that
goes with the participle is also the subject, object or indirect object of
the main verb, since the participle should then itself take the case
(nominative, accusative or dative) of the word with which it agrees,

e.g. Subject　　　　ἐξελθὼν εἶδεν
　　　　　　　　　When he had come out, he saw.

　　　Object　　　　τὸν Πέτρον ἐξερχόμενον εἶδεν ὁ Ἰησοῦς
　　　　　　　　　As Peter came out, Jesus saw him.

　　　Indirect Object　τῷ Πέτρῳ ἐξερχομένῳ εἶπεν ὁ Ἰησοῦς
　　　　　　　　　As Peter came out, Jesus said to him.

This rule is generally adhered to in the New Testament, but by no means strictly, as may be seen in the following example, where a genitive is (by classical standards) 'incorrectly' used:

ἐκπορευομενου αὐτου ἐκ του ἱερου λεγει αὐτῳ εἰς των μαθητων αὐτου (Mark 13. 1)

As he was going out of the temple, one of his disciples says to him.

PERIPHRASTIC TENSES

In Greek, tenses are sometimes formed, as in English, by using a part of the verb 'to be' together with a participle. They are called 'periphrastic tenses' because they show forth (φραζω) their meaning in a roundabout (περι) way.

The common periphrastic tenses are:

The **Periphrastic Imperfect**, formed of the Imperfect of εἰμι and the Present Participle:

καὶ ἠν προαγων αὐτους ὁ Ἰησους (Mark 10. 32)
And Jesus was going ahead of them.

The **Periphrastic Future**, formed of the Future of εἰμι and the Present Participle:

ἀπο του νυν ἀνθρωπους ἐσῃ ζωγρων (Luke 5. 10)
From now on you will catch men.

The periphrastic form of the tense (at least in the Imperfect and Future) tends to emphasise the continuity of the action. Thus

ἠσαν οἱ μαθηται Ἰωανου και οἱ Φαρισαιοι νηστευοντες (Mark 2. 18)

means probably that the disciples of John and the Pharisees *were fasting* at the time in question, not that they *used to fast* from time to time.

This distinction, however, should not be over-pressed, as the unusual frequency of periphrastic tenses in the New Testament may be due to the influence of an Aramaic idiom in which the ordinary Imperfect is expressed periphrastically. In the Perfect and Pluperfect there is in any case little difference in meaning between the periphrastic and the ordinary forms of the tense.

The **Periphrastic Perfect** is formed of the Present of εἰμι and the Perfect Participle:

χαριτι ἐστε σεσωσμενοι (Eph. 2. 5)

By grace you have been saved.

The **Periphrastic Pluperfect** is formed of the Imperfect of εἰμι and the Perfect Participle:

και ἦν ὁ Ἰωανης ἐνδεδυμενος τριχας καμηλου (Mark 1. 6)

And John was clothed with camel's hair.

EXERCISE 37

A

1. Ἐτι δε λαλουντος του Πετρου τα ῥηματα ταυτα, ἐπεσεν το πνευμα το ἁγιον ἐπι παντας τους ἀκουοντας τον λογον. 2. ἐγγυς δε οὐσης Λυδδας τῃ Ἰοππῃ, οἱ μαθηται ἀκουσαντες ὁτι Πετρος ἐστιν ἐκει, ἀπεστειλαν δυο ἀνδρας προς αὐτον. 3. οὗτος ἐστιν ὁ τον λογον ἀκουων, και εὐθυς μετα χαρας λαμβανων αὐτον. 4. ἀλλα λημψεσθε δυναμιν σημερον, ἐλθοντος του ἁγιου πνευματος ἐφ᾽ ὑμας. 5. τοτε ὀψονται τον Υἱον του ἀνθρωπου ἐρχομενον ἐπι των νεφελων του οὐρανου. 6. και ἀπηλθεν κηρυσσων παντοτε ὁσα ἐποιησεν αὐτῳ ὁ Ἰησους. 7. εὐθεως εἰδεν ὁ Ἰησους πνευμα Θεου καταβαινον ὡς περιστεραν ἐπ᾽ αὐτον. 8. και θαυμασαντες ἐπι τῃ ἀποκρισει αὐτου οὐκετι οὐδεν εἰπον. 9. τοτε προσηλθεν αὐτῳ γυνη τις αἰτουσα τι παρ᾽ αὐτου, ὁ δε εἰπεν αὐτῃ Τι νυν θελεις; 10. και παν το πληθος ἦν του λαου προσευχομενον ἐξω. 11. και ἠδη ἦν ὁλη ἡ πολις ἐπισυνηγμενη προς την θυραν. 12. ἡ νυν Ἱερουσαλημ ἐσται πατουμενη παλιν ὑπο των ἐθνων. 13. οὐ γαρ ἐστιν ἐν γωνιᾳ πεπραγμενον τουτο. 14. και ἦσαν οἱ μαθηται Ἰωανου νηστευοντες. 15. ἦν γαρ διδασκων αὐτους ὡς ἐξουσιαν ἐχων και οὐχ ὡς οἱ γραμματεις αὐτων. 16. ἰδε νυν οὐδεν ἀξιον θανατου ἐστιν πεπραγμενον ὑπ᾽ αὐτου. 17. γενομενης δε ἡμερας ἐξελθων ἐπορευθη εἰς ἐρημον τοπον. 18. ὑπαγε εἰς τον οἰκον σου προς τους σους, και ἀπαγγειλον αὐτοις ὁσα ὁ Κυριος σοι πεποιηκεν. 19. νυν κρισις ἐστιν του κοσμου τουτου. 20. ὁπου γαρ ἐστιν ὁ θησαυρος σου ἐκει παντοτε ἐσται και ἡ καρδια σου. 21. ἐν ποιᾳ δυναμει ἠ ἐν ποιῳ ὀνοματι ἐποιησατε τουτο ὑμεις;

22. πως εἰσηλθες ὧδε μη ἐχων ἐνδυμα γαμου;   23. που ἡ πιστις
ὑμων;   24. και ὀψιας γενομενης ἦν το πλοιον ἐν μεσῳ της
θαλασσης, και αὐτος μονος ἐπι της γης.   25. ὁ δε ἐξελθων
ἠρξατο κηρυσσειν παλιν ταυτα, ὥστε μηκετι τον Ἰησουν δυνασθαι
φανερως εἰς την πολιν εἰσελθειν.   26. συ τετηρηκας τον καλον
οἰνον ἑως ἀρτι.   27. λεγω δε ὑμιν ὁτι Ἡλειας ἠδη ἠλθεν.
28. τοτε τῳ πρωτῳ εὐθεως εἰπεν, Σημερον ἐργαζου ἐν τῳ ἀμπελωνι.
29. και τοιαυταις παραβολαις πολλαις ἐλαλει αὐτοις τον λογον.
30. και πληθος πολυ, ἀκουοντες ὁσα ποιει, οὐκετι ἠλθον προς αὐτον.
31. νυνι δε ἐν Χριστῳ Ἰησου ὑμεις ἐγενηθητε ἐγγυς ἐν τῳ αἱματι
του Χριστου.   32. ἐν οἰδα ὁτι τυφλος ὢν ἀρτι βλεπω.   33. γενομενης δε θλιψεως δια τον λογον εὐθυς σκανδαλιζονται.   34. ὁσοι
γαρ εἰς Χριστον ἐβαπτισθητε, Χριστον ἐνεδυσασθε.

B

The clauses marked * should be translated by
a Genitive Absolute.

1. And when the disciples had entered into the boat* Jesus sent the multitudes into the mountains.   2. And a certain man came to him and said, 'What are you doing here?'   3. What power shall we receive when the Holy Spirit has come upon us?*   4. When the day has drawn near* the Son of man will come with the clouds of heaven.   5. But Peter came to him walking upon the water.   6. But when the messengers had gone away* the disciples talked to Jesus privately.   7. But although he sent his own son to them* they were not willing to receive him.   8. And while he was holding my hand* I received power to walk.   9. And while they were drawing near to the city* the whole multitude was rejoicing saying, 'Blessed is he who comes in the name of the Lord'.   10. And now, O Father, glorify me.   11. How can you, being evil, still speak good things?   12. By what authority are you still doing these things?   13. The great tribulation is near.   14. They say to him, 'Where, Lord?' But we shall say to him, 'How, Lord?'   15. Here in Jerusalem is the place where it is necessary to worship.   16. How then does he now see?   17. He who does not believe has been judged already.   18. But who is this of whom I hear such things?

In the following sentences use periphrastic forms:
19. The centurions were eating and drinking.   20. This thing has been done before many witnesses.   21. Here you will always be walking in the way of righteousness.   22. Then all the crowd was gathered together to the sea.

LESSON 38

The Subjunctive mood

THE FORMS OF THE SUBJUNCTIVE

The Subjunctive is much used in Greek and its forms are very simple. There are three points to note:

(1) There is never an augment.

(2) The stem is always the same as in the corresponding tense of the Indicative.

(3) The endings are the same as those of the Present Indicative of λυω except that initial syllables are lengthened where possible and their iotas written subscript.

Thus the **Present Subjunctive Active** is:

λυω
λυῃς
λυῃ
λυωμεν
λυητε
λυωσι(ν)

And the following tenses all have these same endings:

First Aorist Active:	λυσω
Second Aorist Active:	βαλω
First Aorist Passive:	λυθω
Second Aorist Passive:	γραφω
Subjunctive of εἰμι:	ὦ
Subjunctive of οἰδα:	εἰδω.

The **Present Subjunctive Middle and Passive is:**

λυωμαι
λυη
λυηται
λυωμεθα
λυησθε
λυωνται

And the following tenses have the same endings:

First Aorist Middle: λυσωμαι
Second Aorist Middle: γενωμαι

-εω Verbs

Since *all* Subjunctive endings have a long vowel, the ε of -εω verbs will always drop out, and the forms will be the same as those of λυω.

THE USE OF THE SUBJUNCTIVE

Reference may be made here to Introduction: English Grammar, Section 14(3), but it needs to be noted that the use of the Greek Subjunctive is much wider than that of the English Subjunctive. It is therefore better not to learn any one form of words as an equivalent of the Subjunctive.

In general it may be said that the Subjunctive is the *mood of doubtful assertion.* In nearly all its uses there is some element of indefiniteness in the sentence.

There are eight main uses.

(1) **Indefinite clauses.**

(a) *Whoever, whatever.* The Subjunctive is used in clauses introduced by a relative pronoun (e.g. ὅς or ὅστις) which does not refer to a definite person or thing. In these clauses the particle ἀν is placed after the relative pronoun. ἀν is usually untranslatable, but it is introduced to add an element of indefiniteness to the clause:

και ὅς ἀν θελη ἐν ὑμιν εἰναι πρωτος, ἐσται ὑμων δουλος (Matt. 20. 27)
And whoever wishes to be first among you will be your slave.

(b) *Wherever, whenever*. The Subjunctive is used in clauses introduced by ὅπου ἄν or ὅταν (ὅτε + ἄν) which do not refer to a definite place or time:

ἀκολουθήσω σοι ὅπου ἐάν[1] ἀπερχῃ (Luke 9. 57)
I will follow you wherever you go.

καὶ ὅταν προσευχησθε, οὐκ ἐσεσθε ὡς οἱ ὑποκριται (Matt. 6. 5)
And when you pray, you are not to be like the hypocrites.

(In this sentence 'when you pray' does not refer to a single specific, definite act of prayer. The action is conditional and repeated. Hence ὅταν is to be preferred to ὅτε, although the English idiom only requires the translation 'when'.)

(c) *Until* (indefinite). The Subjunctive is used in clauses introduced by ἕως or ἕως ἄν which do not refer to a definite time.

ὅπου ἐάν[1] εἰσελθητε εἰς οἰκιαν, ἐκει μενετε ἕως ἄν ἐξελθητε (Mark 6. 10)
Wherever you go into a house, there stay until you go out.

πορευεται ἐπι το ἀπολωλος ἕως εὑρῃ αὑτο (Luke 15. 4)
He goes after that which is lost, until he finds it.

An indefinite ἕως is frequently followed by ἄν or οὗ (genitive of the relative pronoun) and sometimes by ὅτου (the irregular genitive of ὅστις). Examples can be seen in Exercise 38 A 10, 43 A 20, 40 A 10. The addition of ἄν, οὗ or ὅτου makes no difference to the sense. In the case of οὗ and ὅτου the word χρονου is understood.

Such clauses are usually indefinite because they refer to something future and unfulfilled. If the clause refers to something which has actually happened in the past, it will be in the Indicative:

ὅπου ἄν εἰσεπορευετο (Mark 6. 56)
Wherever he entered.

οὐκ ἐγνωσαν ἕως ἠλθεν ὁ κατακλυσμος (Matt. 24. 39)
They did not know until the flood came.

(2) **Purpose** (or **final**) **clauses.** Purpose clauses are introduced by ἵνα or ὅπως, both of which mean 'in order that' or 'that'. The Sub-

---

[1] ἐάν here is equivalent to ἄν. See also Exercise 38 A 5,12. The commoner use of ἐάν will be dealt with in the next lesson.

junctive (like the imperative, infinitive and participle) is negatived with
μη, so that ἵνα μη and ὅπως μη mean 'in order that not' or 'lest'.[1]

ἦλθεν ἵνα μαρτυρήσῃ περι του φωτος (John 1. 7)

He came $\left\{ \begin{array}{l} \text{that he might} \\ \text{in order to} \\ \text{to} \end{array} \right\}$ bear witness to the light.

ὅπως κἀγω ἐλθων προσκυνήσω αὐτῷ (Matt. 2. 8)
That I also may come and worship him.

μη κρινετε, ἵνα μη κριθητε (Matt. 7. 1)
Do not judge, lest you be judged.

The Aorist is generally used unless there is reason to stress the
continuity or repetition of the action, when the Present will be used.

(3) **Noun clauses introduced by ἵνα.** A noun clause introduced
by ἵνα may be:

(a) The subject of a verb:

ἐμον βρωμα ἐστιν ἵνα ποιω το θελημα του πεμψαντος με (John 4. 34)
To do the will of him who sent me is my food.

(b) The object of a verb:

εἶπε ἵνα οἱ λιθοι οὗτοι ἀρτοι γενωνται (Matt. 4. 3)
Tell these stones to become bread.

(c) In apposition to a noun or pronoun:

ἐν τουτῳ ἐδοξασθη ὁ Πατηρ μου, ἵνα καρπον πολυν φερητε
(John 15. 8)
In this is my Father glorified, that you bear much fruit.

These noun clauses and the purpose clauses of the previous section
should be compared with the uses of the infinitive in Lesson 20. It will
be seen that in Hellenistic Greek ἵνα clauses and the infinitive have
become almost equivalent to one another. In Modern Greek να (an
eroded form of ἵνα) with the Subjunctive has ousted the infinitive.

In this use of the Subjunctive the element of indefiniteness sometimes
seems to have disappeared.

[1] Occasionally μη alone is used for 'lest' in purpose clauses. μη is also
regularly used after verbs of fearing in the sense of 'to fear lest' or 'to fear *that*'.
See Exercise 38A17.

(4) **The Hortatory Subjunctive.** The Subjunctive is used in the first person plural when the speaker is exhorting others to join him in some action:

φαγωμεν και πιωμεν, αυριον γαρ αποθνησκομεν (1 Cor. 15. 32)
Let us eat and drink, for tomorrow we die.

(5) **The Deliberative Subjunctive.** The Subjunctive is used in deliberative questions. In questions, that is, in which a person deliberates before acting, asking himself or others what to do.

τί εἴπω ὑμῖν; (1 Cor. 11. 22)
What am I to say to you?

τί οὖν ποιησωμεν; (Luke 3. 10)
What then shall we do?

(6) **Emphatic negative Future.** The double negative οὐ μη is used with the Aorist Subjunctive in the sense of the Future Indicative with οὐ, but with more emphasis.[1]

ἀμην, ἀμην λεγω ὑμιν, Θανατον οὐ μη θεωρηση εἰς τον αἰωνα (John 8. 51)
Truly, truly I tell you, he will not see death for ever.

ἀμην λεγω ὑμιν ὁτι οὐ μη παρελθῃ ἡ γενεα αὑτη ἑως ἀν παντα ταυτα γενηται (Matt. 24. 34)
Truly, I tell you that this generation will not pass away until all these things come about.

The two further uses:

(7) **Commands not to begin an action;**
(8) **Future conditions,**

will be dealt with under Prohibitions and Conditions in the next lesson.

---

[1] This is the one use of the Subjunctive where it appears totally to have lost its character as the mood of doubtful assertion. A possible explanation of this use is that οὐ negatives the apprehension expressed in early Greek by μη and the subjunctive. θανατον μη θεωρηση = 'perhaps he may see death'. οὐ [μη θανατον θεωρηση] = 'there's *no* perhaps-he-may-see-death', i.e. 'he will certainly not see death'.
An emphatic future negative is also sometimes expressed by οὐ μη and the Future.

EXERCISE 38

A

1. Ἀθετεῖτε τὴν ἐντολὴν τοῦ Θεοῦ, ἵνα τὴν παραδοσιν ὑμων
τηρησητε.   2. ἀγωμεν εἰς τας ἀλλας κωμας, ἵνα και ἐκει κηρυξω.
3. ὃς ἂν ἐν των τοιουτων παιδιων δεξηται ἐπι τῳ ὀνοματι μου, ἐμε
δεχεται· και ὃς ἂν ἐμε δεχηται, οὐκ ἐμε δεχεται, ἀλλα τον ἀποστειλ-
αντα με.   4. και τους ὀφθαλμους αὐτων ἐκαμμυσαν, μη ἰδωσιν
τοις ὀφθαλμοις.   5. ὃ ἐαν δησῃς ἐπι της γης ἐσται δεδεμενον ἐν
τοις οὐρανοις.   6. κυριοι, τί με δει ποιειν ἵνα σωθω;   7. ἀκου-
σεσθε κατα παντα ὅσα ἂν λαλησῃ προς ὑμας.   8. λεγωμεν ἀρα
Ποιησωμεν τα κακα, ἵνα ἐλθῃ τα ἀγαθα;   9. παντοτε γαρ τους
πτωχους ἐχετε, και ὅταν θελητε δυνασθε αὐτοις εὐ ποιησαι.
10. φευγε εἰς Αἰγυπτον και μενε ἐκει ἑως ἂν εἰπω σοι.   11. και
ἐποιησεν δωδεκα ἵνα ὡσιν μετ᾽ αὐτου.   12. ὁπου ἐαν κηρυχθῃ
το εὐαγγελιον τουτο ἐν ὁλῳ τῳ κοσμῳ, λαληθησεται και ὃ ἐποιησεν
αὐτη.   13. ὃς ἂν μη δεξηται την βασιλειαν του Θεου ὡς παιδιον,
οὐ μη εἰσελθῃ εἰς αὐτην.   14. ὁταν ἐν τῳ κοσμῳ ὦ, φως εἰμι του
κοσμου.   15. ἵνα δε μη σκανδαλισωμεν αὐτους, πορευθεις εἰς
θαλασσαν βαλε ἀγκιστρον.   16. Ἀπαγγειλατε μοι, ὁπως κἀγω
ἐλθων προσκυνησω αὐτῳ.   17. ἐφοβουντο γαρ τον λαον, μη
λιθασθωσιν.   18. συμφερει γαρ σοι ἵνα ἀποληται ἐν των μελων
σου και μη ὁλον το σωμα σου βληθῃ εἰς γεενναν.   19. προσευχ-
εσθε δε ἵνα μη γενηται ἡ φυγη ὑμων σαββατῳ.   20. και τινες
των ὡδε ὀντων οὐ μη γευσωνται θανατου ἑως ἂν ἰδωσιν τον Ὑἱον του
ἀνθρωπου.   21. ἐνδυσωμεθα τα ὁπλα του φωτος.   22. ταυτα
ἐγραψα[1] ὑμιν ἵνα εἰδητε ὁτι ζωην ἐχετε αἰωνιον.   23. και παντα
ὅσα ἂν αἰτησητε ἐν τῃ προσευχῃ πιστευοντες λημψεσθε.

B

1. For the Pharisees did not keep the commandment of God that they
might keep their own tradition.   2. Whatever I say to you privately

---

[1] This sentence is from 1 John 5. 13. The verb should probably be taken as
an *Epistolary Aorist* (as in R.S.V.) and be translated 'I write'. With a pleasing
courtesy the Greek writer puts himself in the position of the one who receives
the letter. When the letter is received it will have been written in the past.

proclaim to all the people.　　3. What shall we do then? Shall we remain in sin that grace may abound?　　4. When you see the Gentiles in the Holy Place the end of the age is drawing near.　　5. Wherever the gospel is preached those that believe will be saved.　　6. Send the children to the desert that the priests may not kill them.　　7. Let us eat and drink, for we must depart.　　8. God sent many prophets that they might teach this people. (In this and the next sentence express the verb of the purpose clause in two different ways.)　　9. Let us go to other cities that we may exhort the multitudes.　　10. Whenever we will we can have mercy on the poor.　　11. Remain in the house until I call you.　　12. We took away all the trees so that our enemies might not eat the fruit.　　13. I will not drink wine lest I cause my brother to stumble.　　14. Guard the sheep until I find my little one.　　15. Whoever wishes to be greatest among you let him make himself as a child. 16. Carry the clothes to me that they may be carried to the widows. 17. And he besought him that he might be with him.　　18. Pray that you may not come into temptation.

LESSON 39

Prohibitions
Conditional sentences
The Optative mood

PROHIBITIONS

Negative commands can be stated in two ways.

(a) As we saw in Lesson 18, μη with the **Present Imperative** generally denotes a command **to cease to do** an action already begun, in accordance with the principle that the Present tense denotes action in progress.

> μη μου ἁπτου (John 20. 17)
> Do not continue to hold me.

(b) μη with the **Aorist Subjunctive**, however, generally denotes a command **not to begin** an action.

> και μη εἰσενεγκῃς ἡμας εἰς πειρασμον (Matt. 6. 13)
> And do not lead us into temptation.

An example of both uses in the same verse:

> μη φοβου, ἀλλα λαλει και μη σιωπησῃς (Acts 18. 9)
> Do not be afraid, but speak and do not be silent.

Commands and exhortations (whether expressed by Subjunctive or Imperative) have an element of doubt, since they refer to the future and they may or may not be followed.[1]

CONDITIONAL SENTENCES

The following treatment of conditional sentences is an over-simplification. It gives only the five simplest forms. But when these have been mastered the less straightforward forms will present little difficulty.

Definitions

Conditional sentences have two parts, the protasis and the apodosis.

The **protasis** is the 'if' clause.
The **apodosis** is the 'then' clause.

Classification of conditional sentences

The five types of conditional sentence may be classified as follows:

Conditions of fact

(1) Past.
(2) Present.
(3) Future.

Conditions contrary to fact

(4) Past.
(5) Present.

[1] Commands and prohibitions can also be expressed by the Future Indicative, e.g. οὐκ ἐκπειρασεις (Luke 4. 12), 'You shall not tempt'. This follows a Hebrew idiom.

Mood of conditional sentences

The Indicative is always[1] used, except in Future conditions. Future conditions take the Subjunctive in the protasis.

Conditions of fact

In these sentences a statement is made on the assumption that the given condition is true, or that it will be fulfilled.

Past and Present conditions are introduced by εἰ in the protasis:

(1) *Past*   εἰ ὁ Θεος ἐφιλησεν, δει ἡμας φιλειν
If God loved, we must love.

(2) *Present*   εἰ ὁ Θεος φιλει, δει ἡμας φιλειν
If God loves, we must love.

(3) **Future conditions** have ἐαν (εἰ + ἀν) and the Subjunctive in the protasis:

ἐαν μονον ἁψωμαι του ἱματιου αὐτου, σωθησομαι (Matt. 9. 21)
If I only touch his garment, I shall be made well.[2]

The Subjunctive is appropriate because of the element of doubt in most future conditions.

Conditions contrary to fact

In these sentences a statement is made on the recognition that the given condition is not or was not fulfilled.

Conditions contrary to fact have εἰ in the protasis and ἀν in the apodosis.

(4) **Past uses Aorist:**

εἰ ἐπιστευσατε αὐτῳ, ἐπιστευσατε ἀν ἐμοι
If you had believed him, you would have believed me.

(5) **Present uses Imperfect:**

εἰ ἐπιστευετε αὐτῳ, ἐπιστευετε ἀν ἐμοι
If you believed him (now), you would believe me.

---

[1] In a sentence like: 'If you are the son of God, *command*', the verb in the apodosis will of course be imperative.
[2] Note this common meaning of σωζω.

A sentence can refer to past action in one clause and present action in the other:

εἰ ἐπιστευσατε αὐτῳ, ἐπιστευετε ἀν ἐμοι

If you had believed him, you would believe me.

It will be observed that with conditions contrary to fact, the form of the English sentence is no guide whatever to the way in which it should be translated into Greek. The rules given above must be learnt and applied.

THE OPTATIVE MOOD

The Optative mood, though considerably used in classical times, is rare in the New Testament. It can be described roughly as the *mood of more doubtful assertion*.

Optatives can often be recognised by the presence of the diphthongs οι, ει or αι in or before the personal endings.

There are only two common forms in the New Testament, γενοιτο and εἰη, and these represent the two commonest uses:

(1) To express a wish.
(2) In dependent (indirect) questions.

Expressing a wish

γενοιτο is the third person singular of the Second Aorist Optative Middle of γινομαι, and is found seventeen times mainly in the expression beloved of Paul:

μη γενοιτο   May it not happen! God forbid! (A.V.)

Dependent questions

εἰη (third person singular, occurring eleven times) is the only form of the optative of εἰμι to be found in the New Testament.

και αὐτοι ἠρξαντο συνζητειν προς ἑαυτους το τίς ἀρα εἰη ἐξ αὐτων ὁ τουτο μελλων πρασσειν (Luke 22. 23)

And they began to discuss among themselves which of them it was (N.E.B.: could possibly be) who would do this.

EXERCISE 39

A

1. Ἐαν γαρ εὖ ποιητε τοις εὖ ποιουσιν ὑμιν, τίνα μισθον ἐχετε;
2. ἐφωνησεν δε Παυλος μεγαλη φωνη λεγων Μηδεν πραξῃς σεαυτῳ κακον, ἀπαντες γαρ ἐσμεν ἐνθαδε.   3. ἐαν μη περισσευσῃ ὑμων ἡ δικαιοσυνη πλειον των γραμματεων και Φαρισαιων, οὐ μη εἰσελθητε εἰς την βασιλειαν των οὐρανων.   4. εἰ θελεις εἰσελθειν εἰς την ζωην, τηρει τας ἐντολας.   5. εἰ κακως ἐλαλησα, μαρτυρησον περι του κακου.   6. εἰ ἐτι ἀνθρωποις ἠρεσκον, Χριστου δουλος οὐκ ἀν ἠμην.   7. ἐαν τις θελῃ το θελημα αὐτου ποιειν, γνωσεται περι της διδαχης.   8. μη λεγετε Τί φαγωμεν; ἠ Τί πιωμεν;   9. εἰ του κοσμου τουτου ἠν ἡ βασιλεια ἡ ἐμη, οἱ ὑπηρεται ἀν οἱ ἐμοι ἠγωνιζοντο.   10. εἰ ἠμεθα ἐν ταις ἡμεραις των πατερων ἡμων, οὐκ ἀν ἠμεθα κοινωνοι ἐν τῳ αἱματι των προφητων.
11. και παντες διελογιζοντο ἐν ταις καρδιαις αὐτων περι του Ἰωανου μη ποτε αὐτος εἰη ὁ Χριστος.   12. εἰ ᾐδει ὁ οἰκοδεσποτης ποιᾳ φυλακῃ ὁ κλεπτης ἐρχεται, ἐγρηγορησεν ἀν.   13. ἐαν ᾐ ἐξ ἀνθρωπων ἡ βουλη αὐτη, καταλυθησεται· εἰ δε ἐκ Θεου ἐστιν, οὐ δυνησεσθε καταλυσαι αὐτην.   14. το ἀργυριον σου συν σοι εἰη εἰς ἀπωλειαν.
15. εἰ γαρ ἐγνωκειτε τί ἐστιν Ἐλεος θελω και οὐ θυσιαν, οὐκ ἀν κατεδικασατε τους ἀναιτιους.   16. ἐαν δε εἰπωμεν Ἐξ ἀνθρωπων, ὁ λαος ἁπας καταλιθασει ἡμας, πιστευει γαρ Ἰωανην προφητην εἰναι.
17. μη νομισητε ὁτι ἠλθον καταλυσαι τον νομον ἠ τους προφητας.
18. ἰδου ἡ δουλη Κυριου· γενοιτο μοι κατα το ῥημα σου.   19. οὐαι σοι Χοραζειν· οὐαι σοι Βηθσαϊδαν· ὁτι εἰ ἐν Τυρῳ και Σιδωνι ἐγενοντο αἱ δυναμεις αἱ γενομεναι ἐν ὑμιν, παλαι ἀν ἐν σακκῳ και σποδῳ μετενοησαν.   20. τί οὐν ἐρουμεν; ἐπιμενωμεν τῃ ἁμαρτιᾳ, ἱνα ἡ χαρις πλεοναςῃ; μη γενοιτο.   21. Κυριε, εἰ ἠς ὡδε, οὐκ ἀν ἀπεθανεν ὁ ἀδελφος μου.   22. εἰ ἐγω ἠμην ὁ υἱος αὐτου, αὐτος ἀν ἠν ὁ πατηρ μου.   23. εἰ ἠπιστησαν τινες, μη ἡ ἀπιστια αὐτων την πιστιν του Θεου καταργησει; μη γενοιτο· γινεσθω δε ὁ Θεος ἀληθης, πας δε ἀνθρωπος ψευστης.   24. παντα γαρ ὑμων ἐστιν, εἰτε Παυλος εἰτε Ἀπολλως εἰτε Κηφας, εἰτε κοσμος εἰτε ζωη εἰτε θανατος, παντα ὑμων, ὑμεις δε Χριστου, Χριστος δε Θεου.

B

1. Lord, if you will, you can cleanse me.   2. Do not bring the Gentiles into the temple.   3. Let us not seek the things of this age. 4. Is the law then against the promises of God? God forbid.   5. If you were my mother, he was my brother.   6. If you were my mother, he would be my brother.   7. If you had known me, you would have known my Father also.   8. Do not continue to receive the enemies of the gospel.   9. May it happen to us according to thy will.   10. If you were blind, you would not have sin.   11. If dead men are not raised, neither has Christ been raised.   12. Sin no longer.   13. Do not carry wine to the slaves.   14. If the enemy draws near, I will send the soldiers against him.   15. Do not continue to judge, lest you be judged.

LESSON 40

Contracted verbs in -αω and -οω

In addition to contracted verbs like φιλεω, which have stems ending in ε, there are contracted verbs like τιμαω, 'I honour', which have stems ending in α, and φανεροω, 'I make clear', which have stems ending in ο.

Their **principal parts** follow the pattern of φιλεω:

φιλεω	φιλησω	ἐφιλησα	πεφιληκα	πεφιλημαι	ἐφιληθην
τιμαω	τιμησω	ἐτιμησα	τετιμηκα	τετιμημαι	ἐτιμηθην
φανεροω	φανερωσω	ἐφανερωσα	πεφανερωκα	πεφανερωμαι	ἐφανερωθην

In all the parts except the present,

α lengthens to η,[1]

ο lengthens to ω,

and the tenses are formed as for λυω.

[1] For this lengthening of α to η, cf. p. 53. There are some -αω verbs (including all in which the final α of the stem is preceded by ε, ι or ρ) which do not

Therefore contractions only take place in the tenses of the Present system, i.e. in the Present and Imperfect.

As with φιλεω, there are in each case three **rules of contraction**:

α + O-sound (ο, ω or ου)   → ω
α + E-sound (ε or η)   → α
α + any combination containing ι
(whether subscript or not)   → ᾳ
ο + long vowel   → ω
ο + short vowel or ου   → ου
ο + combination containing ι
(whether subscript or not)   → οι

To these rules there is only one exception, and that is an exception only in appearance. The *Present Infinitive Active* formed from α + ειν and ο + ειν are τιμαν and φανερουν (not τιμᾳν and φανεροιν). These endings contain no ι because -ειν was itself originally a contraction of -εεν. τιμα-εν becomes τιμαν and φανερο-εν becomes φανερουν in strict accordance with the rules.

The conjugations of the tenses of the Present system are set out on pp. 238–41 for the purpose of reference. These need not be learnt. *It is only necessary to learn the principal parts, the six rules of contraction and the infinitive exception,* after which any form may be deduced from λυω.

The peculiarity of ζαω, 'I live' (see p. 239), should be noted. η replaces α in the contracted forms.

EXERCISE 40

A

1. Και ἠρωτησεν παρ' αὐτων που ὁ Χριστος γενναται.   2. Θεος οὐκ ἐστιν νεκρων ἀλλα ζωντων, παντες γαρ αὐτῳ ζωσιν.   3. οὑτος ὁ λογος οὐ φανερουται ἡμιν.   4. ἐλεγον την ἐξοδον αὐτου ἡν ἠμελλεν[1] πληρουν ἐν Ἰερουσαλημ.   5. Σιμων Ἰωανου, ἀγαπᾳς με πλειον τουτων;   6. τοτε ἐσταυρουν συν αὐτῳ δυο λῃστας.

lengthen to η, but retain the α in all the other five parts. The commonest is the deponent Middle ἰαομαι (26) ἰασομαι ἰασαμην — ἰαμαι ἰαθην I heal. (For an initial ι in past tenses, see p. 53 n. 1)

[1] μελλω very often has this lengthened augment.

7. ἀκουσας δε ὀχλου διαπορευομενου ἐπηρωτησεν τί ἀν εἰη τουτο.
8. τί με ἐρωτᾳς περι του ἀγαθου;   9. λεγει αὐτῳ ὁ Ἰησους
Πορευου, ὁ υἱος σου ζῃ.   10. οὐ μη φαγω αὐτο ἑως ὁτου
πληρωθῃ ἐν τῃ βασιλειᾳ του Θεου.   11. ἐαν ἀγαπατε με, τας
ἐντολας τας ἐμας τηρησετε.   12. ἐαν γαρ ἀγαπησητε τους
ἀγαπωντας ὑμας, τίνα μισθον ἐχετε;   13. ὁπως πληρωθῃ το
ῥηθεν¹ δια των προφητων.   14. ἐπηρωτων δε αὐτον οἱ μαθηται
αὐτου τίς αὑτη εἰη ἡ παραβολη.   15. εἰ ἠγαπατε με ἐχαρητε ἀν
ὁτι πορευομαι προς τον πατερα.   16. εἰ ὁ Θεος πατηρ ὑμων ἠν,
ἠγαπατε ἀν ἐμε.   17. πλανασθε μη εἰδοτες τας γραφας μηδε την
δυναμιν του Θεου.   18. οἱ υἱοι του αἰωνος τουτου γεννωνται και
γεννωσιν.   19. ὁρα μηδενι μηδεν εἰπῃς.   20. ὁ μη τιμων τον
υἱον οὐ τιμᾳ τον πατερα.   21. ἐπετιμησεν δε αὐτοις ἱνα μηδενι
λεγωσιν.   22. καυχωμεθα ἐπ᾽ ἐλπιδι της δοξης του Θεου.
23. πας ὁ πιστευων δικαιουται.   24. ὁρατε μηδεις γινωσκετω.
25. και προσκαλεσαμενος ἑνα των παιδων ἠρωτησεν τί ἀν εἰη ταυτα.

B

1. The disciples were making known these things which they had heard.
2. Do not continue to crucify slaves.   3. Are they about to live in our
city?   4. Do you then wish to love the Lord your God?   5. Now
the word of the prophet is being fulfilled.   6. But God justifies the
sons of men by faith and not by works.   7. Your son lives.   8. For
I made your name known to this people and I will make it known to
their children.   9. They beheld the temple filled with² the glory of the
Lord.   10. O Father, make known your power to us that your name
may be glorified.   11. If you do these things you will be loved by
my Father.   12. If we love him we shall keep his commandments.
13. And they went to the priest to ask him about their conscience.
14. I will on no account make myself known to this race.   15. And
one of the scribes, knowing³ that he had answered them well, asked him.
16. The time is fulfilled.   17. But we preach a crucified⁴ Christ.

¹ Participle from ἐρρηθην.
² Use instrumental dative; though genitive is also possible, being a normal
use after verbs of filling.
³ Use οἰδα.   ⁴ Use Perfect Participle Passive.

18. The rich man sees[1] Abraham.   19. Honour your mother.
20. But the disciples were rebuking them.   21. Let no one lead you
astray.   22. He who boasts let him boast in the Lord.   23. Then
the blind man asked what this might be.

REVISION TESTS 5

-ω verbs

These tests are supplementary to the verb tests (3 A and 3 B) on pp. 113 f.
  Allow 1 hour each for Tests A and B. Total number of marks: 70 for
each test.

A

1. Give the principal parts of: τιμαω, κηρυσσω, ἀγγελλω, αἰρω,
ἀνοιγω, βαλλω, γινωσκω, δεχομαι, εὑρισκω, θνησκω, κραζω,
λαμβανω, πινω, σπειρω, σωζω, ἐσθιω, λεγω, φερω. [36 marks]
2. Give the Present Subjunctive Middle and First Aorist Participle
Active (endings in full) of λυω. [2]
3. Give the Periphrastic Imperfect and Periphrastic Perfect of
φιλεω. [2]
4. Give the following tenses or forms of φανεροω. *Active:* Imperfect
Indicative, Perfect Infinitive, First Aorist Subjunctive. *Middle:* Present
Indicative, Present Subjunctive, Present Imperative. *Passive:* Imperfect
Indicative, Present Infinitive, Present Participle (nominative singular
only). [9]
5. Give the rules of contraction for -αω verbs. [3]
6. Give the participle of εἰμι (endings in full). [1]
7. Give the following tenses or forms of γραφω: Perfect Indicative
Active; Second Aorist Subjunctive Passive; nominative singular
Perfect Participle Active. [3]

---

[1] Use ὁραω.

8. Give the following forms of οἶδα: first person singular Pluperfect; first person singular Subjunctive; infinitive; nominative and accusative singular participle. [4]

9. Give the Greek for: I turn (2 words), I return, I love (two words), I question (two words), I honour, I warn, I justify, I make clear. [2]

10. Give eight uses of the Subjunctive. [8]

B

1. Give the principal parts of: φιλεω, φανεροω, πρασσω, ἀγω, ἀκουω, -βαινω, γινομαι, γραφω, ἐγειρω, θελω, καλεω, κρινω, πειθω, πιπτω, -στελλω, ἐρχομαι, ἐχω, ὁραω. [36 marks]

2. Give the Present Subjunctive Active and First Aorist Participle Middle (endings in full) of λυω. [2]

3. Give the Periphrastic Imperfect and Periphrastic Perfect of φιλεω. [2]

4. Give the following tenses or forms of τιμαω. *Active:* Present Indicative, Present Infinitive, Perfect Participle (nominative and accusative singular only). *Middle:* First Aorist Subjunctive, Perfect Infinitive, Present Imperative. *Passive:* Imperfect Indicative, Future, First Aorist Subjunctive. [9]

5. Give the rules of contraction for -οω verbs. [3]

6. Give the Present of κειμαι and the Imperfect of καθημαι. [2]

7. Give the Second Aorist Subjunctive Middle of γινομαι. [1]

8. Give the Present Indicative and Present Infinitive Active of ζαω. [2]

9. Give the Greek for: I turned (two words), I shine, I appeared, I beget, I lead astray, I rebuke, I boast, I fill, I crucify. [2]

10. Give four uses of the participle, other than its use in periphrastic tenses. [4]

11. Give two uses of the Optative. [2]

12. Explain how the five main types of conditional clause are translated into Greek. [5]

LESSON 41

-μι verbs: τίθημι

Besides the verbs in -ω there is a small group of verbs which are called verbs in -μι, from the ending of the first person singular of the Present Indicative Active.

These verbs have endings differing from those of the verbs in -ω in the Present, Imperfect and Second Aorist tenses. In the other tenses their endings are the same as those of the verbs in -ω.

It is especially important, in the case of the verbs in -μι, to remember the distinction laid down in Lesson 22 between the verbal stem, from which most of the tenses of the verb are formed, and the Present stem, from which the Present and Imperfect tenses are formed.

The stems of the three principal verbs in -μι are as follows:

		Verbal stem	Present stem
τίθημι	I place	θε	τιθε
δίδωμι	I give	δο	διδο
ἵστημι	I cause to stand	στα	ἱστα

It will be noticed that the Present stem is a reduplicated form of the verbal stem in all three cases. ἱστα stands for σιστα, the rough breathing taking the place of the σ.

The **principal parts** of τίθημι are:

$$\tau\acute{\iota}\theta\eta\mu\iota \quad \theta\eta\sigma\omega \quad \mathring{\epsilon}\theta\eta\kappa\alpha \quad \tau\acute{\epsilon}\theta\epsilon\iota\kappa\alpha \quad \tau\acute{\epsilon}\theta\epsilon\iota\mu\alpha\iota \quad \mathring{\epsilon}\tau\acute{\epsilon}\theta\eta\nu$$

When λυω is known and the principal parts have been learnt, there remain only quite a small number of new forms to be mastered. The following should be learnt:

PRESENT
Active

Indicative	Subjunctive	Participle	Imperative	Infinitive
τίθημι	τιθω	τιθεις -εισα -εν		
τιθης	τιθης	τιθεντα	τιθει	
τιθησι(ν)	τιθη		τιθετω	τιθεναι
τιθεμεν	τιθωμεν			
τιθετε	τιθητε		τιθετε	
τιθεασι(ν)	τιθωσι(ν)		τιθετωσαν	

It will be noticed that in the Indicative the stem τιθε is lengthened to τιθη in the singular. (This same lengthening is found in δίδωμι and ἵστημι.)

Middle and Passive

The tenses are formed throughout from the Present stem and the endings of the Perfect Passive system of λύω:

τιθε-μαι	τιθε-μενος	τιθε-σθαι

AORIST
Aorist Active

The First Aorist ἔθηκα is found only in the Indicative. In the other moods there are Second Aorist forms.

The Second Aorist of course drops the τι. Otherwise, with the two exceptions given in heavy type, it follows the Present exactly:

Second Aorist Active

Indicative	Subjunctive	Participle	Imperative	Infinitive
Use First	θω	θεις θεισα θεν		
Aorist	θης	θεντα	θες	
	θη		θετω	**θειναι**
	θωμεν			
	θητε		θετε	
	θωσι(ν)		θετωσαν	

Second Aorist Middle

This tense is indistinguishable in meaning from the Active:

ἐθεμην	ἐθεμεθα
ἐθου ← ε(σ)ο	ἐθεσθε
ἐθετο	ἐθεντο

EXERCISE 41

A

1. Οὐ καιουσιν λυχνον και τιθεασιν αὐτον ἐξω της θυρας.   2. και λαβων το σωμα ὁ Ἰωσηφ ἐθηκεν αὐτο ἐν τῳ καινῳ μνημειῳ αὐτου. 3. μητι ἐρχεται ὁ λυχνος ἱνα ἐξω τεθη;   4. και τα παιδια κατευλογει τιθεις τας χειρας ἐπ᾽ αὐτα.   5. ὁ ποιμην ὁ καλος την ψυχην αὐτου τιθησιν ὑπερ των προβατων.   6. ἠραν τον κυριον ἐκ του μνημειου, και οὐκ οἰδαμεν που ἐθηκαν αὐτον.   7. οὐχ ὑμων ἐστιν γνωναι χρονους ἠ καιρους οὑς ὁ πατηρ ἐθετο ἐν τῃ ἰδιᾳ ἐξουσιᾳ.   8. και ἐζητουν αὐτον εἰσενεγκειν και θειναι αὐτον ἐνωπιον αὐτου.   9. και αὐτος θεις τα γονατα προσηυχετο. 10. την ψυχην μου ὑπερ σου θησω.   11. παντοτε προσευχου ἑως ἀν θω τους ἐχθρους σου ὑποποδιον των ποδων σου.   12. οὑτος ἐστιν ὁ θρονος ὁ τεθεις ἐν τῳ ἱερῳ.   13. καταβησομαι ἱνα θω τας χειρας ἐπ᾽ αὐτην και ζησει.   14. τα δικτυα ἐτεθη παρα το πλοιον.   15. χειρας μηδενι ἐπιτιθει.   16. ἐθεωρουν που τεθει- ται.   17. μνημειον καινον, ἐν ᾡ οὐδεπω οὐδεις ἠν τεθειμενος. 18. τί ὁτι ἐθου ἐν τῃ καρδιᾳ σου το πραγμα τουτο;   19. και τον Πετρον ἐθεντο εἰς φυλακην.   20. κατα μιαν σαββατου ἑκαστος ὑμων παρ᾽ ἑαυτῳ τιθετω.   21. ἡ μαχαιρα τιθεται ἐν τῃ χειρι του βασιλεως.

B

τιθημι (or ἐπιτιθημι) is to be used for 'place', 'lay', 'lay down', 'put'.

1. We must place the law of love in our hearts daily.   2. Place joy there similarly.   3. Where have you laid him?   4. How shall we place our daughter at[1] his feet?   5. They put[2] their books in the synagogue.   6. We shall put them there also.   7. You have placed me in a good land.   8. Lay down your lives for the brethren. 9. Do not place this writing upon the cross.   10. Put the body in the tomb.   11. Laying their hands upon us, the apostles blessed us. 12. But the sick man was brought in and placed before him.   13. Come and put your hand upon her.

[1] παρα.   [2] Use Aorist Middle.

LESSON 42

διδωμι

Principal parts:

$$\delta\iota\delta\omega\mu\iota \quad \delta\omega\sigma\omega \quad \check{\epsilon}\delta\omega\kappa\alpha \quad \delta\epsilon\delta\omega\kappa\alpha \quad \delta\epsilon\delta\omega\mu\alpha\iota \quad \check{\epsilon}\delta\omega\theta\eta\nu$$

When θε is replaced by δο the Present and Aorist forms of διδωμι are identical with those of τιθημι, except that:

(1) ου must be written for ει;

(2) there is an ω in all Subjunctive endings. (The ο of the stem prevails over an η in the endings. But the iota subscripts remain.)

PRESENT
Active

Indicative	Subjunctive	Participle	Imperative	Infinitive
διδωμι	διδω			
διδως	διδῳς	διδους -ουσα -ον	διδου	
διδωσι(ν)	διδῳ	διδοντα	διδοτω	διδοναι
διδομεν	διδωμεν			
διδοτε	διδωτε		διδοτε	
διδοασι(ν)	διδωσι(ν)		διδοτωσαν	

Middle and Passive

διδο-μαι		διδο-μενος		διδο-σθαι

SECOND AORIST
Active

Use First	δω			
Aorist	δῳς	δους δουσα δον	δος	
	δῳ	δοντα	δοτω	δουναι
	δωμεν			
	δωτε		δοτε	
	δωσι(ν)		δοτωσαν	

178

Indicative   *Middle*

ἐδομην   ἐδομεθα
ἐδου ← ο(σ)ο   ἐδοσθε
ἐδοτο   ἐδοντο

EXERCISE 42

A

1. Διδωμι δε ὑμιν ἐξουσιαν ἐκβαλλειν πνευματα ἀκαθαρτα.   2. ὁ γαρ Θεος διδωσιν το πνευμα το ἁγιον τοις αἰτουσιν αὐτον.   3. τίς ἐστιν ὁ δους σοι την ἐξουσιαν ταυτην;   4. θελω ἱνα δῳς μοι την κεφαλην Ἰωανου.   5. και δια τί οὐκ ἐδωκας μου το ἀργυριον τοις πτωχοις;   6. ὑμιν δεδοται γνωναι τα μυστηρια της βασιλειας. 7. ἀποδος μοι εἰ τι ὀφειλεις.   8. ὁ δε οὐκ ἠθελεν, ἀλλα ἀπελθων ἐβαλεν αὐτον εἰς φυλακην ἑως ἀποδῳ το ὀφειλομενον.   9. ἐξεστιν δουναι κηνσον Καισαρι ἠ οὐ; δωμεν ἠ μη δωμεν;   10. ἐδοθη μοι πασα ἐξουσια ἐν οὐρανῳ και ἐπι γης.   11. ὁ πατηρ ἀγαπᾳ τον υἱον, και παντα δεδωκεν ἐν τῃ χειρι αὐτου.   12. μακαριον ἐστιν μαλλον δουναι ἠ λαμβανειν.   13. τίς ἡ σοφια ἡ δοθεισα τουτῳ; 14. εἰπε μοι εἰ το χωριον ἀπεδοσθε.   15. ταυτα παντα σοι δωσω ἐαν πεσων προσκυνησῃς μοι.   16. και ὁταν ἀγωσιν ὑμας παραδιδοντες, μη προμεριμνατε τί λαλησητε, ἀλλ᾽ ὁ ἐαν δοθῃ ὑμιν ἐν ἐκεινῃ τῃ ὡρᾳ, τουτο λαλειτε.   17. οἰδατε γαρ δοματα ἀγαθα διδοναι τοις τεκνοις ὑμων.   18. δεδωκεισαν δε οἱ ἀρχιερεις ἐντολας.

B

1. Always pay all that you have.   2. Give to the poor today.   3. We wish to give it to the high-priests.   4. It was given to me by my father.   5. Do not give good things to the evil men.   6. And they walked about giving clothes to the lepers.   7. I will on no account give what is yours to the Lord.   8. But you gave me water.   9. Let us keep the commands which are being given[1] to us.   10. He who gives bread to the sick will have his reward.   11. The king has given us this city; let us not betray it to his enemies.   12. Forgiveness is being given to us.

[1] Use participle.

179

ἵστημι

ἵστημι and its compounds have two peculiarities in the use of tenses.

(1) They have one set of transitive and one set of intransitive tenses.

(2) The Perfect tense is Present in meaning and the Pluperfect is Imperfect in meaning.

The **transitive tenses** of the principal parts are:

Present Active	ἵστημι	I cause to stand
Future Active	στησω	I shall cause to stand
First Aorist Active	ἐστησα	I caused to stand

ἵστημι has two Aorists which are distinct in meaning. The Second Aorist is intransitive.

The **intransitive tenses** of the principal parts are:

Second Aorist Active	ἐστην	I stood
Perfect Active	ἐστηκα	I stand (N.B. Present in meaning)
First Aorist Passive	ἐσταθην	I stood (usually indistinguishable in meaning from ἐστην)

This use of tenses can easily be remembered if the principal parts of the verb are carefully set out in two lines:

Transitive: ἵστημι στησω ἐστησα
Intransitive: ἐστην ἐστηκα — ἐσταθην

In the **Present and Second Aorist,** when θε is replaced by στα, the needed forms of ἵστημι are identical with those of τιθημι, except that:

(1) the Active Participles end in -ας -ασα -αν;

(2) there is a Second Aorist Indicative Active ἐστην (like -εβην, ἐλυθην);

(3) the Second Aorist Infinitive is στηναι.

PRESENT
Active

Indicative	Subjunctive	Participle	Infinitive
ἱστημι	ἱστω		
ἱστης	ἱστῃς	ἱστας ἱστασα ἱσταν	
ἱστησι(ν)	ἱστῃ	ἱσταντα	ἱσταναι
ἱσταμεν	ἱστωμεν		
ἱστατε	ἱστητε		
ἱστασι(ν)	ἱστωσι(ν)		

Middle and Passive

ἱσταμαι	ἱσταμενος	ἱστασθαι

AORIST
Second Aorist Active

ἐστην	στω		
ἐστης	στῃς	στας στασα σταν	
ἐστη	στῃ	σταντα	στηναι
ἐστημεν	στωμεν		
ἐστητε	στητε		
ἐστησαν	στωσι(ν)		

Note. (1) The third person plural of the First and Second Aorists are the same: ἐστησαν. When this word is met its meaning must be inferred from the context. Examples are given in Exercise 43 A 22, 23, 24.

(2) The *Perfect Participle Active* has two forms:

         First Perfect: ἐστηκως -υια -ος
                       ἐστηκοτα
         Second Perfect: ἐστως -ωσα -ος
                       ἐστωτα

ἐστως is the commoner of the two. Both are Present in meaning: 'standing'.

(3) The Pluperfect Active, which is Imperfect in meaning, 'I was standing', is εἱστηκειν.

EXERCISE 43

A

1. Τοτε παραλαμβανει αυτον ὁ διαβολος εἰς την ἁγιαν πολιν και ἐστησεν αυτον ἐπι το πτερυγιον του ἱερου. 2. ταυτα δε αὐτων λαλουντων αὐτος ἐστη ἐν μεσῳ αὐτων. 3. ἐβλεψαν συν αὐτοις ἑστωτα τον ἀνθρωπον τον τεθεραπευμενον. 4. ἀνθρωπε, τίς με κατεστησεν κριτην ἐφ᾽ ὑμας; 5. τα νυν παραγγελλει ὁ Θεος τοις ἀνθρωποις παντας πανταχου μετανοειν, καθ᾽ ὅτι ἐστησεν ἡμεραν ἐν ᾗ μελλει κρινειν την οἰκουμενην ἐν δικαιοσυνῃ. 6. ὁ Φαρισαιος σταθεις ταυτα προς ἑαυτον προσηυχετο. 7. ὁ δε τελωνης μακροθεν ἑστως οὐκ ἠθελεν οὐδε τους ὀφθαλμους ἐπαραι εἰς τον οὐρανον. 8. ὁ δε Ἰησους ἐσταθη ἐμπροσθεν του ἡγεμονος. 9. θεις δε τα γονατα ἐκραξεν φωνῃ μεγαλῃ Κυριε, μη στησῃς αὐτοις ταυτην την ἁμαρτιαν. 10. μετα ταυτα ἀνεστη Ἰουδας ὁ Γαλιλαιος ἐν ταις ἡμεραις της ἀπογραφης. 11. εἰ Μωϋσεως και των προφητων οὐκ ἀκουουσιν, οὐδ᾽ ἐαν τις ἐκ νεκρων ἀναστῃ πεισθησονται. 12. και ἀναστησω αὐτον ἐν τῃ ἐσχατῃ ἡμερᾳ. 13. ἡ μητηρ και οἱ ἀδελφοι αὐτου εἱστηκεισαν ἐξω ζητουντες αὐτῳ λαλησαι. 14. οἱ ὑποκριται φιλουσιν ἐν ταις συναγωγαις ἑστωτες προσευχεσθαι. 15. δους δε αὐτῃ την χειρα ἀνεστησεν αὐτην. 16. και ἐπιστας ἐπανω αὐτης ἐπετιμησεν τῳ πυρετῳ. 17. ἐν μιᾳ των ἡμερων ἐπεστησαν οἱ ἀρχιερεις και εἰπαν. 18. ὁ δε Ἰησους ἐπιλαβομενος παιδιον ἐστησεν αὐτο παρ᾽ ἑαυτῳ. 19. πορευεσθε και σταθεντες λαλειτε ἐν τῳ ἱερῳ παντα τα ῥηματα της ζωης ταυτης. 20. μηδενι εἰπητε το ὁραμα ἑως οὗ ὁ Υἱος του ἀνθρωπου ἐκ νεκρων ἀναστῃ. 21. οἷς και παρεστησεν ἑαυτον ζωντα μετα το παθειν αὐτον. 22. και προσελθων ἡψατο της σορου, οἱ δε βασταζοντες ἐστησαν. 23. και ἐστησαν μαρτυρας ψευδεις λεγοντας Ὁ ἀνθρωπος οὗτος οὐ παυεται λαλων ῥηματα κατα του τοπου του ἁγιου. 24. ἀγαγοντες δε αὐτους ἐστησαν ἐν τῳ συνεδριῳ. 25. ἐνδυσασθε την πανοπλιαν του Θεου προς το δυνασθαι ὑμας στηναι.

B

1. I will cause you to stand in darkness.   2. There are certain of those standing here.   3. Paul therefore must stand in the council. 4. The priests stood the publican there.   5. But Peter stood up and preached the word to the crowd.   6. He is not here, for he has risen from the dead.   7. Who appointed you a ruler of this people? 8. Then we arose and departed from the city.   9. You made the king to stand in the Holy Place.   10. How shall we stand in the day of his wrath?   11. We stood outside wishing to see her husband. 12. After these things there arose many evil men.   13. We hope to stand in that day.   14. Then the Spirit of the Lord appointed me a light to the multitudes.   15. If anyone believes in me I will raise him up on the last day.   16. But his mother was standing outside.

LESSON 44

Other -μι verbs

ἀφιημι, συνιημι

The verb ἵημι, meaning 'I send', occurs in the New Testament only in compounds, the most common of which are:

> ἀφιημι   I send away, I forgive.
> συνιημι   *lit.* I send together; *hence*, I understand.

The verbal stem of ἵημι is ἑ.
The Present stem of ἵημι is ἱε.

With few exceptions its forms follow τίθημι exactly. The principal parts of ἀφιημι are:

> ἀφιημι   ἀφησω   ἀφηκα   —   ἀφεωνται   ἀφεθην

ἀφεωνται (third person plural) is the only Perfect Passive form in the New Testament.

δεικνυμι: I SHOW

Verbs in -υμι tend generally in the New Testament to assimilate themselves to verbs in -ω. Such -μι forms as do occur are almost always the
same as those of τιθημι allowing for the stem vowel υ instead of ε.

φημι: I SAY

The following forms are found in the New Testament:

Present: φημι I say   φησι(ν) he says   φασι(ν) they say
Imperfect: ἐφη   he said.

We have now given all the common forms of the -μι verbs. For a
complete list reference must be made to the larger works. But some of
the less common forms can be easily recognised. For example,

Future Middles will always follow the Future Actives:

$$\theta\eta\sigma o\mu\alpha\iota \qquad \delta\omega\sigma o\mu\alpha\iota \qquad \sigma\tau\eta\sigma o\mu\alpha\iota^1$$

Future Passives will always follow the First Aorist Passives:

$$\tau\epsilon\theta\eta\sigma o\mu\alpha\iota \quad \delta o\theta\eta\sigma o\mu\alpha\iota \quad \sigma\tau\alpha\theta\eta\sigma o\mu\alpha\iota \quad \dot{\alpha}\phi\epsilon\theta\eta\sigma o\mu\alpha\iota$$

Imperfects will have the Present stem together with an augment:

$$\dot{\epsilon}\text{-}\tau\iota\theta\epsilon \qquad \dot{\epsilon}\text{-}\delta\iota\delta o \qquad \dot{\iota}\sigma\tau\alpha^2$$

EXERCISE 44

1. Τοτε ἀφιησιν αὐτον ὁ διαβολος.   2. ὁ δε φησιν Πασα ἁμαρτια
και βλασφημια ἀφεθησεται τοις ἀνθρωποις.   3. ἀφετε τα παιδια
και μη κωλυετε αὐτα ἐλθειν προς με.   4. ὁ δε Ἰησους παλιν
κραξας ἀφηκεν το πνευμα.   5. ἐν δε παραβολαις τα παντα
γινεται μηποτε ἐπιστρεψωσιν και ἀφεθη αὐτοις.   6. και οὐκετι
ἀφιετε αὐτον οὐδεν ποιησαι τῳ πατρι.   7. φημι σοι Ἀφεωνται αἱ
ἁμαρτιαι αὐτης αἱ πολλαι.   8. τίς οὑτος ἐστιν ὁς και ἁμαρτιας
ἀφιησιν;   9. ἰδου ἀφιεται ὑμιν ὁ οἰκος ὑμων.   10. ἀφιετε εἰ

---

¹ The middle of ἱστημι, like the passive, is intransitive.
² See p. 53 n. 1.

τι ἐχετε κατα τινος. 11. οὐκ ἀφησουσιν λιθον ἐπι λιθον ἐν σοι.
12. ἐαν τινων ἀφητε τας ἁμαρτιας ἀφεωνται αὐτοις. 13. οὑτος
ἐστιν ὁ τον λογον ἀκουων και συνιεις. 14. ἀκουσατε μου παντες
και συνετε. 15. ὁ δε ἐφη Κυριε, σωσον, ἀπολλυμεθα. 16. μελλει
γαρ Ἡρῳδης ζητειν το παιδιον του ἀπολεσαι αὐτο. 17. πορευεσθε δε μαλλον προς τα προβατα τα ἀπολωλοτα. 18. ὁ εὑρων
την ψυχην αὐτου ἀπολεσει αὐτην. 19. παντες γαρ οἱ λαβοντες
μαχαιραν ἐν μαχαιρῃ¹ ἀπολουνται. 20. μη δυναται προφητης
ἀπολεσθαι ἐξω Ἱερουσαλημ; 21. ὁ λογος γαρ ὁ του σταυρου
τοις ἀπολλυμενοις μωρια ἐστιν. 22. ἀπολω την σοφιαν των
σοφων. 23. τί οὐν φημι; 24. καθως φασιν τινες ἡμας λεγειν.
25. Ἀφες ἀρτι, φησιν, οὑτως γαρ πρεπον ἐστιν ἡμιν πληρωσαι πασαν
δικαιοσυνην. τοτε ἀφιησιν αὐτον. 26. τοτε συνηκαν οἱ μαθηται
ὁτι περι Ἰωανου του βαπτιστου εἰπεν αὐτοις. 27. τίς δυναται
ἀφιεναι ἁμαρτιας εἰ μη εἱς, ὁ Θεος; 28. οἱ δε εὐθεως ἀφεντες τα
δικτυα ἠκολουθησαν αὐτῳ. 29. και ἀφες ἡμιν τα ὀφειληματα
ἡμων, ὡς και ἡμεις ἀφηκαμεν τοις ὀφειλεταις ἡμων. 30. ἐαν γαρ
ἀφητε τοις ἀνθρωποις τα παραπτωματα αὐτων, ἀφησει και ὑμιν ὁ
πατηρ ὑμων ὁ οὐρανιος. 31. τοτε δεικνυσιν αὐτῳ ὁ διαβολος
πασας τας βασιλειας του κοσμου. 32. ἐκεινοις δε τοις ἐξω ἐν
παραβολαις τα παντα γινεται, ἱνα ἀκουοντες ἀκουωσιν και μη
συνιωσιν. 33. ὁ δε Ἰησους ἐδιδου τον ἀρτον τοις μαθηταις ἱνα
διδωσιν αὐτον τοις ὀχλοις. 34. και ὁπου ἀν εἰσεπορευετο ἐν ταις
ἀγοραις ἐτιθεσαν² τους ἀσθενουντας. 35. και το ἀργυριον ἐτιθουν
παρα τους ποδας των ἀποστολων. 36. και τους ἀρτους ἐδιδου
τοις μαθηταις ἱνα παρατιθωσιν αὐτοις. 37. πως οὐν σταθησεται
ἡ βασιλεια αὐτου; 38. διδοτε και δοθησεται ὑμιν. 39. ὁ δε
Ἰησους ἐφη Ἐγειρε. και ἀναστας ἐστη.

---

¹ μαχαιρα forms its genitive and dative singular: μαχαιρης, μαχαιρῃ.
² ἐτιθεσαν and ἐτιθουν (in the next sentence) are alternative forms of the
third person plural Imperfect Active.

REVISION TESTS 6

-μι verbs

Allow 45 minutes each for Tests A and B. Total number of marks: 50 for each test.

A

1. Give the principal parts of: τιθημι, ἐφιστημι, ἀποδιδωμι, ἀφιημι. [8 marks]
2. Describe the use of tenses in ἱστημι. [4]
3. Without repeating the stems, write out in full the First Perfect Participle Active of ἱστημι. [2]
4. Write out the following tenses of τιθημι: Second Aorist Subjunctive Active, Second Aorist Indicative Middle, Present Indicative Middle. [3]
5. Write out the following tenses of διδωμι: Present Indicative Passive, Present Imperative Active. [2]
6. Write out the Present Subjunctive Active of ἱστημι. [1]
7. Parse: τιθετε (2), ἐτιθετε, τιθητε, θετε, τιθετω, τιθεσθαι, τεθησῃ, θησεσθε, δωσεις, διδως, διδῷς, διδωσιν (2), διδουσιν, διδομενη, δοθησεται, ἱστασιν (2), ἐστησαν (2), στασης, στησῃ (2), ἐπεστησεν, ἀφησω, φησιν, ἀπολουμεν, ἀπωλου, ἀπολλυμενος. [30]

B

1. Give the principal parts of: ἐπιτιθημι, ἱστημι, ἀφιημι, ἀπολλυμι. [8 marks]
2. Write out the following tenses of τιθημι: Present Subjunctive Active, Second Aorist Imperative Active. [2]
3. Write out the following tenses of διδωμι: Present Subjunctive Active, Second Aorist Indicative Middle. [2]
4. Write out the Second Aorist Indicative Active of ἱστημι. [1]
5. Write out the Present Indicative Active of δεικνυμι. [1]
6. Without repeating the stems, write out in full the Second Perfect Participle Active of ἱστημι. [2]

186

7. Parse: τιθεντα, τιθεναι, θεντι, τεθεντι, θωσιν, θεισιν, τεθεισιν, τιθεται, τεθειται, ἐθου, τιθεμενων, ἐδοθης, δεδοται, ἐδιδοντο, δωῃ, δος, δουναι, δον, ἱσταναι, ἱστασθαι, στασων, στηναι, ἱστασαι, ἱσταντι, ἀφεθη, ἀφεθη, ἀφεθησῃ, ἐφη, φημι, φασιν, σταθησῃ, ἐφεστηκεν, ἀπολουνται, ἀπωλετο. [34]

GENERAL REVISION TESTS 7

Earlier revision tests will be found on pp. 43, 76 ff., 113 f., 134 f., 173 f., 186 f.

The tests which follow are based solely upon the vocabularies, the list of principal parts and the summary of grammar (morphology and syntax). These are to be found on pp. 193–249. The Greek–English Index and the English–Greek Vocabulary may also be found useful as a means of revision.

Allow 1½ hours each for Tests 7A, 7B, 7C. Total marks: 100 for each test.

7A

1. Decline in the singular: Ἰησους, πολις, first personal pronoun, μεγας (all genders). [5 marks]

2. Decline in the plural: οὐς, ὁς (all genders), indefinite pronoun (all genders), reciprocal pronoun. [6]

3. Give the nominative singular, genitive singular, article and dative plural of the words meaning: righteousness, steadfastness, sea, vineyard, resurrection. [5]

4. Give the comparative and superlative of δικαιως. [1]

5. Write out the following tenses or forms of λυω: *Active:* nominative singular of Present Participle (all genders). *Middle:* Aorist Subjunctive. *Passive:* nominative singular of Aorist Participle (all genders). [3]

6. Give the table of contractions of θ with mutes. [1]

7. Give the rules of contraction for -οω verbs. [1]

8. Give the Imperfect Indicative Active of ἐρωταω. [1]

9. Give the Imperfect, Infinitive and nominative singular of the Participle (all genders) of εἰμι. [3]

10. Give the Perfect Infinitive Active of γραφω. [1]

11. Give the principal parts of: ἀγγελλω, ἀνοιγω, -βαινω, δεχομαι, ἐγειρω, κραζω, πειθω, πιπτω, σωζω, ἐχω, φερω, ἱστημι, ἀπολλυμι. [26]

12. Give the Second Aorist Indicative Middle of διδωμι. [1]

13. Parse: ἐπεστησαν (2 ways), ἐρωτησω (2 ways). [4]

14. Give the nominative singular masculine of the word meaning: sufficient, young, one, six. [2]

15. Give the Greek for: I persecute, I injure, I buy, I belong to, I owe, I understand. [3]

16. Give the Greek for: not even (four words), even as (two words), worse, woe, still, why? [5]

17. Give three ways of expressing 'from' and three of 'to'. [6]

18. Give two uses of μετα, two of κατα, and three of ὁτι. [7]

19. Give six uses of the accusative. [6]

20. Give eight uses of the Subjunctive. [8]

21. Give five types of conditional clause. [5]

7B

1. Decline in the singular: Σατανας, ἰχθυς, μηδεις (all genders). [4 marks]

2. Decline in the plural: μητηρ, ὁρος. [2]

3. Decline in the singular and plural: ἀληθης (all genders). [3]

4. Give the vocative and accusative singular of πατηρ, γυνη, βασιλευς, χαρις. [4]

5. Give the nominative singular, genitive singular, article and dative plural of the words meaning: prayer, coming, husband, light, year. [5]

6. Give the comparative and superlative of δικαιος. [1]

7. Give of λυω: *Active:* Pluperfect Indicative. *Middle:* Aorist Imperative. *Passive:* Perfect Infinitive. [3]

8. Give the table of contractions of σ with mutes. [1]

9. Give the rules of contraction for -αω verbs. [1]

10. Give the Present Indicative Passive of φανεροω. [1]

11. Give the Aorist Indicative Active of γινωσκω. [1]

12. Give the Present Indicative Active of ζαω. [1]

13. Give the principal parts of λυω, πρασσω, αἰρω, γινωσκω, εὑρισκω, θνησκω, καλεω, λαμβανω, πινω, -στελλω, ἐσθιω, διδωμι. [24]

14. Give the Second Aorist Subjunctive Active of τιθημι. [1]

15. Parse: ἑστωτα, εὑαγγελιζομενου. [2]

16. Give the nominative singular masculine of the word meaning: free, weak. [1]

17. Give the nominative plural masculine of the word meaning: old, few. [1]

18. Give the Greek for: outside, therefore (three words), greater, more (adverb), hundred, thousand (two forms), alas, behold (two forms). [6]

19. Give the Greek for: I weep, I worship, I cleanse, I begin, I sow, I boast, I justify, I hope. [4]

20. Give two uses of ὑπερ and two of ὑπο. [4]

21. Give four ways of expressing 'with' and three of 'before'. [7]

22. Give six uses of the dative. [6]

23. Give seven uses of the article. [7]

24. How may time clauses be translated? [6]

25. Explain the use of οὐ and μη in questions. [2]

26. Give two uses of the Optative. [2]

7C

1. Decline in the singular: δοξα, μερος; all genders of ἀλλος, πολυς. [6 marks]

2. Decline in the plural: πλοιον, second personal pronoun. [2]

3. Decline in the singular and plural: γραμματευς. [2]

4. Give the nominative singular, genitive singular, article and dative plural of the word meaning: temptation, sacrifice, soldier, hand, judgement (two words). [6]

5. Give the comparative and superlative of σοφος. [1]

6. Write out the following tenses of λυω: *Active:* Aorist Imperative. *Middle:* Present Subjunctive. *Passive:* Future. [3]

7. Give the three rules of reduplication. [2]

8. Give the rules of contraction for -εω verbs. [1]

9. Give the Present Infinitive Active of πληροω. [1]
10. Give the Present Subjunctive Middle of ἀγαπαω. [1]
11. Give the Future of εἰμι. [1]
12. Give the Aorist Subjunctive Active of ἁμαρτανω. [1]
13. Give the Aorist Imperative Passive of κρυπτω. [1]
14. Give the principal parts of τιμαω, ἀγω, ἀκουω, βαλλω, γινομαι, κρινω, σπειρω, ἐρχομαι, λεγω, ὁραω, τιθημι, ἀφιημι. [24]
15. Give of ἱστημι: Second Aorist Infinitive Active; all genders of the nominative singular of the Present Participle Middle and of the two Perfect Participles Active. [4]
16. Parse: ἀποκτεινωμεν, λαβοντες. [2]
17. Give nominative singular masculine of the word meaning: each, rich, full, different. [2]
18. Give the Greek for: I read, I am ill, I am about, I wonder at, I reckon, I lie, I rebuke, I clothe. [4]
19. Give the Greek for: until (two words), better, five, forty, similarly, as much as, today. [4]
20. Give two uses of δια and three of παρα. [5]
21. Give three ways of expressing 'for' and three of 'by'. [6]
22. Give six uses of the infinitive. [6]
23. Describe the uses of the participle. [7]
24. Give eight uses of the genitive. [8]

THE NEXT STEP

The student has now traversed the elements of New Testament Greek and is in a position to tackle the text of the New Testament with confidence. What further help does he need?

The fullest and most up-to-date lexicon is *A Greek–English Lexicon of the New Testament* by W. Bauer, translated by Arndt and Gingrich (Cambridge). For the student who expects to do advanced work, this is unquestionably the best lexicon. The beginner may find it rather overwhelming.

G. Abbott-Smith's *A Manual Greek Lexicon of the New Testament* (T. and T. Clark) is a good lexicon at this stage. It has two most useful appendices: Irregular Verbs and an Alphabetical List of Verbal Forms. Even for advanced students it has one advantage over Arndt–Gingrich, in that it gives not only the Septuagint uses of Greek words, but also the Hebrew words which they translate.

An excellent small lexicon is B. M. Newman's *A Concise Greek–English Dictionary of the New Testament* (United Bible Societies).

MORPHOLOGY

From time to time the student will meet rare forms of words which he has not learnt. They can almost always be identified in Newman or Abbott–Smith, but for serious work it is more satisfactory to have a text-book which sets out the complete morphology. The advanced book is Moulton and Howard, *A Grammar of New Testament Greek*, vol. 2 (T. and T. Clark). J. H. Moulton, *An Introduction to the Study of New Testament Greek* (Epworth) gives a concise, but adequate, summary.

A newcomer to the field is Ward Powers, *Learn to Read the Greek New Testament* (Paternoster and Eerdmans, 3rd ed., 1982) which is based on the principles of scientific linguistics. It has a complete morphology and much additional information. Because of its fresh angle it could provide a most stimulating refresher course.

SYNTAX

The syntax covered so far has been rather slight. It would probably be wise to study H. P. V. Nunn's *A Syntax of New Testament Greek* (Cambridge) or Moulton's *Introduction* (see above) or A. C. M. Hargreaves' *Notes on the Translation and Text of St Mark's Gospel in Greek and on New Testament Greek Syntax* (Christian Literature Society, Madras), before using H. E. Dana and J. R. Mantey's *A Manual Grammar of the Greek New Testament* (Macmillan, New York), C. F. D. Moule's *An Idiom Book of New Testament Greek* (Cambridge) and the large standard works: *A Grammar of New Testament Greek* by J. H. Moulton, vol. 3, 'Syntax', by N. Turner (T. and T. Clark), Blass–Debrunner–Funk, *A Greek Grammar of the New Testament* (Cambridge) and A. T. Robertson, *A Grammar of the Greek New Testament in the Light of Historical Research* (Hodder and Stoughton, out of print).

NOTE ON THE VOCABULARIES OPPOSITE

It needs to be stressed that words in one language seldom have a precise equivalent in another language. Any word has a *range* of meanings and the nearest equivalent word in another language will have a range of meanings which overlaps but does not exactly coincide with it. The English equivalents chosen in the vocabularies introduce the student to the commonest meaning or meanings of the Greek word.

VOCABULARIES

*The figure following the Greek word shows the approximate number
of times it occurs in the New Testament*

βαλλω (122)	I throw. [ballistic]
βλεπω (132)	I see.
γινωσκω (221)	I know. [The Gnostics claimed secret γνωσις, 'knowledge' (Vocab. 31)]
γραφω (190)	I write. [geography: writing about γη, 'the earth' (Vocab. 8)]
ἐγειρω (143)	I raise.
ἐσθιω (65)	I eat. [Cf. com*est*ibles]
εὑρισκω (176)	I find.
ἐχω (705)	I have.
θεραπευω (43)	I heal. [therapy]
κρινω (114)	I judge. [critic]
λαμβανω (258)	I take.
λεγω (1318)	I say. [Cf. lecture]
λυω (42)	I loose. [ἀναλυσις, 'analysis', the loosening up (ἀνα) of something into its elements]
μενω (118)	I remain. [The '-main' of 'remain' comes from the same root as μενω]
πεμπω (79)	I send.
σωζω (106)	I save. [σωτηρια, 'salvation' (Vocab. 9) comes from the same root. Soteriology deals with the doctrine of salvation]

LESSON 4

αἰτεω (70)	I ask, ask for.
βλασφημεω (34)	I blaspheme.
εὐλογεω (42)	I bless. [eulogise]
ζητεω (117)	I seek.
θεωρεω (58)	I look at, see. [A 'theory' is something to look at, pending acceptance or rejection]
καλεω (148)	I call.
λαλεω (298)	I speak. [glosso*lalia*: speaking in tongues; γλωσσα 'tongue' (Vocab. 9)]
μαρτυρεω (76)	I bear witness. [martyr]

μετανοεω (34) I repent.
μισεω (39) I hate. [misogynist: woman-hater; γυνη, 'woman' (Vocab. 28)]
ποιεω (565) I do, make. [poem; pharmaco*poeia*: making of drugs]
τηρεω (70) I keep.
φιλεω (25) I love. [philosophy: love of σοφια, 'wisdom' (Vocab. 9); a bibliophile is a lover of βιβλια, 'books' (Vocab. 7)]

LESSON 5

ὠ (17) O!
και (8947) and; (sometimes) even, also.
Ἰσραηλ (68) Israel (indeclinable masculine noun).
Ἰουδαιος (194) Jew. [I.e. member of the tribe of Judah]
Φαρισαιος (97) Pharisee.
Χριστος (529) Christ. [Hebrew: Messiah, i.e. Anointed One]
ἀγγελος (175) messenger, angel.
ἀγρος (35) field. [Cf. agriculture]
ἀδελφος (343) brother. [Christadelphians: a Christian brotherhood]
ἀνθρωπος (548) man. [anthropology: the word (λογος) or science of Man]
ἀποστολος (79) apostle.
διακονος (29) servant, deacon. [diaconate]
διδασκαλος (59) teacher. [didactic]
ἐχθρός (32) enemy.
θανατος (120) death. [euthanasia: death induced εὐ ('well', Vocab. 33), i.e. gently and easily]
θρονος (62) throne.
κοσμος (185) world. [cosmos, cosmic]
κυριος (718) lord, the Lord. [Kyrie: name given to the liturgical response, 'Lord (vocative Κυριε), have mercy upon us'] Κυριος with a capital letter means 'The Lord'. It is the word used in the Septuagint to denote the sacred name of Jehovah. It sometimes has the definite article and sometimes not—see next lesson.
λαος (141) people. [The laity are the people of God]
λεπρός (9) leper.
λιθος (58) stone. [Palaeolithic, Mesolithic, Neolithic: belonging to the Old, Middle, New Stone Ages; monolith: see also Vocabs. 11, 12]
λογος (331) word [Same root as λεγω, 'I say']
νομος (191) law. [Deuteronomy: The Second Law. δευτερος, 'second' (Vocab. 12)]

194

VOCABULARIES 5, 6

ὀφθαλμός (100) eye. [ophthalmic]
παραλυτικός (10) paralytic, paralysed man.
ποταμός (17) river. [hippopotamus: river horse; Mesopotamia: the land in the middle (lying between) the Rivers (Euphrates and Tigris)]
πρεσβύτερος (65) presbyter, elder.
τόπος (95) place. [topography]
φίλος (29) friend. [Cf. φιλεω]
φόβος (47) fear. [phobia]

LESSON 6

ἐστί(ν) (891) is
Ἰησους (905) Jesus.
Ἰακωβος (42) James. [Jacobite: supporter of King James]
ἁμαρτωλός (47) sinner.
ἄνεμος (31) wind. [The wind-flower is an anemone. An anemometer measures wind speed]
ἄρτος (97) bread, loaf.
διάβολος (37) (the) devil. [diabolical]
δοῦλος (124) slave.
ἥλιος (32) sun. [helium: an element first known through studying the spectrum of the sun. Heliopolis: city of the sun (πολις, Vocab. 31)]
Θεός (1314) God. [theology]
καρπός (66) fruit.
μισθός (29) reward, pay.
ναός (45) temple; especially the shrine of the temple.
οἶκος (112) house.
οἶνος (34) wine.
οὐρανός (272) heaven. [The element uranium; the planet Uranus] Though there are many exceptions, οὐρανος usually takes the article and is usually put in the plural, e.g. 'the kingdom of heaven', ἡ βασιλεια των οὐρανων.
ὄχλος (174) crowd. [ochlocracy: mob rule]
πειρασμός (21) temptation.
σταυρός (27) cross.
υἱός (375) son

Two words for time

καιρός (85) fitting season, opportunity, time.
χρόνος (54) time. [chronology]

Three feminine nouns

ἐρημος (47)   desert. [eremite = hermit]

ὁδος (101)   way. [exodus; ἐξ 'out of' (Vocab. 10)]

παρθενος (15)   virgin. [parthenogenesis: virgin birth]

LESSON 7

ἀργυριον (21)   silver, money. [Cf. French and heraldic 'argent']

βιβλιον (34)   book. [Bible]

δαιμονιον (63)   demon.

δενδρον (25)   tree. [rhododendron: lit. rose-tree]

ἐργον (169)   work. [energy; erg is the physical unit of work]

εὐαγγελιον (76)   gospel. [evangel]

ἱερον (70)   temple. [A hierarchy is a system of sacred rulers (cf. ἀρχω 'I rule', Vocab. 23)] Usually ναος would refer to the sanctuary, whereas ἱερον would include the precincts as a whole. Note that the breathing is on the ι not on the ε. Whereas αι, ει, οι are diphthongs (pronounced as a single syllable), ια, ιε, ιο form two separate syllables. Hence σοφ-ι-α (Vocab. 9), ἱματ-ι-ον, ἱ-ερ-ον.

ἱματιον (60)   garment; pl. clothes.

μνημειον (37)   tomb. [Thought of as something by which to remember (μνημονευω) the dead. A mnemonic is an aid to memory]

μυστηριον (27)   mystery.

παιδιον (52) ⎫
τεκνον (99) ⎭   child. [paediatrics, Paedo-baptist] In origin the -ιον ending was a diminutive, so that ἀργυριον was a small piece of silver, δαιμονιον a lesser demon, παιδιον a little παις ('child', Vocab. 28). But in many cases the diminutive force has disappeared. παιδιον and τεκνον are used of children of all ages. [A pedagogue is one who leads (ἀγω, Vocab. 13) a child]

πλοιον (66)   boat.

ποτηριον (31)   cup.

προβατον (37)   sheep.

προσωπον (74)   face.

σημειον (77)   sign. [semaphore carries (φερω, Vocab. 13) a sign]

συνεδριον (22)   council, the Sanhedrin. (Sanhedrin is one of the rare instances of Hebrew borrowing a Greek word.)

σαββατον (68)   Sabbath. (The Aramaic for Sabbath was 'Shabbata'.
So the plural form σαββατα (as well as the singular
form σαββατον) is often used with singular meaning.)

The Greek form of the word for 'Jerusalem' is also Second Declension
neuter plural:

(τα) Ἱεροσολυμα (63)

There is also a Hebrew form which is feminine singular and indeclinable:

(ἡ) Ἱερουσαλημ (76)

LESSON 8

ὁ ἡ το (19,734)	the.
ἀγάπη (116)	love. [The Agape in the Early Church was a love feast]
ἀρχή (55)	beginning. [archaic]
γῆ (248)	earth, land. [geography, geology]
γραφή (50)	writing, Scripture (cf. γραφω). [autograph: writing of the man 'himself', αὐτος (Vocab. 15)]
διαθήκη (33)	covenant (ἡ καινη διαθηκη: 'The New Testament').
διδαχή (30)	teaching (cf. διδασκαλος). ['The Didache' is the name by which an early Christian writing, The Teaching of the Twelve Apostles, is generally known.]
δικαιοσύνη (91)	righteousness.
εἰρήνη (91)	peace. [eirenical]
ἐντολή (68)	commandment.
ἐπιστολή (24)	letter. [epistle]
ζωή (135)	life. [zoology]
κεφαλή (75)	head. [cephalic; autocephalous: self-governing]
κώμη (27)	village.
νεφέλη (25)	cloud. [Cf. nebula, a cloudy star-cluster; nebulous]
ὀργή (36)	anger.
παραβολή (50)	parable.
προσευχή (36)	prayer.
συναγωγη (56)	synagogue.
τιμή (41)	honour, price. [Timothy: honouring God]
ὑπομονή (32)	steadfastness (remaining (μενω) steadfast under (ὑπο, Vocab. 16) trial).
φυλακή (46)	guard, prison. [A phylactery was a guard against evil; prophylactic: preventative]
φωνή (137)	sound, voice. [phonetic; telephone: voice at a distance]
ψυχή (101)	soul, life. [psychology]

There are about 137,500 words in the New Testament. We are now
familiar with one-third of them.

LESSON 9
Stems ending in vowel or ρ

ἀδικία (25)	unrighteousness. (Same root as δικαιοσυνη, δικαιος 'righteous' (Vocab. 12). ἀ- is a negative prefix which will be seen again in Vocab. 11.)
ἀλήθεια (109)	truth.
ἁμαρτία (173)	sin (cf. ἁμαρτωλος).
βασιλεία (162)	kingdom, sovereignty, royal rule.
γενεά (43)	generation. [genealogy]
ἐκκλησία (114)	assembly, congregation, church. [ecclesiastic]
ἐξουσία (102)	authority.
ἐπαγγελία (52)	promise.
ἡμέρα (388)	day. [ephemeral: for a day]
θύρα (39)	door. [θυρα and 'door' come from the same root. The θ and the d have a common origin]
θυσία (28)	sacrifice.
καρδία (156)	heart. [cardiac]
μαρτυρία (37)	witness (cf. μαρτυρεω). The neuter form μαρτυριον is also common: 20 times.
μετάνοια (22)	repentance (cf. μετανοεω).
οἰκία (94)	house. (οἰκ-ι-α is in form a diminutive of οἰκος, but there is now no sharp distinction between the two words. Cf. note on παιδ-ι-ον, Vocab. 7.)
παρουσία (24)	coming.
πέτρα (15)	rock. [petrify. Cf. Πετρος below]
σοφία (51)	wisdom. [philosophy]
σωτηρία (45)	salvation (cf. σωζω). [soteriology]
χαρά (59)	joy.
χήρα (26)	widow.
χρεία (49)	need.
ὥρα (106)	hour. [ὡρα and 'hour' come from the same root. Horoscope: prediction based on person's hour of birth]
Γαλιλαία (61)	Galilee.
Ἰουδαία (44)	Judaea.

Stems ending in consonant other than ρ

γλῶσσα (50)	tongue. [glossolalia: speaking with tongues]
δόξα (165)	glory. [doxology]
θάλασσα (91)	sea.

Names (*Second Declension*)

Παῦλος (158)   Paul.
Πέτρος (154)   Peter.

LESSON 10

Nouns ending in ης

'Ιωάνης (134)   John (sometimes spelt 'Ιωαννης).
βαπτιστής (12)   baptist.
ἐργάτης (16)   workman (cf. ἐργον).
κριτής (19)   judge [critic] (cf. κρινω).
μαθητής (a6a)   disciple (cf. μανθανω, 'I learn' (Vocab. 25)). [Mathe-
                matics is a basic form of learning]
προφήτης (144)   prophet.
στρατιώτης (26)   soldier. [Strategy is concerned with the way in which
                an army (στρατος) is led (ἀγω, Vocab. 13)]
τελώνης (21)   tax-collector.
ὑποκριτής (18)   hypocrite.

Nouns ending in -ας: -ε -ι or -ρ stem, Genitive in -ου

νεανίας -ου (4)   young man (cf. νεος, 'new', 'young', Vocab. 12).
'Ανδρέας -ου (13)   Andrew.
'Ηλείας -ου (29)   Elijah. 'Elijah' comes from the Hebrew; 'Elias' (the
                New Testament form in the Authorised Version)
                from the Greek.

Nouns ending in -ας: consonant stem, 'Doric' Genitive in -α

Σατανᾶς -α (36)   Satan.
'Ιούδας -α (44)   Judas, Judah.

Prepositions
taking accusative

εἰς (1753)   to, into.
πρός (696)   to, towards.

taking genitive

ἀπο, ἀπ', ἀφ' (645)   from, away from. [Apocalypse = Revelation, i.e.
                taking the veil *away from*] It is usually written ἀπ'
                when the word which follows begins with a vowel
                which has a smooth breathing; ἀφ' before a rough
                breathing.

ἐκ, ἐξ (915)   from, out of [Exodus] (ἐξ is used before a vowel).

taking dative

ἐν (2713)   in.

Adverb

οὐ, οὐκ, οὐχ (1619)   not (οὐκ before smooth, οὐχ before rough breathing).

Conjunctions

ἀλλά (635)   but (often written ἀλλ' before a vowel).

The three small conjunctions (often called *particles*) which follow never stand as the first word of a sentence or clause. They are usually written second.

γάρ (1036)   for. (The conjunction 'for', which is virtually equivalent to 'because', must be distinguished from the preposition 'for', which represents the dative.)

οὖν (493)   therefore, then (in a logical, not a temporal, sense).

δέ (2771)   but, and (lighter than ἀλλα and και).

In Greek, particles and conjunctions are used to bind one sentence to another more frequently than in English. It is the exception rather than the rule to start a sentence without one. So much so that it is a matter for note if two sentences are *not-bound-together*. There is said to be an *asyndeton*. (See δεω, Vocab. 14.) και and δε in particular are lavishly used, sometimes with very little force. As a discipline in accuracy the beginner should always translate these words, though an expert might at times be justified in considering it more idiomatic to leave such a word untranslated.

οὐ and δε combine to make:

οὐδέ (139)   and not, not even, neither, nor. (It can stand first in the sentence.)

ἄρα (49)   also means 'therefore, then'. It is a little lighter than οὖν and is sometimes found first in the sentence.

LESSON 11

Adjectives with consonant stems (other than ρ), declined like
ἀγαθος -η -ον

ἀγαθος (104)   good.

ἀγαπητος (61)   beloved (cf. ἀγαπη).

δυνατός (32)   powerful, possible. [dynamite]

ἕκαστος (81)   each, every.

ἔσχατος (52)   last. [eschatology]

ἱκανός (40)   sufficient. *worthy, enough*

καινός (42)   new ('Η ΚΑΙΝΗ ΔΙΑΘΗΚΗ: 'The New Testament').

κακός (50)   bad. [cacophony: bad sound (φωνη)]

καλός (99)   beautiful, good. [calligraphy is beautiful writing, though notice that καλος has only one λ.]

λοιπός (55)   remaining; as a noun in the plural, '(the) rest'.

μέσος (56)   middle. The commonest expression is ἐν μεσῳ, 'in the midst'. [Mesopotamia; mesolithic: belonging to the Middle Stone Age]

μόνος (112)   alone, only. [monologue; monolith] The neuter accusative μονον is frequently used as an adverb.

Examples of the use of μονος

   Adjectivally

   Attributive position: ὁ μονος Θεος or ὁ Θεος ὁ μονος the-only-God

   Predicative position: μονος ὁ Θεος or ὁ Θεος μονος { God-only, God-alone
   (see further next Lesson).

   Adverbially

   μονον πιστευει   he only-believes
   οὐ μονον...ἀλλα και   not only...but also

ὀλίγος (40)   little, pl. few. [oligarchy: rule of a few. See ἀρχω, Vocab. 23]

πιστός (67)   believing, faithful.

πρῶτος (152)   first. [prototype] The neuter accusative πρωτον is frequently used as an adverb.

τρίτος (48)   third. [Deutero- and Trito-Isaiah are the hypothetical second and third prophets held to be responsible for the later parts of the Book of Isaiah. For δευτερος see next vocabulary.]

πτωχός (34)   poor.

σοφός (20)   wise (cf. σοφια).

τυφλός (50)   blind.

Adjectives with no separate feminine endings

Compound adjectives use λογος endings for feminine as well as masculine. Among these are all adjectives with the negative prefix ἀ-, including:

ἄπιστος ον (23)   unbelieving, faithless.

ἀκάθαρτος ον (31)   unclean [catharsis] (cf. καθαρος, 'clean' (Vocab. 12) and καθαριζω, 'I cleanse' (Vocab. 22)).

Though not a compound adjective, also of this type is:

αἰώνιος ον (70)   eternal, everlasting. [aeon] 'Eternal life' is αἰώνιος
                   ζωη.[1]

LESSON 12

Adjectives with vowel or ρ stems, declined like ἁγιος -α -ον

ἁγιος (233)   holy; as noun, saint. [hagiographer: writer of lives of
                   saints]

ἀξιος (41)   worthy.

δεξιος (54)   right, as distinguished from left. [Cf. dexterous]

δευτερος (44)   second. [Deuteronomy; Deutero-Isaiah]

δικαιος (79)   just, righteous (cf. δικαιοσυνη, ἀδικια).

ἐλευθερος (23)   free.

ἑτερος (98)   different, other. [heterodox]

ἰδιος (113)   one's own. [idiosyncrasy]. Normally it is used with the
                   article and without a personal pronoun. Thus ὁ ἰδιος
                   means 'my own', 'your own', etc., according to the
                   context.

ἰσχυρος (28)   strong.

καθαρος (26)   clean, pure [catharsis] (cf. ἀκαθαρτος, Vocab. 11).

μακαριος (50)   blessed, happy. *macarism*

μικρος (30)   small. [microscope; omicron is a short (small) 'o']

νεκρος (128)   dead. [A necropolis is a cemetery, a city, πολις (Vocab.
                   31), of the dead; necromancy is prediction through
                   communication with the dead] *necrophilia necrology*

νεος (23)   new, young (cf. νεανιας). [neolithic: belonging to New
                   Stone Age; neo-orthodox] *cf. νεος -temple*

παλαιος (19)   old. [palaeolithic: belonging to Old Stone Age]

πλουσιος (28)   rich. [plutocrat]

πονηρος (78)   evil.

ὁμοιος (45)   like (takes dative. This word was famous in the Arian
                   controversy. Was the Son of 'like' (ὁμοιος) substance
                   with or of the 'same' (ὁμος) substance as the Father?)

εἰμι (1556)   I am.

---

[1] With αἰωνιος, however, separate feminine endings are occasionally found.
As the stem αἰωνι- ends in a vowel, the feminines in these cases have -α
endings, like ἁγιος -α -ον (next lesson).

VOCABULARY 13

LESSON 13

Verbs compounded with a preposition

ἄγω (66)   I lead, bring. Intransitive, I go.

From the simple verb ἄγω are derived the following compound verbs:

ἀπάγω (15)   I lead away.

συνάγω (59)   I bring or gather together (cf. συναγωγη).

ὑπάγω (79)   I depart (intransitive).

φέρω (68)   I carry. [Christopher: carrying Christ. Cf. transfer, refer]

From φερω is derived:

προσφέρω (17)   I bring, offer.

ἀκούω (427)   I hear. [acoustics] Usually takes accusative of thing heard, but *genitive* of the person heard.

From ἀκουω is derived:

ὑπακούω (21)   I obey (takes dative).

Other compound verbs:

ἀναγινώσκω (32)   I read.

ἐπιγινώσκω (44)   I perceive, recognise.

ἀποθνήσκω (113)   I die.

ἀπολύω (65)   I release.

ἐκβάλλω (81)   I throw out, send out.

ἐνδύω (28)   I put on, clothe. [Cf. endue]

παραλαμβάνω (49)   I receive.

Other verbs

ἀνοίγω (78)   I open.

διδάσκω (95)   I teach (cf. διδαχη).

διώκω (44)   I pursue, persecute.

κλαίω (38)   I weep.

πείθω (52)   I persuade.

περισσεύω (39)   I abound.

πιστεύω (241)   I believe (takes dative. Cf. πιστος, ἀπιστος).

προφητεύω (28)   I prophesy.

χαίρω (74)   I rejoice (cf. χαρα).

We are now familiar with more than half the words in the New ← N.B Testament.

LESSON 14
-εω verbs compounded with a preposition

κατοικέω (44)   I inhabit, dwell (followed by accusative or ἐν with dative; from οἶκος).

παρακαλέω (109)   I beseech, exhort, encourage. [Paraclete]

περιπατέω (95)   I walk. [peripatetic]

προσκυνέω (59)   I worship (usually takes <u>dative</u>; sometimes accusative).

Other -εω verbs

ἀδικέω (27)   I do wrong to, injure (cf. δικαιος, ἀδικια).

ἀκολουθέω (90)   I follow (takes <u>dative</u>). [acolyte: one who follows. The grammatical term 'anacoluthon' is made up of ἀν- (the full form of the negative prefix) and ἀκολουθεω. It is used of a sentence which *does not follow on* properly: for instance, when a new construction is begun before the old one is completed, e.g. Exod. 32. 32: 'But now, if thou wilt forgive their sin—and if not....' See also Mark 7. 19 (R.V.) ἀν- comes from the same root as *un-* in 'unlike' and *in-* in 'injustice'.]

ἀσθενέω (33)   I am weak, ill. [neurasthenia: nervous debility]

γαμέω (28)   I marry. [monogamy]

δέω (41)   I bind. [asyndeton: ἀ + συν ('with', Vocab. 16) + δεω: where a sentence has no conjunction or particle to bind it with the previous sentence. Cf. Vocab. 10]

διακονέω (36) διηκονουν (Imperf.)   I wait upon, serve, minister. (Takes dative. Cf. διακονος. The δι- of διακονεω is not in fact a preposition, but the augment is inserted as though it were.)

δοκέω (62)   I think, seem. [Docetism taught that Christ was only *seemingly* human.]

ἐλεέω (32)   I have mercy on. [eleemosynary, which is derived from the same root as 'alms']

εὐχαριστέω (38)   I give thanks. [Eucharist] (The prefix εὐ, 'well' (Vocab. 33) has already been met in εὐλογεω; and the stem in χαρα and χαιρω.)

κρατέω (47)   I take hold of, hold. *seize*

οἰκοδομέω (40)   I build (cf. οἶκος).

φωνέω (42)   I call (cf. φωνη).

The following three words are put in the predicative position:

οὗτος (1388)   this.
ἐκεῖνος (243)   that. } Occasionally these are used for 'he', 'she', 'it'.

ὅλος -η -ον (108)   whole. [holocaust: a whole burnt-offering]

We saw in Lesson 10 that the *dative is the case of personal interest*. We have now had five verbs which usually take the dative:

5 {
ὑπακουω	I obey
πιστευω	I believe
προσκυνεω	I worship
ἀκολουθεω	I follow
διακονεω	I serve

It will be noticed that they all involve a close personal relationship between the subject and the person referred to in the dative case.

We have had one verb which often takes the genitive: ἀκουω, 'I hear'.

LESSON 15

ἀλλος -η -ο (155) other, another. [allotropic: another form of the same substance. Diamond is an allotropic form of ordinary carbon]

ἀλληλους (100)   one another. [parallel: lines beside (παρα, Vocab. 16) one another]

αὐτος -η -ο (5534)   personal pronoun: he; emphasising pronoun: himself; identical adjective: same. [autograph]

ἑαυτόν -ην -ο (320)   reflexive pronoun: himself.

LESSON 16

Prepositions with three cases

Study 17 prepos [handwritten]

With most prepositions elision usually takes place before a vowel. There are, however, many exceptions, e.g. ὑπο ἐξουσιαν is the form always found in the New Testament. In the case of ἐπι, μετα, ὑπο, κατα (like ἀπο, Vocab. 10), there are different forms before the smooth and the rough breathing. περι and προ never elide. Cf. p. 55 n. 1.

παρά, παρ'   beside. [parallel] (παραβολη, putting (βαλλω) two things side by side.)

(acc. 60)   to beside, alongside, beside.
(gen. 79)   from beside, from. (Used of persons.)
(dat. 52)   (rest) beside, with.

ἐπί, ἐπ', ἐφ' (878) upon, on. [epitaph: inscription upon a tomb (τάφος); epiclesis: calling (καλεω) down the Holy Spirit upon the sacramental elements or upon the worshippers] (One meaning of genitive: in the time of.)

Prepositions with two cases

διά, δι' (acc. 280) because of.
  (gen. 386) through. [diameter: measure through centre]

μετά, μετ', μεθ' (acc. 103) after. (usually of time)
  (gen. 364) with.

ὑπέρ (acc. 19) above. [hypersensitive]
  (gen. 130) on behalf of, for.

ὑπο, ὑπ', ὑφ' (acc. 50) under. [hypodermic: under the skin]
  (gen. 167) by. (Used for an agent, not an instrument.)

κατά, κατ', καθ' (acc. 398) according to.
  (gen. 73) against.

(Note two other common phrases in the accusative:

κατ' ἰδιαν privately.
καθ' ἡμεραν daily.)

περί about.
  (acc. 38) round, around, approximately. [perimeter, periphrasis: roundabout way of saying something]
  (gen. 293) concerning.

Prepositions with one case: taking genitive

πρό (47) before (of place or time). [prologue]
ἐνώπιον (93)
ἔμπροσθεν (48) before (usually of place).
ὀπίσω (35) after (usually of place).
ἔξω (62) outside, out of (from ἐκ).
χωρίς (41) apart from.
ἄχρι (48)
ἕως (145) until, as far as.

ἐνωπιον, ἐμπροσθεν, ὀπισω, ἐξω, χωρις are usually classified as adverbs, but they are frequently used as prepositions.

ἀχρι, ἑως are sometimes prepositions, sometimes conjunctions.

Prepositions with one case: taking dative

σύν (127)   with (closely similar in use to μετα with genitive). [There are many words transliterated 'syn-' or 'sym-', e.g. sympathy, suffering with.]

It will be useful to collect the examples so far met of English prepositions which can have more than one Greek translation.

After: μετα + accusative (usually time)
ὀπίσω + genitive (usually place)

Before: προ (time or place)
ἐνώπιον
ἐμπροσθεν } (usually place) } + genitive

By: instrument—dative
agent—ὑπο + genitive
time during which—genitive

For: indirect object—dative
on behalf of—ὑπερ + genitive
length of time—accusative

From: ἀπο (away from)
ἐκ (out of)
παρα (from beside—but only of persons) } genitive/ablative

On: ἐπι—all cases: accusative, genitive or dative
time at which—dative/locative, with or without ἐν

Out of: ἐκ, ἐξω—genitive/ablative

To: indirect object—dative
εἰς (into)
προς (towards) } accusative

With: instrument—dative
παρα (rest beside)—dative/locative
μετα + genitive
σύν + dative } (in company with)

LESSON 18

ὅς, ἥ, ὅ (1369)   who, which, that (relative).
διό (53)   therefore (i.e. δι' ὅ 'because of which').

μή (1055)   not (with all moods except the Indicative).

Questions expecting the answer 'no' and hesistant questions use μή or:

μήτι (16)

Questions expecting the answer 'yes' use οὐ or:

οὐχί (53)

δε may be added to μη (as to οὐ, Vocab. 10) giving:

οὐδέ (with Indicative)
μηδέ (57) (with other moods) } and not, neither, nor, not even.

Another common particle (also never coming first in a sentence) is

τε (201) and (but denoting a closer connection than και) (cf. Latin -que).

This too forms a pair of conjunctions similar in meaning to οὐδε and μηδε:

οὔτε (91) (with Indicative)
μήτε (34) (with other moods) } and not, neither, nor.

They never mean 'not even' and are most common in the form οὔτε...
οὔτε and μήτε...μητε meaning 'neither...nor'.

NB   We are now familiar with more than 60 per cent of the words of the New
Testament.

With ὅς ἥ ὅ we have now had seven words with the -ο ending in the
neuter singular:

ὁ ἡ το	the
ἐκεινος -η -ο	that
οὗτος αὗτη τουτο	this
ἀλλος -η -ο	other
αὐτος -η -ο	he, etc.
ἑαυτον -ην -ο	himself, etc.
ὅς ἥ ὅ	who, etc.

LESSON 19

ὡς (505)   as. (This very common word has various other
meanings.)

καθώς (178)   as, even as (=κατα ὡς: slightly stronger in feeling
than ὡς).

ὥσπερ (36)   just as, even as (περ is a suffix which can add force to a
word).

μέν (181)   For meaning, see Lesson. Like δε never the first,
usually the second, word in the sentence.

First and second person personal pronouns

ἐγώ (1713)　　　I. [egoist]

ἐγω provides the commonest example of *crasis*, i.e. of two words being joined together, a smooth breathing being placed over the vowel at the point of union:

κἀγώ = καὶ ἐγω (84)　and I.
κἀκεῖνος = καὶ ἐκεῖνος (22)　and that.
σύ (1057)　　　you (singular).
ἡμεῖς (856)　　we.
ὑμεῖς (1830)　you (plural).

First and second person singular possessive adjectives and pronouns

ἐμός (76)　　　my, mine.
σός (27)　　　　your, yours.

First and second person singular reflexive pronouns

ἐμαυτον (37)　myself.
σεαυτόν (43)　yourself.

LESSON 20

δύναμαι (209)　I am able, can (cf. δυνατος).
θέλω (207)　　I will, wish. [A monothelite believes that Christ has
　Imperf. ἤθελον　only one will]
μέλλω (110)　　I am about.
δει (Impf. ἐδει) (102)　it is necessary. (δει as an impersonal verb is usually treated separately from δεω, but the meanings 'it is binding' and 'it is necessary' probably come from the same root.)
ἐξεστι(ν) (31)　it is lawful (takes dative).
ὥστε (84)　　with the result that, so that.

LESSON 22

-πτω verbs with labial (π) stem

ἀπο-καλύπτω (26)　I reveal. [apocalypse]
κρύπτω (19)　　I hide. [crypt, cryptic]

-ιζω *verbs* (all have dental (δ) stems)

βαπτίζω (77)	I baptise.
ἐγγίζω (42)	I draw near (usually takes dative).
ἐλπίζω (31)	I hope.
καθαρίζω (31)	I cleanse (cf. καθαρος, ἀκαθαρτος).
καθίζω (45)	I seat, sit.
σκανδαλίζω (29)	I cause to stumble. [scandalise] (σκανδαλον (15) is a 'trap', 'snare', 'stumbling-block'.)

-αζω *verbs with dental* (δ) *stem*

ἁγιαζω (27)	I sanctify (cf. ἁγιος).
ἀγοράζω (30)	I buy.
βασταζω (27)	I carry.
δοξαζω (61)	I glorify (cf. δοξα).
ἑτοιμαζω (41)	I prepare.
θαυμαζω (42)	I wonder at. [thaumaturge: a wonder-worker]
πειραζω (38)	I test, tempt (cf. πειρασμος).

-αζω *verb with guttural* (γ) *stem*

κραζω (55)	I cry out.

-σσω *verbs with guttural* (γ or κ) *stem*

κηρυσσω (61)	I proclaim, preach.
πρασσω (39)	I do, practise.
φυλασσω (31)	I guard (cf. φυλακη).

LESSON 23

Verb with an important Middle use

ἀρχω (2)	I rule (takes genitive). The Indicative is very rare, but the Present Participle ἀρχων, 'ruler' (Vocab. 28), which is used and regarded as a noun, is common. [Patriarch: father and ruler of a family (πατηρ, Vocab. 31); monarchy: rule by only one person; oligarchy: rule by a few.]
ἀρχομαι (83)	I begin (cf. ἀρχη).

ἄρχω has one common compound:

√ ὑπάρχω (60)   I am, exist, belong to. ὑπάρχω, when it means 'I am' or 'I exist', and γίνομαι, 'I become' (see below), take the <u>same case before and after</u>, like εἰμί.

Deponent Middle verbs

ἅπτομαι (39)   I take hold <u>of,</u> touch (takes <u>genitive</u>).

ἀρνέομαι (32)   I deny.

ἀσπάζομαι (59)   I greet. - *passive in form, active in meaning*

δέχομαι (56)   I receive. (δέχομαι and παραλαμβανω are similar in use, but (as its form suggests) παραλαμβανω can mean 'I take with me'.)

ἐργάζομαι (41)   I work (cf. ἔργον, ἐργάτης).

ἔρχομαι, Fut. ἐλεύσομαι (631)   I come (I go) (cf. πορεύομαι below).

  ἀπέρχομαι (116)   I go away.

  διέρχομαι (42)   I go through.

  εἰσέρχομαι (192)   I go into, come into.

  ἐξέρχομαι (216)   I go out.

  προσέρχομαι (87)   I come to (takes <u>dative</u>).

  συνέρχομαι (30)   I come together.

εὐαγγελίζομαι (54)   I bring good news, preach the gospel (cf. εὐαγγελιον) [evangelise].

Impf. εὐηγγελιζομην: note the augment.

  εὖ 'well' is treated like a compounding preposition.

λογίζομαι (40)   I reckon (i.e. make a λογος, λογος sometimes meaning 'an account'). [Cf. logic, logistics, logarithm]

προσεύχομαι (86)   I pray (cf. προσευχη).

Deponent Passive verbs

βούλομαι (37)   I will, wish. (It is doubtful whether any distinction in meaning from θελω can be maintained.)

φοβέομαι (95)   I fear, am afraid (cf. φοβος).

Deponent verbs with some Middle and some Passive forms

ἀποκρίνομαι (231)   I answer (usually takes dative; cf. κρινω: an *answer* is made after the matter <u>has been</u> *judged*).

γίνομαι, Fut. γενησομαι (667)   I become; sometimes, I am.

  παραγίνομαι (36)   I am beside, I come.

πορεύομαι (150)   I go (I come).

  ἐκπορεύομαι (33)   I go out.

In Greek the distinction between coming and going is not as clear as in English, but ἔρχομαι more often means 'come' than 'go' and πορεύομαι more often means 'go' than 'come'. In compounds, however, ἔρχομαι is often more readily translated 'go'.

There are three possible ways of expressing compound verbs, such as 'go through':

(1) The compound verb followed by the accusative, e.g.

διηρχοντο την τε Φοινικην και Σαμαριαν (Acts 15. 3)
They went through both Phoenicia and Samaria.

(2) The compound verb with its preposition repeated after the verb, e.g.
ἔδει δε αὐτον διερχεσθαι δια της Σαμαριας (John 4. 4)
And it was necessary for him to go through Samaria.

(3) In the case of εἰς and προς the simple verb is often used, and the only preposition follows the verb, e.g.

και συ ἐρχῃ προς με; (Matt. 3. 14) And do you come to me?

The use varies somewhat from verb to verb.

προσερχομαι, it will be noticed, takes the dative.

Note. This classification of Deponent verbs into Middle and Passive must be taken on trust for the time being. Whether a Deponent verb is Middle or Passive is discovered by looking at the forms of the Aorist, which are different for the two voices. They are dealt with in Lessons 27 and 35.

LESSON 25

In the following table of verbs the Aorist Infinitive has been added in those cases where there may be doubt about the form of the Aorist stem. The beginner might not know, for instance, whether ἤγαγον was derived from ἀγαγ- or ἐγαγ-. The Aorist stem (without augment) is needed in order to form the infinitive and the Imperative.

Verbs whose first three principal parts should now be learnt

Present	Future	Aorist	
ἀγω	ἀξω	ἤγαγον ✓	I lead, bring. Intr. I go.
		Inf. ἀγαγειν	
-βαινω	-βησομαι	-εβην	I go (used only in compounds):
ἀναβαινω (81)[1]			I go up.
καταβαινω (81)			I go down.
γινωσκω	γνωσομαι	ἐγνων	I know.

[1] The numbers in brackets refer to the occurrences of new words, or (in the case of ἐσθιω and λεγω) to the occurrences of the new Aorist (and Future) forms.

ἔρχομαι	ἐλευσομαι	ἦλθον Inf. ἐλθειν	I come (I go).
ἐσθιω (94)	φαγομαι	ἐφαγον	I eat. [anthropophagous: man-eating].
εὑρισκω	εὑρησω	εὑρον	I find. (The Aorist is εὑρον, the Imperfect is ηὑρισκον. Cf. p. 53 n. 2)
ἐχω Imperf. εἰχον	ἐξω	ἐσχον	I have.
λαμβανω	λημψομαι	ἐλαβον	I take.
ὁραω (450)	ὀψομαι	εἰδον Inf. ἰδειν	I see. (With ὀψομαι, cf. ὀφθαλμος. For ὁραω, see further Lesson 40.)
πινω (73)	πιομαι	ἐπιον	I drink.
φερω	οἰσω	ἠνεγκον Inf. ἐνεγκειν	I carry.

Verbs whose Second Aorists should now be learnt

ἁμαρτανω (42)	ἠμαρτον	I sin (cf. ἁμαρτωλος, ἁμαρτια).
ἀποθνησκω	ἀπεθανον	I die.
βαλλω	ἐβαλον	I throw.
καταλειπω (23)	κατελιπον	I leave.
λεγω (925)	εἰπον Inf. εἰπειν	I say.
μανθανω (25)	ἐμαθον	I learn (cf. μαθητης).
πασχω (40)	ἐπαθον	I suffer [sympathy].
πιπτω (90)	ἐπεσον	I fall.
φευγω (29)	ἐφυγον	I flee [cf. fugitive].

ἰδε (29) ⎫ behold, lo.
ἰδου (200) ⎭

Though regarded as an interjection, rather than a verb, ἰδε is in fact the second person singular of the Imperative Active and ἰδου of the Imperative Middle of εἰδον. For Second Aorist Imperative Middle, see Lesson 27.

W.B.

We are now familiar with 70 per cent of the words of the New Testament.

LESSON 26

αἰρω (101)	ἀρω	ἠρα	I lift up, I take away.
σπειρω (52)	(σπερω)	ἐσπειρα	I sow. (The Future is not actually found in the New Testament.)
ἐγειρω	ἐγερω	ἠγειρα	I raise, rouse (cf. Ex. 17 B 12).

ἀποκτεινω (74)	ἀποκτενω	ἀπεκτεινα	I kill.
ἀποστελλω (131)	ἀποστελω	ἀπεστειλα	I send (with a commission, cf. ἀποστολος).
ἀγγελλω (1) ἀπαγγελλω (46)	ἀγγελω	ἠγγειλα }	I announce.
παραγγελλω (30)			I command (takes dative; see Lesson 20).
μενω	μενῶ	ἐμεινα	I remain.
κρινω	κρινῶ	ἐκρινα	I judge.
βαλλω	βαλω	ἐβαλον	I throw.
ἀποθνησκω	ἀποθανουμαι	ἀπεθανον	I die.
πιπτω	πεσουμαι	ἐπεσον	I fall.
λεγω	ἐρω (96)	εἰπον	I say. (Has a Future with a liquid stem.)
ὀφειλω (35)	—	—	I owe, ought. (Only found in Present and Imperfect.)
ὁτι (1285)	because; that; *recitative* (introducing a direct statement).		

To be carefully distinguished from:

ὁτε (102)	when.
ἑως	as a conjunction can mean 'while' as well as 'until'.

Verbs which take dative

We have now had ten verbs which usually take the dative:

ἀκολουθεω	I follow	παραγγελλω	I command
ἀποκρινομαι	I answer	πιστευω	I believe
διακονεω	I serve	προσερχομαι	I come to
ἐγγιζω	I draw near	προσκυνεω	I worship
ἐξεστιν	it is lawful	ὑπακουω	I obey

(One more: ἐπιτιμαω, 'I rebuke', 'warn' will be found in Vocab. 40.)

Verbs which take genitive

ἀρχω	I rule	ἁπτομαι	I touch
ἀκουω	I hear (usually takes genitive of the person heard).		

LESSON 27

δεχομαι	δεξομαι	ἐδεξαμην	I receive
γινομαι	γενησομαι	ἐγενομην	I become
(ἀπολλυμι) (90) (Lesson 44)		ἀπωλομην Inf. ἀπολεσθαι	I perish

LESSON 28

Nouns declined like ἀστηρ

ἀνηρ ἀνδρος ὁ (216)
dat. pl.:
ἀνδρασιν

man, husband. [polyandry: culture where women may have more than one husband] (ἀνηρ is man as opposed to woman, ἀνθρωπος man as opposed to beast.)

ἀστηρ ἀστερος ὁ (23)

star. [aster, asteroid, asterisk, astronomy, astronaut]

μαρτυς μαρτυρος ὁ (35)

witness (cf. μαρτυρεω; μαρτυρια and μαρτυριον refer to witness in the abstract, whereas a μαρτυς is a person).

σωτηρ σωτηρος ὁ (24)

saviour (cf. σωτηρια, σωζω).

χειρ χειρος ἡ (176)
dat. pl. χερσιν

hand. [chiropodist: strictly, one who treats defects of hands and feet. See πους below]

Nouns with stems ending in a guttural

γυνη γυναικος ἡ (209)
voc. sing. γυναι

woman, wife. [gynaecology, misogynist]

σάρξ σαρκος ἡ (147)

flesh. [sarcophagus: a coffin which 'eats' the flesh within; sarcasm is from σαρκαζω, 'I eat flesh', i.e. I speak bitterly]

Nouns with stems ending in a dental or in ν

Dentals

ἐλπις ἐλπιδος ἡ (53)

hope (cf. ἐλπιζω).

νυξ νυκτος ἡ (61)

night. [cf. nocturnal]

παις παιδος ὁ or ἡ (24)

boy, girl, child, servant (cf. παιδιον).

πους ποδος ὁ (93)

foot. [chiropodist; tripod: see τρεις, τρια, 'three', Vocab. 32]

χαρις χαριτος ἡ (155)
acc. sing. χαριν

grace. [Grace is bestowed on those in whom the giver finds joy, χαρα]

ν endings

αἰων αἰωνος ὁ (123)
εἰς τον αἰωνα
εἰς τους αἰωνας των αἰωνων
ἀμπελων ἀμπελωνος ὁ (23)
εἰκων εἰκονος ἡ (23)

age [aeon] (cf. αἰωνιος).
for ever.
for ever and ever.
vineyard.
image. [ikon; iconoclasm: breaking of images]

Ἕλλην Ἕλληνος ὁ (26) (a) Greek. [King of the Hellenes; Hellenistic Greek]
μήν μηνος ὁ (18) month. [Cf. menstrual]
Σιμων Σιμωνος ὁ (75) Simon.

Noun with -οντ- stem

ἀρχων -οντος ὁ (37) ruler (cf. ἀρχω of which ἀρχων is a Present Participle. See Vocab. 23 and Lesson 36).

Nouns like πατηρ πατρος

θυγατηρ ἡ (28) daughter.
μητηρ ἡ (84) mother. [metropolis, cf. maternal; but, note, this word is μητηρ, not ματηρ like the Latin]
πατηρ ὁ (415) father. [Cf. paternal, Patristics]
voc. πατερ

LESSON 29

Neuter nouns declined like σωμα σωματος το

There is a big group of words with nominative singular in -μα and genitive singular in -ματος:[1]

αἱμα (97) blood. [anaemic, without blood; leukaemia, white blood; haemorrhage]
βαπτισμα (20) baptism.
θελημα (62) will (cf. θελω).
κριμα (27) judgement (cf. κρινω, κριτης).
ὀνομα (228) name. [An onomatopoeic word is one which is 'named' after, i.e. it imitates, the natural sound denoted (e.g. moo, phizz)]
πνευμα (379) spirit. [pneumatic]
ῥημα (68) word. [rhetoric]
σπερμα (44) seed [sperm] (cf. σπειρω).
στομα (78) mouth. [Stomach was used of the mouth of the digestive organ, and then of the organ itself]

[1] The declension of nouns with nominative singular ending in -α may be determined by the following rules. Those in which the -α is preceded by

a vowel or ρ	are declined like ἡμερα -ας ἡ
μ	„ „ „ σωμα -ατος το
any other consonant „	„ „ δοξα -ης ἡ

σῶμα (142)   body. [psycho-somatic treatment deals with mind and
               body together]

There are a few third declension neuter nouns with consonant stems of
which both nominative and genitive singular have to be separately learnt.
But in all of them the case endings from the genitive singular onwards
are exactly the same as those of σῶμα:

οὖς ὠτός[1] (36)   ear. [otitis: inflammation of the ear]
πῦρ πυρός (71)   fire. [pyre; pyrotechnics: fireworks]
τέρας τέρατος (16) a wonder.
ὕδωρ ὕδατος (76)   water. [hydrant, hydro-electric]
φῶς φωτός (73)   light. [phosphorus: a light-bearing substance; photo-
                   graph]

Neuter nouns declined like γενος γενους το

γένος (20)   race, kind. [cf. genus] A large number of words are
               derived from the root γεν which means 'beget',
               'become'; e.g. γινομαι, γενησομαι; γενεα. Those of
               one race or kind have a common begetting. See
               also γενναω Vocab. 40.
ἔθνος (162)   nation; pl. τα ἔθνη: the Gentiles. [ethnology]
ἔλεος (27)   mercy, compassion (cf. ἐλεεω).
ἔτος (49)   year. [There are Etesian winds in the Mediterranean
               which blow from the North-west annually]
μέλος (34)   member.
μέρος (42)   part. [In botany -merous is a suffix indicating the
               number of parts. Pentamerous: having five parts.]
ὄρος (62)   mountain. [orology: study of mountains]
πλῆθος (31)   multitude. [plethora]
σκεῦος (23)   vessel (a utensil, not a ship).
σκότος (30)   darkness. [scotoscope: instrument for seeing in the
               dark]
τέλος (41)   end. [teleology: view that developments are due to the
               ends which they serve]

Indeclinable nouns

πασχα το (29)   Passover. [Paschal]
'Αβρααμ ὁ (73) Abraham.

[1] The full declension is: οὖς ὠτος ὠτι ὠτα ὠτων ὠσιν.

LESSON 30
Like πλειων

κρεισσων (19)	better.	Where English uses 'than' after a compara-
μειζων (48)	greater.	tive, Greek normally uses a genitive: the
πλειων (55)	more.	Genitive of Comparison, e.g. μειζων τουτων
χειρων (11)	worse.	ἀλλη ἐντολη οὐκ ἐστιν (Mark 12. 31) 'There is no other commandment greater than these'.

Like ἀληθης

ἀληθης (26)	true (cf. ἀληθεια).
ἀσθενης (25)	weak, ill, sick (cf. ἀσθενεω).
πληρης (16)	full (cf. πληθος).

Pronouns

τίς τί (552)	who? (masculine and feminine); what? (neuter). τί also means 'why?'
τις τι (518)	someone, anyone, a certain one, something, etc. (τις is never the first word of a sentence.)
ὁστις ἡτις ὁτι (154)	who, whoever.

LESSON 31

ἰχθυς -υος ὁ (20)   fish. [ichthyology] The fish was a favourite Christian symbol, representing the acrostic:

᾽Ιησους	Jesus
Χριστος	Christ
Θεου	God's
Ὑιος	Son
Σωτηρ	Saviour

Feminine nouns like πολις πολεως ἡ

ἀναστασις (42)	resurrection (ἀνα, 'up'; ἱστημι, 'I cause to stand', Vocab. 43).
ἀποκαλυψις (18)	revelation [Apocalypse] (cf. ἀποκαλυπτω).
ἀφεσις (17)	forgiveness.
γνωσις (29)	knowledge (cf. γινωσκω).
δυναμις (118)	power [dynamic, dynamite] (cf. δυναμαι, δυνατος).

θλιψις (45)   tribulation, trouble, hardship.
κρισις (47)   judgement [crisis] (cf. κρινω, κριτης, κριμα¹).
παραδοσις (13)   tradition.
πιστις (243)   faith (cf. πιστευω, πιστος, ἀπιστος).
πολις (161)   city. [necropolis; politics, originally concerned with the
                        government of the Greek city-state]
συνειδησις (30)   conscience.

                    Masculine nouns like βασιλευς βασιλεως ὁ

βασιλευς (115)   king. *BASIL*
  voc. βασιλευ
γραμματευς (62)   scribe (cf. γραφω).
ἱερευς (31)   priest (cf. ἱερον).
ἀρχιερευς (122)   high-priest, chief priest (cf. ἀρχω).

We can now collect the Third Declension forms which have merited
special mention:

Vocative singular

                    πατερ   γυναι   βασιλευ

Accusative singular

                    χαριν
Dative plural
                    ἀνδρασιν   χερσιν

IMPORTANT NOTE

**From this point a lexicon will be needed to look up the less
common words in the Greek-to-English exercises.** The vocabularies
will continue to give all the common words, and only these will be used
in the English-to-Greek exercises. It is not intended that the less common
words should be systematically memorised, but if they stick in the memory
so much the better. The recitation of the Greek alphabet should be revised at this point.

When translating from Greek, difficulty may sometimes be found in
identifying a verb, because verbs are given in a lexicon under the first
person singular Present Indicative. If a verb begins with ἐ, it probably
means that there is an augment to subtract. If it begins with a long vowel,

---

¹ Often -σις is an action ending and -μα a result ending. κρισις would then
be the *act of judging* and κριμα the *judicial verdict*. But this distinction is not
always maintained.

it probably means that an initial vowel has been lengthened. In this case the table in Lesson 13 can be put into reverse, thus:

$$\eta \leftarrow a \text{ or } \epsilon \qquad \eta \leftarrow a\iota \text{ or } \epsilon\iota \qquad \eta\upsilon \leftarrow a\upsilon \text{ or } \epsilon\upsilon$$
$$\omega \leftarrow o \qquad \qquad \omega \leftarrow o\iota$$

Therefore a word beginning (for example) with η may have to be looked for under a or ε.

For guidance in the choice of a lexicon, see p. 191.

Greater use will now be made of sentences direct from the New Testament. The student will be able to observe for himself various idioms and turns of phrase which are not of sufficient difficulty or importance to require comment, yet which will increase his knowledge of the forms of the living language. It will also be found that from now on rather greater freedom will be needed in translating Greek words. The vocabularies give the most generally useful translations, but often there is a better, idiomatic English rendering, which will usually be clear enough from the context. The 'Key' will of course help to check your translations.

LESSON 32

πας πασα παν (1226)   every, all. [Pan-African]

ἁπας ἁπασα ἁπαν (32)   all (a slightly more literary word, found chiefly in Luke and Acts).

Note. There is a good deal of overlap in the meanings of ὁλος, πας and ἁπας. ὁλος (Vocab. 14) is often translated 'all'; πας and ἁπας are occasionally translated 'whole'. πας and ἁπας are often used without an article. When used with the article they are usually put in the predicative position.

We have now had five adjectives which *normally stand in the predicative position*:

ἐκεινος
ουτος
ὁλος
πας
ἁπας

πολυς πολλη πολυ (353)   much; pl. many. [polytheism]

μεγας μεγαλη μεγα (194)   great. [megaphone, megalomania. Omega is long (great) 'o'.]

Numerals

εἱς μια ἑν (337)   one. [henotheism: belief in one tribal God without denying the existence of other gods]

οὑδεις (226)   no one (with Indicative);

μηδεις (85)   no one (with other moods).

δυο (136)   two. (Cf. δευτερος, dual. Apart from the dative plural,
dat. δυσιν   δυο is indeclinable.)
τρεις τρια (67)   three (cf. τριτος, tripod).

The complete declension of τρεις is as follows:

	M.F.	N.
N.A.	τρεις	τρια
G.	τριων	
D.	τρισι(ν)	

τεσσαρες -α (41)   four. [Tatian's Diatessaron was a second-century
harmony of the gospels. Lit. 'through four']

The numbers 5 to 100 are indeclinable:

πεντε (38)   five. [Pentateuch, pentagon, pentameter, pentathlon,
pentamerous]
ἑξ (13)   six. [hexagon, hexameter. Origen's six-column Old
Testament was called the Hexapla]
ἑπτα (87)   seven. [heptagon; heptane is C_7H_{16}]
δεκα (25)   ten. [decathlon; Decapolis: region with 10 cities S.E. of
Sea of Galilee; Decalogue]
δωδεκα (75)   twelve. [Dodecanese: group of 12 Aegean islands]
τεσσαρακοντα (22) forty.
ἑκατον (17)   hundred.
χιλιοι -αι -α (11) or ⎱ thousand. [Chiliasm: belief in a reign of Christ on
χιλιας -αδος ἡ (23) ⎰ earth of literally 1000 years]

From ἑκατον and χιλιοι we get the military terms:

ἑκατονταρχης -ου ὁ (20)   centurion. Roughly, sergeant-major.
χιλιαρχος -ου ὁ (21)   military tribune, commander of a cohort, chiliarch.
(A.V. usually 'chief captain'.) Roughly, colonel.

LESSON 33

Superlative adjective

μικρος   small, little.
ἐλαχιστος (14)   smallest, least.

Comparative and superlative adverbs of degree

μαλλον (80)   more, rather.
μαλιστα (12)   most, most of all, specially.

Adverbs of manner

ἀληθῶς (18)	truly.
καλῶς (37)	well.
ὁμοίως (31)	in like manner, similarly.
οὕτως (208)	in this manner, thus, so.
ἀμήν (126)	truly, Amen.
εὖ (6)	well. (Many compounds: εὐαγγελιον, εὐλογεω, εὐχαριστεω.)
ναι (34)	yes.

Interjection

οὐαι (45)	alas, woe.

Comparative and disjunctive particle

ἤ (342)	than (comparative); or (disjunctive).

We are now familiar with more than 80 per cent of the words of the New Testament.

LESSON 34

A verb Perfect Active in form but Present in meaning:

οἶδα (321) I know. (The Old English *wot* comes from the same root. οἶδα originally contained a digamma, which is equivalent to *w*. Cf. Ϝοινος, wine; Ϝεργον, work.)

Pluperfect	ἤδειν	I knew
Infinitive	εἰδεναι	to know

(For future reference)

Participle εἰδως εἰδυια εἰδος
εἰδοτα
Subjunctive εἰδω

The use of the Perfect in Greek for *I know* is logical—it represents a present state resulting from acquisition of knowledge in the past.
In the New Testament there is no sharp distinction in meaning between γινωσκω and οἶδα. The full range of uses can be seen in the lexicon.

Two verbs conjugated like δυναμαι:

κᾰθημαι (91)   I sit.

κειμαι (24)   I lie. (The compounds of κειμαι are often used for
                  reclining at meals, so that the A.V. translates 'I sit at
                  meat'. But in fact it is καθημαι that means 'I sit' and
                  κειμαι 'I lie'. Reclining may be thought of as lying
                  down on to one's elbow, κατα-κειμαι (12), or as
                  propping oneself *up* on one's elbow, ἀνα-κειμαι (14).
                  συν-ανα-κειμαι (7) is 'I sit at table with'.)

Learn the principal parts (pp. 227 8) of the following verbs:

λυω and φιλεω; κηρυσσω to -θνησκω

The Aorist Passives should be learnt along with the other parts. Their
forms are dealt with in the next lesson.

LESSON 35

στρεφω (21)   ⎫ I turn. The Aorist Passive is deponent: I
2nd Aor. Pass. ἐστραφην ⎬ turned. [Cf. catastrophe. Καταστροφη is
ἐπιστρεφω (36)   ⎭ an overturning; lit. a turning down]

ὑποστρεφω (35)   I return.
φαινω (31)   I shine. Passive, I appear. [phantom]
2nd Aor. Pass. ἐφανην

Learn the principal parts (p. 228): καλεω to φερω.

LESSON 36

Note again the participle of οἰδα referred to in Vocab. 34:

εἰδως εἰδυια εἰδος
εἰδοτα

LESSON 37

ὁσος -η -ον (110) as much as; pl., as many as.

τοιουτος (56)   of such a kind, such. (The last two syllables are declined
-αυτη -ουτο   like οὑτος, except that any initial τ in the declension
                   of οὑτος is omitted.)

ποιος -α -ον (32) of what sort? what?

223

Adverbs of Place

ὧδε (61)   here.
ἐκεῖ (95)   there.
ὅπου (82)   where, whither.
ἐγγύς (31)   near (cf. ἐγγίζω).

Adverbs of Time

νῦν (148), νυνί (18)   now, at the present time.
ἤδη (60)   now, already, by this time.
ἄρτι (36)   now, just now.
τότε (159)   then.
πάντοτε (41)   always (cf. πᾶς πᾶσα πᾶν).
πάλιν (139)   again. [palimpsest: a manuscript which has been used
                      again]
ἔτι (92)   yet, still.
    οὐκέτι (48) ⎫
    μηκέτι (21) ⎭   no longer ⎰ with Indicative;
                                ⎱ with other moods.
εὐθύς (54)   ⎫   at once. (As an adjective, εὐθύς means 'straight', cf.
εὐθέως (33) ⎭   'straightway'.)
σήμερον (41)   today.

Interrogative adverbs

πῶς (104)   how?
ποῦ (47)   where?

LESSON 38

ἵνα (673)   ⎫
ὅπως (53)   ⎭   in order that, etc.
ἄν (166)   A particle which usually adds an element of indefinite-
                    ness to a clause.
ὅταν (ὅτε + ἄν) (123) whenever, when.

Note again the subjunctive of οἶδα referred to in Vocab. 34: εἰδῶ, εἰδῇς, etc.

LESSON 39

εἰ (513)   if.
ἐάν (εἰ + ἄν) (343) if (but less definite than εἰ). Sometimes ἐάν is equivalent
                    to ἄν. See Lesson 38, p. 161 n. 1.)
εἴτε (εἰ + τε) (65) εἴτε...εἴτε: 'whether...or'.

LESSON 40
-αω verbs

ἀγαπαω (141)	I love (cf. ἀγαπη, ἀγαπητος).
γενναω (97)	I beget, bear. Passive, am born (cf. γινομαι). [Hydrogen (with oxygen) begets water, ὑδωρ]
ἐρωταω (62) ἐπερωταω (56)	I ask, question. (αἰτεω is not used of asking questions.)
ὁραω	I see (met already in Vocab. 25).
πλαναω (39)	I cause to wander, lead astray. [A 'planet' is a wandering star]
τιμαω (21)	I honour (cf. τιμη).
ἐπιτιμαω (29)	I rebuke, warn.[1] (Takes dative. With those listed at the end of Vocab. 26, this completes eleven verbs which take the dative.)
καυχαομαι (37)	I boast (deponent Middle).
ζαω (140)	I live.

-οω verbs

δικαιοω (39)	I justify (cf. δικαιος).
πληροω (86)	I fill, fulfil (cf. πληρης, πληθος).
σταυροω (46)	I crucify (cf. σταυρος).
φανεροω (49)	I make clear, make known (cf. φαινω, ἐφανην).

LESSON 41

τιθημι (101)	I place.
ἐπιτιθημι (40)	I place upon.

LESSON 42

διδωμι (416)	I give.
ἀποδιδωμι (47)	I give back, pay; Middle, sell.
παραδιδωμι (120)	I hand over, betray (cf. παραδοσις).

LESSON 43

ἱστημι (152)	Trans., I cause to stand. Intrans., I stand.
ἀνιστημι (107)	Trans., I raise up. Intrans., I rise (cf. ἀναστασις).
ἐφιστημι (21)	Intrans., I stand by, come up.

[1] Note the sharp difference in meaning between τιμαω and ἐπιτιμαω. τιμη can be used of a price paid as a penalty. ἐπιτιμαω is used with regard to someone judged worthy of a penalty.

καθιστημι (21) Trans., I appoint.

παριστημι (41) Trans., I cause to stand beside, present. Intrans., I stand by.

Note that with words like ἐφιστημι, καθιστημι and ἀφιημι (below), it is the rough breathing which gives the aspirated forms ἐφ-, καθ- and ἀφ-. (Cf. Vocab. 16.) When the preposition is prefixed to a form with a smooth breathing, e.g. -ἐστη, we get forms like ἐπεστη. When it is prefixed to a form with no initial vowel, e.g. -στασα, we get ἐπιστασα, ἀναστασα (cf. Luke 2. 9, 38; 1. 39).

LESSON 44

ἀφιημι (142)   I forgive, leave, allow (cf. ἀφεσις).
συνιημι (26)   I understand.
δεικνυμι (32) I show.
φημι (66)   I say.
ἀπ-ολλυμι   I destroy, lose; Middle and Perfect Active, perish (cf. Vocab. 27).

The principal parts of ἀφιημι and ἀπολλυμι, which are given on p. 228, should be learnt. Those parts of ἀπολλυμι which mean 'destroy' or 'lose' and those parts which mean 'perish' have been set out on separate lines. It is probably best to learn the ἀπολλυμι and ἀπολλυμαι lines separately.

PRINCIPAL PARTS

Except for those in brackets, the parts given below are those which actually occur in the New Testament. In the case of the bracketed words, it seems easier to learn the word than the blank. A hyphen before a word indicates that it is only found in a compound form of the verb.

Present   Future   Aorist A.   Perfect A.   Perfect P.   Aorist P.

The following are the principal parts of the standard regular verbs:

λυω	λυσω	ἐλυσα	λελυκα	λελυμαι	ἐλυθην	loose
φιλεω	φιλησω	ἐφιλησα	πεφιληκα	πεφιλημαι	ἐφιληθην	love
τιμαω	τιμησω	ἐτιμησα	τετιμηκα	τετιμημαι	ἐτιμηθην	honour
φανεροω	φανερωσω	ἐφανερωσα	πεφανερωκα	πεφανερωμαι	ἐφανερωθην	make clear

Apart from the 'aspirated Perfect' (χ instead of κ) the following are also quite regular:

| κηρυσσω | κηρυξω | ἐκηρυξα | (κεκηρυχα) | -κεκηρυγμαι | ἐκηρυχθην | proclaim |
| πρασσω | πραξω | ἐπραξα | πεπραχα | πεπραγμαι | (ἐπραχθην) | do |

The following have various irregularities:

ἀγγελλω	-ἀγγελω	-ἠγγειλα	-ἠγγελκα	-ἠγγελμαι	-ἠγγελην	announce
ἀγω	ἀξω	ἠγαγον[1]	—	-ἠγμαι	ἠχθην	lead
αἰρω	ἀρω	ἠρα	ἠρκα	ἠρμαι	ἠρθην	lift up
ἀκουω	ἀκουσω	ἠκουσα	ἀκηκοα	—	ἠκουσθην	hear
ἀνοιγω	ἀνοιξω	ἠνοιξα	ἀνεωγα	ἀνεωγμαι	ἠνοιχθην	open[2]
-βαινω	-βησομαι	-ἐβην	-βεβηκα	—	—	go
βαλλω	βαλω	ἐβαλον	βεβληκα	βεβλημαι	ἐβληθην	throw
γινομαι	γενησομαι	ἐγενομην	γεγονα[3]	γεγενημαι	ἐγενηθην	become
γινωσκω	γνωσομαι	ἐγνων	ἐγνωκα	ἐγνωσμαι	ἐγνωσθην	know
γραφω	γραψω	ἐγραψα	γεγραφα	γεγραμμαι	ἐγραφην	write
δεχομαι	δεξομαι	ἐδεξαμην	—	δεδεγμαι	-ἐδεχθην	receive
ἐγειρω	ἐγερω	ἠγειρα	—	ἐγηγερμαι	ἠγερθην	raise

[1] The First Aorist form -ἠξα is found in 2 Pet. 2. 5.
[2] A number of other forms are found: Aorist Active, ἠνεῳξα, ἀνεῳξα; Perfect Passive, ἠνεῳγμαι, ἠνοιγμαι; Aorist Passive, ἀνεῳχθην, ἠνεῳχθην, ἠνοιγην. These are easily recognised when the six forms above are known.
[3] Note this Second Perfect Active form. The other forms, Middle and Passive, are deponent. Therefore all the forms are Active in meaning; both Aorists mean 'I became' and both Perfects 'I have become'.

εὑρισκω	εὑρησω	εὑρον	εὑρηκα	—	εὑρεθην	find
θελω	θελησω	ἠθελησα	—	—	—	will
-θνησκω	-θανουμαι	-ἐθανον	τεθνηκα	—	—	die[1]
καλεω	καλεσω	ἐκαλεσα	κεκληκα	κεκλημαι	ἐκληθην	call
κραζω	κραξω	ἐκραξα	κεκραγα	—	—	cry out
κρινω	κρινῶ	ἐκρινα	κεκρικα	κεκριμαι	ἐκριθην	judge
λαμβανω	λημψομαι	ἐλαβον	εἰληφα	-εἰλημμαι	ἐλημφθην	take
πειθω	πεισω	ἐπεισα	πεποιθα[2]	πεπεισμαι	ἐπεισθην	persuade
πινω	πιομαι	ἐπιον	πεπωκα	—	-ἐποθην	drink
πιπτω	πεσουμαι	ἐπεσον	πεπτωκα	—	—	fall
σπειρω	(σπερω)	ἐσπειρα	—	ἐσπαρμαι	ἐσπαρην	sow
-στελλω	-στελω	-ἐστειλα	-ἐσταλκα	-ἐσταλμαι	-ἐσταλην	send[3]
σωζω	σωσω	ἐσωσα	σεσωκα	σεσωσμαι	ἐσωθην	save

The following have stems derived from more than one verb:

ἐρχομαι	ἐλευσομαι	ἠλθον	ἐληλυθα	—	—	come
ἐσθιω	φαγομαι	ἐφαγον	—	—	—	eat
ἐχω	ἑξω	ἐσχον	ἐσχηκα	—	—	have
λεγω	ἐρω	εἰπον	εἰρηκα	εἰρημαι	ἐρρηθην ἐρρεθην	say[4]
ὁραω	ὀψομαι	εἰδον	ἑωρακα ἑορακα	—	ὠφθην	see
φερω	οἰσω	ἠνεγκον	-ἐνηνοχα	—	ἠνεχθην	carry

-μι verbs

τιθημι	θησω	ἐθηκα	τεθεικα	τεθειμαι	ἐτεθην	place
διδωμι	δωσω	ἐδωκα	δεδωκα	δεδομαι	ἐδοθην	give
-ἰστημι	στησω	ἐστησα				cause to stand
		ἐστην	ἐστηκα	—	ἐσταθην	stand
ἀφιημι	ἀφησω	ἀφηκα		ἀφεωνται	ἀφεθην	forgive
ἀπολλυμι	ἀπολεσω ἀπολω	ἀπωλεσα	—	—	—	destroy
ἀπολλυμαι	ἀπολουμαι	ἀπωλομην	ἀπολωλα	—	—	perish

---

[1] θνησκω is used in Perf. and Pluperf., ἀποθνησκω in all other tenses. Cf. Mk. 15. 44.

[2] πεποιθα has a present sense, and it means 'I trust', not 'I have persuaded'. It takes dative.

[3] -στελλω is never found as a simple verb. But there are various other compounds in addition to ἀποστελλω.

[4] The forms -λεξω -ἐλεξα -λελεγμαι -ἐλεχθην are also found, but only in compounds.

SUMMARY OF GRAMMAR: MORPHOLOGY

NOUNS

First Declension

	Feminine				Masculine	
N.	ἀρχη	ἡμερα	δοξα	προφητης	νεανιας	Σατανας
V.	ἀρχη	ἡμερα	δοξα	προφητα	νεανια	Σατανα
A.	ἀρχην	ἡμεραν	δοξαν	προφητην	νεανιαν	Σαταναν
G.	ἀρχης	ἡμερας	δοξης	προφητου	νεανιου	Σατανα
D.	ἀρχῃ	ἡμερᾳ	δοξῃ	προφητῃ	νεανιᾳ	Σατανᾳ
N.V.	ἀρχαι	ἡμεραι	δοξαι	προφηται	νεανιαι	
A.	ἀρχας	ἡμερας	δοξας	προφητας	νεανιας	
G.	ἀρχων	ἡμερων	δοξων	προφητων	νεανιων	
D.	ἀρχαις	ἡμεραις	δοξαις	προφηταις	νεανιαις	

Second Declension

N.	λογος	λογοι	ἐργον	ἐργα	Ἰησους
V.	λογε	λογοι	ἐργον	ἐργα	Ἰησου
A.	λογον	λογους	ἐργον	ἐργα	Ἰησουν
G.	λογου	λογων	ἐργου	ἐργων	Ἰησου
D.	λογῳ	λογοις	ἐργῳ	ἐργοις	Ἰησου

Third Declension

N.	ἀστηρ	πατηρ	σωμα	γενος	ἰχθυς	πολις	βασιλευς
A.	ἀστερα	πατερα	σωμα	γενος	ἰχθυν	πολιν	βασιλεα
G.	ἀστερος	πατρος	σωματος	γενους	ἰχθυος	πολεως	βασιλεως
D.	ἀστερι	πατρι	σωματι	γενει	ἰχθυϊ	πολει	βασιλει
N.	ἀστερες	πατερες	σωματα	γενη	ἰχθυες	πολεις	βασιλεις
A.	ἀστερας	πατερας	σωματα	γενη	ἰχθυας	πολεις	βασιλεις
G.	ἀστερων	πατερων	σωματων	γενων	ἰχθυων	πολεων	βασιλεων
D.	ἀστερσιν	πατρασιν	σωμασιν	γενεσιν	ἰχθυσιν	πολεσιν	βασιλευσιν

Rules for formation of dative plural with consonant stems:

$$\kappa \ \gamma \ \chi \ + \sigma\iota\nu \rightarrow \xi\iota\nu \qquad \alpha\nu\tau + \sigma\iota\nu \rightarrow \alpha\sigma\iota\nu$$
$$\pi \ \beta \ \phi \ + \sigma\iota\nu \rightarrow \psi\iota\nu \qquad \epsilon\nu\tau + \sigma\iota\nu \rightarrow \epsilon\iota\sigma\iota\nu$$
$$\tau \ \delta \ \theta \ \nu + \sigma\iota\nu \rightarrow \sigma\iota\nu \qquad \quad o\nu\tau + \sigma\iota\nu \rightarrow o\upsilon\sigma\iota\nu$$

Note vocative singular: πατερ, γυναι, βασιλευ; accusative singular: χαριν; dative plural: ἀνδρασιν, χερσιν.

ADJECTIVES, ARTICLE, PRONOUNS

Adjectives of First and Second Declension

Consonant stem (not ρ)			Vowel or ρ stem			Definite Article		
N.	ἀγαθος	η	ον	ἁγιος	α	ον			
V.	ἀγαθε	η	ον	ἁγιε	α	ον	N. ὁ	ἡ	το
A.	ἀγαθον	ην	ον	ἁγιον	αν	ον	A. τον	την	το
G.	ἀγαθου	ης	ου	ἁγιου	ας	ου	G. του	της	του
D.	ἀγαθῳ	ῃ	ῳ	ἁγιῳ	ᾳ	ῳ	D. τῳ	τῃ	τῳ
N.V.	ἀγαθοι	αι	α	ἁγιοι	αι	α	N. οἱ	αἱ	τα
A.	ἀγαθους	ας	α	ἁγιους	ας	α	A. τους	τας	τα
G.	ἀγαθων	ων	ων	ἁγιων	ων	ων	G. των	των	των
D.	ἀγαθοις	αις	οις	ἁγιοις	αις	οις	D. τοις	ταις	τοις

Demonstratives

	'that'				'this'		
N.	ἐκεινος	η	ο	οὑτος	αὑτη	τουτο	
A.	ἐκεινον	ην	ο	τουτον	ταυτην	τουτο	
G.	ἐκεινου	ης	ου	τουτου	ταυτης	τουτου	
D.	ἐκεινῳ	ῃ	ῳ	τουτῳ	ταυτῃ	τουτῳ	
N.	ἐκεινοι	αι	α	οὑτοι	αὑται	ταυτα	
A.	ἐκεινους	ας	α	τουτους	ταυτας	ταυτα	
G.	ἐκεινων	ων	ων	τουτων	τουτων	τουτων	
D.	ἐκεινοις	αις	οις	τουτοις	ταυταις	τουτοις	

Like ἐκεινος: αὐτος, ἀλλος, ὁς (Relative)

	Reflexive 'himself', 'herself', 'itself'			Reciprocal 'one another'
A.	ἑαυτον	ην	ο	
G.	ἑαυτου	ης	ου	
D.	ἑαυτῳ	ῃ	ῳ	
A.	ἑαυτους	ας	α	ἀλληλους
G.	ἑαυτων	ων	ων	ἀλληλων
D.	ἑαυτοις	αις	οις	ἀλληλοις

Similarly: ἐμαυτον ην 'myself'
σεαυτον ην 'yourself'

Personal pronouns

	Singular		Plural	
N.	ἐγω	συ	ἡμεις	ὑμεις
A.	(ἐ)με	σε	ἡμας	ὑμας
G.	(ἐ)μου	σου	ἡμων	ὑμων
D.	(ἐ)μοι	σοι	ἡμιν	ὑμιν

Adjectives of First and Third Declension

N.	εἷς	μια	ἑν
A.	ἑνα	μιαν	ἑν
G.	ἑνος	μιας	ἑνος
D.	ἑνι	μιᾳ	ἑνι
cf.	οὐδ|εις	οὐδε|μια	οὐδ|εν
	μηδ|εις	μηδε|μια	μηδ|εν

N.	πολυς	πολλη	πολυ	μεγας	μεγαλη	μεγα
A.	πολυν	πολλην	πολυ	μεγαν	μεγαλην	μεγα
G.	πολλου	πολλης	πολλου	μεγαλου	μεγαλης	μεγαλου
D.	πολλῳ	πολλῃ	πολλῳ	μεγαλῳ	μεγαλῃ	μεγαλῳ
N.	πολλοι	πολλαι	πολλα	μεγαλοι	μεγαλαι	μεγαλα
A.	πολλους	πολλας	πολλα	μεγαλους	μεγαλας	μεγαλα
G.	πολλων	πολλων	πολλων	μεγαλων	μεγαλων	μεγαλων
D.	πολλοις	πολλαις	πολλοις	μεγαλοις	μεγαλαις	μεγαλοις

Adjectives and Pronouns of Third Declension

N.	πλειων	πλειον	τις	τι	ἀληθης	ἀληθες
A.	πλειονα	πλειον	τινα		ἀληθη	ἀληθες
G.	πλειονος	πλειονος			ἀληθους	ἀληθους
D.	πλειονι	πλειονι			ἀληθει	ἀληθει
N.	πλειονες	πλειονα			ἀληθεις	ἀληθη
A.	πλειονας	πλειονα			ἀληθεις	ἀληθη
G.	πλειονων	πλειονων			ἀληθων	ἀληθων
D.	πλειοσιν	πλειοσιν			ἀληθεσιν	ἀληθεσιν

COMPARISON OF ADJECTIVES AND ADVERBS

Regular comparison:

δικαιος	δικαιοτερος	δικαιοτατος
σοφος	σοφωτερος	σοφωτατος
δικαιως	δικαιοτερον	δικαιοτατα

Irregular comparison:

ἀγαθος	κρεισσων	—
κακος	χειρων	—
μεγας	μειζων	—
πολυς	πλειων	—
μικρος	μικροτερος	ἐλαχιστος
εὐ	κρεισσον	—
—	μαλλον	μαλιστα

231

Principal parts	λυω				λυσω		ἐλυσα	
		Present	Imperfect					
Present	Imperfect	Middle &	Middle &	Future	Future		Aorist	Aorist
Active	Active	Passive	Passive	Active	Middle		Active	Middle

Indicative

λυω	ἐλυον	λυομαι	ἐλυομην	λυσω	λυσομαι		ἐλυσα	ἐλυσαμην
λυεις	ἐλυες	λυῃ	ἐλυου	λυσεις	λυσῃ		ἐλυσας	ἐλυσω
λυει	ἐλυεν	λυεται	ἐλυετο	λυσει	λυσεται		ἐλυσεν	ἐλυσατο
λυομεν	ἐλυομεν	λυομεθα	ἐλυομεθα	λυσομεν	λυσομεθα		ἐλυσαμεν	ἐλυσαμεθα
λυετε	ἐλυετε	λυεσθε	ἐλυεσθε	λυσετε	λυσεσθε		ἐλυσατε	ἐλυσασθε
λυουσιν	ἐλυον	λυονται	ἐλυοντο	λυσουσιν	λυσονται		ἐλυσαν	ἐλυσαντο

Subjunctive

λυω		λυωμαι					λυσω	λυσωμαι
λυῃς		λυῃ					λυσῃς	λυσῃ
λυῃ		λυηται					λυσῃ	λυσηται
λυωμεν		λυωμεθα					λυσωμεν	λυσωμεθα
λυητε		λυησθε					λυσητε	λυσησθε
λυωσιν		λυωνται					λυσωσιν	λυσωνται

Imperative

λυε		λυου					λυσον	λυσαι
λυετω		λυεσθω					λυσατω	λυσασθω
λυετε		λυεσθε					λυσατε	λυσασθε
λυετωσαν		λυεσθωσαν					λυσατωσαν	λυσασθωσ

Infinitive

λυειν		λυεσθαι					λυσαι	λυσασθαι

Participle

λυων ουσα ον		λυομενος η ον					λυσας ασα αν	λυσαμενος
λυοντα							λυσαντα	η ον

λελυκα		λελυμαι		ἐλυθην	
Perfect Active	Pluperfect Active	Perfect Middle & Passive	Pluperfect Middle & Passive	Aorist Passive	Future Passive
λελυκα	(ἐ)λελυκειν	λελυμαι	(ἐ)λελυμην	ἐλυθην	λυθησομαι
λελυκας	(ἐ)λελυκεις	λελυσαι	(ἐ)λελυσο	ἐλυθης	λυθηση
λελυκεν	(ἐ)λελυκει	λελυται	(ἐ)λελυτο	ἐλυθη	λυθησεται
λελυκαμεν	(ἐ)λελυκειμεν	λελυμεθα	(ἐ)λελυμcθα	ἐλυθημεν	λυθησομεθα
λελυκατε	(ἐ)λελυκειτε	λελυσθε	(ἐ)λελυσθε	ἐλυθητε	λυθησεσθε
λελυκασιν	(ἐ)λελυκεισαν	λελυνται	(ἐ)λελυντο	ἐλυθησαν	λυθησονται

λυθω
λυθης
λυθη
λυθωμεν
λυθητε
λυθωσιν

λυθητι
λυθητω
λυθητε
λυθητωσαν

λελυκεναι   λελυσθαι   λυθηναι

λελυκως υια ος   λελυμενος η ον   λυθεις εισα εν
λελυκοτα   λυθεντα

Like λελυμαι: δυναμαι, κειμαι, καθημαι.

VOWEL AND CONSONANT CHANGES IN THE VERB

Initial vowel changes in formation of Past Tenses

$a \to \eta$	$a\iota \to \eta$	$a\upsilon \to \eta\upsilon$
$\epsilon \to \eta$	$\epsilon\iota \to \eta$	$\epsilon\upsilon \to \eta\upsilon$ (or $\epsilon\upsilon$)
$o \to \omega$	$o\iota \to \omega̧$	
	$\iota \to \bar{\iota}$	

With compound verbs, prepositions (except $\pi\epsilon\rho\iota$ and $\pi\rho o$) drop final vowel.

Formation of Perfect stem

(1) Initial consonant is repeated $+\epsilon$, e.g. $\lambda\epsilon\lambda\upsilon$-.
(2) $\chi \, \phi \, \theta \to \kappa\epsilon\chi, \, \pi\epsilon\phi, \, \tau\epsilon\theta$.
(3) $\sigma, \, \zeta$ or ξ merely add ϵ.
(4) Initial vowel is lengthened.

Addition of σ to Mutes	*Addition of θ to Mutes*
$\kappa \, \gamma \, \chi + \sigma \to \xi$	$\kappa \, \gamma \, \chi + \theta \to \chi\theta$
$\pi \, \beta \, \phi + \sigma \to \psi$	$\pi \, \beta \, \phi + \theta \to \phi\theta$
$\tau \, \delta \, \theta + \sigma \to \sigma$	$\tau \, \delta \, \theta + \theta \to \sigma\theta$

VERB: TABLE OF SECOND TENSES

	Indicative	Imperative	Subjunctive	Infinitive	Participle
Aorist	ἔβαλον		βαλω		
Active	ἔβαλες	βαλε	βαλης		
	ἔβαλεν	βαλετω	βαλη	βαλειν	βαλων
	ἐβαλομεν		βαλωμεν		
	ἐβαλετε	βαλετε	βαλητε		
	ἔβαλον	βαλετωσαν	βαλωσιν		
Middle	ἐγενομην		γενωμαι		
	ἐγενου	γενου	γενῃ		
	ἐγενετο	γενεσθω	γενηται	γενεσθαι	γενομενος
	ἐγενομεθα		γενωμεθα		
	ἐγενεσθε	γενεσθε	γενησθε		
	ἐγενοντο	γενεσθωσαν	γενωνται		
Passive	ἐγραφην		γραφω		
	ἐγραφης	σπαρηθι	γραφῃς		
	ἐγραφη	σπαρητω	γραφῃ	γραφηναι	γραφεις
	ἐγραφημεν		γραφωμεν		
	ἐγραφητε	σπαρητε	γραφητε		
	ἐγραφησαν	σπαρητωσαν	γραφωσιν		
Future	γραφησομαι				
Passive	γραφησῃ				
	γραφησεται				
	γραφησομεθα				
	γραφησεσθε				
	γραφησονται				
Perfect	γεγραφα				
Active	γεγραφας				
	γεγραφεν				γεγραφεναι γεγραφως
	γεγραφαμεν				
	γεγραφατε				
	γεγραφασιν				

Aorist Active of γινωσκω: ἐγνων ως ω ωμεν ωτε ωσαν

-βαινω: -εβην ης η ημεν ητε ησαν

Forms not listed in Principal Parts:

Second Aorist Active: ἡμαρτον, κατελιπον, ἐμαθον, ἐφυγον, ἐπαθον.

Second Aorist Passive: ἐκρυβην, ἐστραφην, ἐφανην.

Second Aorist Middle: Third singular optative, γενοιτο.

-εω VERBS

Rules of Contraction: $\epsilon + \epsilon \rightarrow \epsilon\iota$

$\epsilon + o \rightarrow ov$

$(\epsilon) +$ long vowel or diphthong.

Present system of φιλεω

Present Active		Imperfect Active	
Indicative			
φιλεω →	φιλω	ἐφιλεον →	ἐφιλουν
φιλεεις	φιλεις	ἐφιλεες	ἐφιλεις
φιλεει	φιλει	ἐφιλεε	ἐφιλει
φιλεομεν	φιλουμεν	ἐφιλεομεν	ἐφιλουμεν
φιλεετε	φιλειτε	ἐφιλεετε	ἐφιλειτε
φιλεουσιν	φιλουσιν	ἐφιλεον	ἐφιλουν
Subjunctive			
φιλεω	φιλω		
φιλεῃς	φιλῃς		
φιλεῃ	φιλῃ		
φιλεωμεν	φιλωμεν		
φιλεητε	φιλητε		
φιλεωσιν	φιλωσιν		
Imperative			
φιλεε	φιλει		
φιλεετω	φιλειτω		
φιλεετε	φιλειτε		
φιλεετωσαν	φιλειτωσαν		
Infinitive			
φιλεειν	φιλειν		
Participle			
φιλεων ουσα ον	φιλων ουσα ουν		

Present Middle and Passive		Imperfect Middle and Passive	
Indicative			
φιλεομαι →	φιλουμαι	ἐφιλεομην →	ἐφιλουμην
φιλεῃ	φιλῃ	ἐφιλεου	ἐφιλου
φιλεεται	φιλειται	ἐφιλεετο	ἐφιλειτο
φιλεομεθα	φιλουμεθα	ἐφιλεομεθα	ἐφιλουμεθα
φιλεεσθε	φιλεισθε	ἐφιλεεσθε	ἐφιλεισθε
φιλεονται	φιλουνται	ἐφιλεοντο	ἐφιλουντο

Subjunctive

φιλεωμαι	φιλωμαι
φιλεῃ	φιλῃ
φιλεηται	φιληται
φιλεωμεθα	φιλωμεθα
φιλεησθε	φιλησθε
φιλεωνται	φιλωνται

Imperative

φιλεου	φιλου
φιλεεσθω	φιλεισθω
φιλεεσθε	φιλεισθε
φιλεεσθωσαν	φιλεισθωσαν

Infinitive

φιλεεσθαι	φιλεισθαι

Participle

φιλεομενος	φιλουμενος

LIQUID VERBS: STEMS ENDING IN λ μ ν OR ρ

Liquid Futures (e.g. ἀρω) are formed with -ε(σ)- and the endings are as for the present of φιλεω.

-αω VERBS

Rules of contraction: α + O-sound (o, ω or ου) → ω
α + E-sound (ε or η) → α
α + any combination containing ι (whether subscript or not) → ᾳ (except present infinitive
active)

Present system of τιμαω

	Present Active		Imperfect Active
Indicative			
τιμαω →	τιμω	ἐτιμαον →	ἐτιμων
τιμαεις	τιμᾷς	ἐτιμαες	ἐτιμας
τιμαει	τιμᾷ	ἐτιμαε	ἐτιμα
τιμαομεν	τιμωμεν	ἐτιμαομεν	ἐτιμωμεν
τιμαετε	τιματε	ἐτιμαετε	ἐτιματε
τιμαουσιν	τιμωσιν	ἐτιμαον	ἐτιμων

Subjunctive

τιμαω	τιμω
τιμαῃς	τιμᾷς
τιμαῃ	τιμᾷ
τιμαωμεν	τιμωμεν
τιμαητε	τιματε
τιμαωσιν	τιμωσιν

Imperative

τιμαε	τιμα
τιμαετω	τιματω
τιμαετε	τιματε
τιμαετωσαν	τιματωσαν

Infinitive

τιμαειν	τιμ<u>αν</u>

Participle

τιμαων ουσα ον	τιμων ωσα ων

Present Middle and Passive		Imperfect Middle and Passive	

Indicative

τιμαομαι	→	τιμωμαι	ἐτιμαομην	→	ἐτιμωμην
τιμαῃ		τιμᾳ	ἐτιμαου		ἐτιμω
τιμαεται		τιμαται	ἐτιμαετο		ἐτιματο
τιμαομεθα		τιμωμεθα	ἐτιμαομεθα		ἐτιμωμεθα
τιμαεσθε		τιμασθε	ἐτιμαεσθε		ἐτιμασθε
τιμαονται		τιμωνται	ἐτιμαοντο		ἐτιμωντο

Subjunctive

τιμαωμαι	τιμωμαι
τιμαῃ	τιμᾳ
τιμαηται	τιμαται
τιμαωμεθα	τιμωμεθα
τιμαησθε	τιμασθε
τιμαωνται	τιμωνται

Imperative

τιμαου	τιμω
τιμαεσθω	τιμασθω
τιμαεσθε	τιμασθε
τιμαεσθωσαν	τιμασθωσαν

Infinitive

τιμαεσθαι	τιμασθαι

Participle

τιμαομενος	τιμωμενος

ζαω (properly ζηω)

ζαω, I live: Present Indicative   ζω ζῃς ζῃ ζωμεν ζητε ζωσιν
Present Infinitive   ζην

239

-οω VERBS

Rules of contraction: ο + long vowel   → ω
ο + short vowel or ου   → ου
ο + combination containing ι → οι
(except present infinitive active)

Present system of φανεροω

Present Active		Imperfect Active	
Indicative			
φανεροω →	φανερω	ἐφανεροον →	ἐφανερουν
φανεροεις	φανεροις	ἐφανεροες	ἐφανερους
φανεροει	φανεροι	ἐφανεροε	ἐφανερου
φανεροομεν	φανερουμεν	ἐφανεροομεν	ἐφανερουμεν
φανεροετε	φανερουτε	ἐφανεροετε	ἐφανερουτε
φανεροουσιν	φανερουσιν	ἐφανεροον	ἐφανερουν

Subjunctive

φανεροω	φανερω
φανεροῃς	φανεροις
φανεροῃ	φανεροι
φανεροωμεν	φανερωμεν
φανεροητε	φανερωτε
φανεροωσιν	φανερωσιν

Imperative

φανεροε	φανερου
φανεροετω	φανερουτω
φανεροετε	φανερουτε
φανεροετωσαν	φανερουτωσαν

Infinitive

φανεροειν	φανερου̲ν̲

Participle

φανεροων	φανερων
ουσα ον	ουσα ουν

Present Middle and Passive   Imperfect Middle and Passive

Indicative

φανερουμαι →	φανερουμαι	ἐφανεροομην	ἐφανερουμην
φανεροῃ	φανεροι	ἐφανεροου	ἐφανερου
φανεροεται	φανερουται	ἐφανεροετο	ἐφανερουτο
φανεροομεθα	φανερουμεθα	ἐφανεροομεθα	ἐφανερουμεθα
φανεροεσθε	φανερουσθε	ἐφανεροεσθε	ἐφανερουσθε
φανεροονται	φανερουνται	ἐφανεροοντο	ἐφανερουντο

Subjunctive

φανεροωμαι	φανερωμαι
φανεροῃ	φανεροι
φανεροηται	φανερωται
φανεροωμεθα	φανερωμεθα
φανεροησθε	φανερωσθε
φανεροωνται	φανερωνται

Imperative

φανεροου	φανερου
φανεροεσθω	φανερουσθω
φανεροεσθε	φανερουσθε
φανεροεσθωσαν	φανερουσθωσαν

Infinitive

φανεροεσθαι	φανερουσθαι

Participle

φανεροομενος	φανερουμενος

-μι VERBS

Principal parts:	τιθημι	θησω	ἔθηκα	τεθεικα	τεθειμαι	ἐτεθην
	διδωμι	δωσω	ἔδωκα	δεδωκα	δεδομαι	ἐδοθην
(Transitive)	ἱστημι	στησω	ἔστησα			
(Intransitive)			ἔστην	ἔστηκα		ἐσταθην

Stems	Verbal	Present	Perfect
	θε	τιθε	τεθε
	δο	διδο	δεδο
	στα	ἱστα	ἑστα

Active

Indicative	Imperative	Subjunctive	Infinitive	Participle

Present

Indicative	Imperative	Subjunctive	Infinitive	Participle
τιθη-μι		τιθω	τιθε-ναι	τιθεις εισα εν
s	τιθει	ῃς		εντα
σιν	τιθε-τω	ῃ		
τιθε-μεν		ωμεν		
τε	τε	ητε		
ασιν	τωσαν	ωσιν		

Second Aorist

Indicative	Imperative	Subjunctive	Infinitive	Participle
		θω	θειναι	θεις εισα εν
	θες	ῃς		εντα
—	θε-τω	ῃ		
		ωμεν		
	τε	ητε		
	τωσαν	ωσιν		

Present

Indicative	Imperative	Subjunctive	Infinitive	Participle
διδω-μι		διδω	διδο-ναι	διδους ουσα ον
s	διδου	ῳς		οντα
σιν	διδο-τω	ῳ		
διδο-μεν		ωμεν		
τε	τε	ωτε		
ασιν	τωσαν	ωσιν		

Second Aorist

Indicative	Imperative	Subjunctive	Infinitive	Participle
		δω	δουναι	δους ουσα ον
	δος	ῳς		οντα
—	δο-τω	ῳ		
		ωμεν		
	τε	ωτε		
	τωσαν	ωσιν		

Present

ἱστη-μι		ἱστω	ἱστα-ναι	ἱστας ασα αν
s		ῃς		αντα
σιν	—	ῃ		
ἱστα-μεν		ωμεν		
τε		ητε		
ἱστα-σιν		ωσιν		

Second Aorist

ἐστην		στω	στηναι	στας ασα αν
ης		ῃς		αντα
η	—	ῃ		
ημεν		ωμεν		
ητε		ητε		
ησαν		ωσιν		

Middle and Passive

Present Middle and Passive

Present forms consist of: Present stem + perfect passive endings of λυω.

Indicative		Infinitive		Participle	
τιθε ⎫		τιθε ⎫		τιθε ⎫	
διδο ⎬ μαι		διδο ⎬ σθαι		διδο ⎬ μενος	
ἱστα ⎭		ἱστα ⎭		ἱστα ⎭	

Second Aorist Middle

Only Indicative need be learnt:

augment + verbal stem + Pluperfect endings of λυω, with contraction in second singular:

ἐ-θε-μην	ἐ-δο-μην
ἐ-θου ← ε(σ)ο	ἐ-δου ← ο(σ)ο
ἐ-θε-το	ἐ-δο-το
ἐ-θε-μεθα	ἐ-δο-μεθα
ἐ-θε-σθε	ἐ-δο-σθε
ἐ-θε-ντο	ἐ-δο-ντο

Additional notes on ἱστημι

(1) The Perfect tense is Present in meaning and the Pluperfect (εἱστηκειν) is Imperfect in meaning.

(2) There are two forms of the *Perfect Participle Active:*

First Perfect:	ἐστηκως	υια	ος
		οτα	
Second Perfect:	ἐστως	ωσα	ος
		ωτα	

243

εἰμί

Indicative

Present	Future	Imperfect	Sub-junctive	Infini-tive	Participle	Opta-tive
εἰμί	ἔσομαι	ἤμην	ὦ	εἶναι	ὢν οὖσα ὄν	
εἶ	ἔσῃ	ἦς or ἦσθα	ἦς		ὄντα	
ἐστιν	ἔσται	ἦν	ᾖ			εἴη
ἐσμεν	ἐσόμεθα	ἦμεν or ἤμεθα	ὦμεν			
ἐστε	ἔσεσθε	ἦτε	ἦτε			
εἰσιν	ἔσονται	ἦσαν	ὦσιν			

Imperative is usually expressed by the Present Imperative of γίνομαι. For other -μι forms see Lesson 44.

SUMMARY OF GRAMMAR: SYNTAX

The numbers in parentheses refer to the lesson in which the subject is treated.

I. WORDS NEVER USED FIRST IN A SENTENCE
γαρ, οὖν, μεν, δε; τε, τις (indefinite) and other enclitics (p. 121 n. 1).

2. NUMBER
Verbs agree with subject (5), except

(a) neuter plural nouns take singular verb (7);

(b) collective nouns may use a construction according to sense (p. 127 n. 1).

3. CASES
Nominative: Subject of verb (5), other than infinitive (20).
Vocative: case of address, with or without ὦ (5).
Accusative: case of extension.
1. Direct object (5).
2. Motion to (10). So with προς, εἰς, παρα ('to beside' or 'alongside').
3. Time How Long (16).
4. 'Subject' of infinitive (20), properly an example of:
5. Adverbial accusative, acc. of general reference or acc. of respect. μονον, πρωτον (Vocab. 11); comparative and superlative adverbs (p. 131 n. 2).
6. For various uses with δια, μετα, ὑπερ, ὑπο, κατα, περι, ἐπι (16, esp. Vocab.).

Genitive

1. Case of genus or kind of thing; possessive (6).
2. Kind of time: Time During Which (16).
3. *Ablative:* case of separation; motion from (10). So with ἐκ, ἀπο, παρα ('from beside').
4. Genitive of comparison (Vocab. 30, Lesson 33).
5. Genitive absolute (37).
6. After προ, ἐνωπιον, ἐμπροσθεν, ὀπισω, ἐξω, χωρις, ἀχρι, ἑως.
7. For various uses with δια, μετα, ὑπερ, ὑπο. κατα, περι, ἐπι (16, esp. Vocab.)
8. After ἀκουω, ἁπτομαι, ἀρχω.

Dative

1. Case of personal interest: indirect object (6).
2. *Locative:* place in space (10). So with ἐν, παρα ('rest beside').
3. Point in time: Time At Which (16).
4. *Instrumental* (10, 17).
   Note. Instrument: dative.
   Agent: ὑπο + genitive.
5. After συν.
6. After ἀκολουθεω, ἀποκρινομαι, διακονεω, ἐγγιζω, ἐξεστιν, παραγγελλω, πιστευω, προσερχομαι, προσκυνεω, ὑπακουω, ἐπιτιμαω, πεποιθα (p. 228 n. 2).

Summary of time uses (16)

Time how long: accusative.
Time during which: genitive.
Time at which: dative.

4. PREPOSITIONS

1. See Lesson 16, esp. Vocab.
2. Compound verbs; perfective use (13); prepositions after compound verbs (Vocab. 23).

5. ARTICLE

1. Usual with Θεος, Ἰησους, words indicating a whole class, e.g. ἀνθρωπος; often with abstract nouns and proper names (6).
2. Complement usually without article and placed before verb (6).
3. Making an adjective equivalent to a noun (11).
4. With δε making a personal pronoun; with μεν...δε..., 'some... others...' (19).

5. Articular infinitive (20).
6. τοῦ with infinitive for purpose (20).
7. Articular participle (36).
8. To make a prepositional phrase equivalent to an adjective (p. 71 n. 1).

6. ATTRIBUTIVE AND PREDICATIVE USE OF ADJECTIVES

1. Attributive: ὁ ἀγαθος προφητης or ὁ προφητης ὁ ἀγαθος
   Predicative: ὁ προφητης ἀγαθος or ἀγαθος ὁ προφητης (12)
2. Normally in predicative position: ἐκεινος, οὑτος, ὁλος, πας, ἁπας.

7. USES OF αὐτος (15)

1. Third personal pronoun.
2. Predicative: emphasising pronoun.
3. Attributive: identical adjective.

8. TENSE

1. Linear: Present, Imperfect (3, 13, 18).
2. Punctiliar: Aorist (24). Epistolary Aorist (38 n.)
3. Completed action: Perfect, Pluperfect.
   Comparative table of uses of Perfect, Past Simple and Aorist (34).
4. Conditions contrary to fact: Past—Aorist;
   Present—Imperfect (39).

Tenses of ἱστημι (43)

1. Perfect: Present in meaning.
   Pluperfect: Imperfect in meaning.
2. Transitive: ἱστημι, στησω, ἐστησα.
   Intransitive: ἐστην, ἐστηκα, ἐσταθην.

9. SUBJUNCTIVE (38, 39)

1. Indefinite clauses: 'whoever', 'wherever', 'whenever', 'until'.
2. Purpose: ἱνα or ὁπως.
3. Noun clauses: ἱνα.
4. Hortatory.
5. Deliberative.
6. Emphatic negative future.
7. Command not to begin.
8. Future condition.

10. OPTATIVE (39)

1. To express a wish.
2. Dependent (indirect) question.

11. INFINITIVE (20)

1. A neuter verbal noun.
2. As a noun can be subject or object of a sentence.
3. Its 'subject' is accusative.
4. Consequence: ὥστε.
5. Articular infinitive:

> ἐν—time at which.
> προ—'before'.
> μετα (with accusative)—'after'.
> δια (with accusative)—'because'.
> εἰς, προς—purpose.

6. Infinitive alone or with του for purpose.

12. PARTICIPLE (36, 37)

1. Adjectival: articular, usually translated by relative clause.
2. Adverbial: temporal, causal, concessive clauses.
3. Present: usually action at same time as action of main verb.
4. Aorist: usually action before action of main verb.
5. Aorist can be used for Attendant Circumstances.
6. Genitive absolute; noun in genitive not usually subject, object or indirect object of main verb.
7. Periphrastic tenses:

Imperfect:	Imperfect of εἰμι + Present Participle.
Future:	Future of εἰμι + Present Participle.
Perfect:	Present of εἰμι + Perfect Participle.
Pluperfect:	Imperfect of εἰμι + Perfect Participle.

13. COMMANDS, PROHIBITIONS

1. Commands.

Present Imperative: continue to do an action or do it repeatedly (18).
Aorist Imperative: simple command without regard to continuity or repetition (24).

2. Prohibitions (39).

μη + Present Imperative: do not continue an action.
μη + Aorist Subjunctive: do not begin an action.
οὐ + Future (Hebrew idiom): 'you shall not'.

SUMMARY OF GRAMMAR

14. QUESTIONS (18)

1. Expecting answer 'Yes': οὐ, οὐχί.
2. Expecting answer 'No', or hesitant question: μη, μητι.

15. NEGATIVES

1. οὐ: Indicative.

   μη: Imperative, Infinitive, Participle, Subjunctive, Optative.
2. Two negatives do not cancel out (32).

16. USES OF ὅτι (26)

1. 'Because'.
2. Recitative.
3. Introducing dependent statements.

   Note. The tense used by the original speaker is retained.

17. PURPOSE CLAUSES

1. Infinitive alone (20).
2. τον + infinitive (20).
3. εἰς or προς with articular infinitive (20).
4. ἱνα or ὁπως with Subjunctive (38).

18. CONSEQUENCE CLAUSES (20)

ὡστε with accusative and infinitive.

19. CAUSAL CLAUSES

1. ὅτι (26).
2. δια το + infinitive (20).
3. Participle (36).

20. TIME CLAUSES

1. Infinitive (20).

   ἐν τῳ—'while', 'when'.
   προ του—'before'.
   μετα το—'after'.

SYNTAX

2. Participle (36).
3. Conjunctions:
   (a) 'When' (definite): ὅτε + Indicative.
   (b) 'When' (indefinite), 'whenever': ὅταν + Subjunctive (38).
   (c) 'Until' (definite: usually past): ἕως + Indicative (38).
   (d) 'Until' (indefinite: usually future): ἕως (ἄν, οὗ, ὅτου) + Subjunctive (38).

21. RELATIVE CLAUSES

1. ὅς (definite): Indicative (18).
2. ὅς ἄν (indefinite): Subjunctive (38).

22. CONDITIONAL CLAUSES (39)

Conditions of fact

	Protasis
Past:	εἰ + Indicative.
Present:	εἰ + Indicative.
Future:	ἐάν + Subjunctive.

Conditions contrary to fact

εἰ + Indicative; add ἄν in apodosis.

Past:	Aorist.
Present:	Imperfect.

Also participle (p. 152).

ENGLISH–GREEK VOCABULARY

The numeral after the Greek word refers to the vocabulary in which it is treated. Fuller references to the forms and uses of some words will be found in the Greek Index.

able, am, δυναμαι 20
abound, περισσευω 13
about (prep.), περι 16
about, am, μελλω 20
above, ὑπερ 16
Abraham, Ἀβρααμ 29
according to, κατα 16
afraid, am, φοβεομαι 23
after, see Vocab. 16
again, παλιν 37
against, κατα 16
age, αἰων 28
alas, οὐαι 33
all, πας, ἁπας 32
allow, ἀφιημι 44
alone, μονος 11
alongside, παρα 16
already, ἠδη 37
also, και 5
always, παντοτε 37
am, εἰμι p. 244: ὑπαρχω, γινομαι 23
Amen, ἀμην 33
and, και 5; δε 10; τε 18
Andrew, Ἀνδρεας 10
angel, ἀγγελος 5
anger, ὀργη 8
announce, ἀγγελλω, ἀπαγγελλω 26
another, ἑτερος 12; ἀλλος 15
(one) another, ἀλληλους 15
answer, ἀποκρινομαι 23
anyone, anything, τις, τι 30
apart from, χωρις 16
apostle, ἀποστολος 5
appear, φαινω (passive) 35

appoint, καθιστημι 43
approximately, περι 16
around, περι 16
as, ὡς, καθως 19
as far as, ἀχρι, ἑως 16
as much (many) as, ὁσος 37
ask, ask for, αἰτεω 4
ask (esp. a question), ἐρωταω, ἐπερωταω 40
assembly, ἐκκλησια 9
astray, lead, πλαναω 40
at once, εὐθυς, εὐθεως 37
authority, ἐξουσια 9
away from, ἀπο 10

bad, κακος 11
baptise, βαπτιζω 22
baptism, βαπτισμα 29
baptist, βαπτιστης 10
bear (children), γενναω 40
bear witness, μαρτυρεω 4
beautiful, καλος 11
because (conj.), ὁτι 26
because of (prep.), δια 16
become, γινομαι 23
before, see Vocab. 16
beget, γενναω 40
begin, ἀρχομαι 23
beginning, ἀρχη 8
(on) behalf of, ὑπερ 16
behold, ἰδε, ἰδου 25
believe, πιστευω 13
believing πιστος 11
belong to ὑπαρχω 23

beloved ἀγαπητος 11
beseech, παρακαλεω 14
beside (prep.), παρα 16
beside, am, παραγινομαι 23
betray, παραδιδωμι 42
better κρεισσων 30
bind δεω 14
blaspheme, βλασφημεω 4
bless, εὐλογεω 4
blessed, μακαριος 12
blind, τυφλος 11
blood, αἱμα 8
boast, καυχαομαι 40
boat, πλοιον 7
body, σωμα 29
book, βιβλιον 7
born, am, γενναομαι 40
boy, παις 28
bread, ἀρτος 6
bring, ἀγω, προσφερω 13
bring together, συναγω 13
brother, ἀδελφος 5
build, οἰκοδομεω 14
but, ἀλλα, δε 10
buy, ἀγοραζω 22
by, see Vocab. 16

call, καλεω 4; φωνεω 14
can, δυναμαι 20
carry, φερω 13; βασταζω 22
centurion ἑκατονταρχης 32
(a) certain man, τις 30
chief priest, ἀρχιερευς 31
child, παιδιον, τεκνον 7; παις 28
Christ, Χριστος 5
church, ἐκκλησια 9
city, πολις 31
clean, καθαρος 12
cleanse, καθαριζω 22
clear, make, φανεροω 40
clothe, ἐνδυω 13
clothes, ἱματια 7

cloud, νεφελη 8
colonel, χιλιαρχος 32
come, ἐρχομαι, πορευομαι, παραγινομαι 23
come into, εἰσερχομαι 23
come to, προσερχομαι 23
come to pass, γινομαι 23
come together, συνερχομαι 23
come up, ἐφιστημι (intrans.) 43
coming, παρουσια 9
command, παραγγελλω 26
commandment, ἐντολη 8
compassion, ἐλεος 29
concerning, περι 16
congregation, ἐκκλησια 9
conscience, συνειδησις 31
council, συνεδριον 7
covenant, διαθηκη 8
cross, σταυρος 6
crowd, ὀχλος 6
crucify, σταυροω 40
cry out, κραζω 22
cup, ποτηριον 7

daily, καθ' ἡμεραν 16
darkness, σκοτος 29
daughter, θυγατηρ 28
day, ἡμερα 9
deacon, διακονος 5
dead, νεκρος 12
death, θανατος 5
demon, δαιμονιον 7
deny, ἀρνεομαι 23
depart, ὑπαγω 13
desert, ἐρημος 6
destroy, ἀπολλυμι 44
devil, διαβολος 6
die, ἀποθνησκω 13
different, ἑτερος 12
disciple, μαθητης 10
do, ποιεω 4; πρασσω 22
door, θυρα 9

down, κατα p. 66 n. 1
draw near, ἐγγιζω 22
drink, πινω 25
dwell, κατοικεω 14

each, ἑκαστος 11
ear, οὐς 29
earth, γη 8
eat, ἐσθιω 3
elder, πρεσβυτερος 5
Elijah, Ἡλειας 10
encourage, παρακαλεω 14
end, τελος 29
enemy, ἐχθρος 5
eternal, αἰωνιος 11
even, και 5
even as, καθως, ὡσπερ 19
ever, for, εἰς τον αἰωνα 28
everlasting, αἰωνιος 11
every, ἑκαστος 11; πας 32
evil, πονηρος 12
exhort, παρακαλεω 14
exist, ὑπαρχω 23
eye, ὀφθαλμος 5

face, προσωπον 7
faith, πιστις 31
faithful, πιστος 11
faithless, ἀπιστος 11
fall, πιπτω 25
father, πατηρ 28
fear (n.), φοβος 5
fear (vb.), φοβεομαι 23
few, ὀλιγοι 11
field, ἀγρος 5
fill, πληροω 40
find, εὑρισκω 3
fire, πυρ 29
first, πρωτος 11
fish, ἰχθυς 31
fitting season, καιρος 6
five, πεντε 32

flee, φευγω 25
flesh, σαρξ 28
follow, ἀκολουθεω 14
foot, πους 28
for (conj.), γαρ 10
for (prep.), see Vocab. 16
forgive, ἀφιημι 44
forgiveness, ἀφεσις 31
forty, τεσσαρακοντα 32
four, τεσσαρες 32
free, ἐλευθερος 12
friend, φιλος 5
from, see Vocab. 16
fruit, καρπος 6
fulfil, πληροω 40
full, πληρης 30

Galilee, Γαλιλαια 9
garment, ἱματιον 7
gather together, συναγω 13
generation, γενεα 9
Gentiles, ἐθνη 29
girl, παις 28
give, διδωμι 42
give back, ἀποδιδωμι 42
glorify, δοξαζω 22
glory, δοξα 9
go, ἐρχομαι, πορευομαι 23; ἀγω 13
go away, ἀπερχομαι 23
go down, καταβαινω 25
go into, εἰσερχομαι 23
go out, ἐξερχομαι, ἐκπορευομαι 23
go through, διερχομαι 23
go up, ἀναβαινω 25
God, Θεος 6
good, ἀγαθος, καλος 11
good news, bring, εὐαγγελιζομαι 23
gospel, εὐαγγελιον 7
gospel, preach the, εὐαγγελιζομαι 23
grace, χαρις 28
great, μεγας 32
greater, μειζων 30

Greek, a, Ἑλλην 28
greet, ἀσπαζομαι 23
guard (n.), φυλακη 8
guard (vb.), φυλασσω 22

hand, χειρ 28
hand over, παραδιδωμι 42
happy, μακαριος 12
hardship, θλιψις 31
hate, μισεω 4
have, ἐχω 3
he, she, it, αὐτος η ο 15
head, κεφαλη 8
heal, θεραπευω 3 ; ἰαομαι p. 170 n. 1
hear, ἀκουω 13
heart, καρδια 9
heaven, οὐρανος 6
here, ὡδε 37
hide, κρυπτω 22
high-priest, ἀρχιερευς 31
himself, etc., αὐτος, ἑαυτον 15
hold, take hold of, κρατεω 14;
    ἁπτομαι 23
holy, ἁγιος 12
honour (n.), τιμη 8
honour (vb.), τιμαω 40
hope (n.), ἐλπις 28
hope (vb.), ἐλπιζω 22
hour, ὡρα 9
house, οἰκος 6; οἰκια 9
how?, πως 37
hundred, ἑκατον 32
husband, ἀνηρ 28
hypocrite, ὑποκριτης 10

I, ἐγω 19
if, εἰ, ἐαν 39
ill, ἀσθενης 30
ill, am, ἀσθενεω 14
image, εἰκων 28
in, ἐν 10
inhabit, κατοικεω 14

injure, ἀδικεω 14
into, εἰς 10
Israel, Ἰσραηλ 5

James, Ἰακωβος 6
Jerusalem, Ἱεροσολυμα, Ἱερουσα-
    λημ 7
Jesus, Ἰησους 6
Jew, Ἰουδαιος 5
John, Ἰωανης 10
joy, χαρα 9
Judaea, Ἰουδαια 9
Judah, Judas, Ἰουδας 10
judge (n.), κριτης 10
judge (vb.), κρινω 3
judgement, κριμα 29; κρισις 31
just, δικαιος 12
just as, ὡσπερ 19
just now, ἀρτι 37
justify, δικαιοω 40

keep, τηρεω 4
kill, ἀποκτεινω 26
kind, γενος 29
king, βασιλευς 31
kingdom, βασιλεια 9
know, γινωσκω 25; οἰδα 34
knowledge, γνωσις 31
known, make, φανεροω 40

land, γη 8
last, ἐσχατος 11
law, νομος 5
lawful, it is, ἐξεστιν 20
lead, ἀγω 13
lead astray, πλαναω 40
lead away, ἀπαγω 13
learn, μανθανω 25
least, ἐλαχιστος 33
leave, καταλειπω 25; ἀφιημι 44
leper, λεπρος 5
letter, ἐπιστολη 8

lie, κειμαι 34
life, ζωη, ψυχη 8
lift up, αἰρω 26
light, φως 29
like, ὁμοιος 12
like manner, in, ὁμοιως 33
little, ὀλιγος 11; μικρος 33
live, ζαω 40
lo, ἰδε, ἰδου 25
loaf, ἀρτος 6
(no) longer, οὐκετι, μηκετι 37
look at, θεωρεω 4
loose, λυω 3
lord, Lord, κυριος, Κυριος 5
lose, ἀπολλυμι 44
love (n.), ἀγαπη 8
love (vb.), φιλεω 4; ἀγαπαω 40

make, ποιεω 4
man, ἀνθρωπος 5; ἀνηρ 28
(young) man, νεανιας 10
many, πολλοι 32
marry, γαμεω 14
member, μελος 29
mercy, ἐλεος 29
mercy on, have, ἐλεεω 14
messenger, ἀγγελος 5
middle, midst, μεσος 11
minister (vb.), διακονεω 14
money, ἀργυριον 7
month, μην 28
more (adj.), πλειων 30
more (adv.), μαλλον 33
most, μαλιστα 33
mother, μητηρ 28
mountain, ὀρος 29
mouth, στομα 29
much, πολυς 32
multitude, πληθος 29
must, see necessary
my, ἐμος, μου 19
myself, ἐμαυτον 19

mystery, μυστηριον 7

name, ὀνομα 29
nation, ἐθνος 29
near, draw, ἐγγιζω 22
necessary, it is, δει 20
need, χρεια 9
neither, see Vocab. 18
new, καινος 11; νεος 12
night, νυξ 28
no longer, οὐκετι, μηκετι 37
no one, οὐδεις, μηδεις 32
nor, see Vocab. 18
not, οὐ 10; μη 18
(and) not, see Vocab. 18
not even, see Vocab. 18
now, νυν, νυνι, ἀρτι, ἠδη 37

O, ὠ 5
obey, ὑπακουω 13
offer, προσφερω 13
old, παλαιος 12
on, see Vocab. 16
one, εἰς μια ἑν 32
one another, ἀλληλους 15
one's own, ἰδιος 12
only, μονος 11
open, ἀνοιγω 13
opportunity, καιρος 6
or, ἠ 33; εἰτε 39
(in) order that, ἰνα, ὁπως 38
other, ἑτερος 12; ἀλλος 15
ought, ὀφειλω 26
our, ἡμων p. 80
out of, ἐκ 10; ἐξω 16
outside, ἐξω 16
owe, ὀφειλω 26
own, ἰδιος 12

parable, παραβολη 8
paralytic (man), παραλυτικος 5
part, μερος 29
Passover, πασχα 29

Paul, Παυλος 9
pay (n.), μισθος 6
pay (vb.), αποδιδωμι 42
peace, ειρηνη 8
people, λαος 5
perceive, επιγινωσκω 13
perhaps, *see* Hesitant questions, Lesson 18
perish απολλυμαι 27, 44
persecute, διωκω 13
persuade, πειθω 13
Peter, Πετρος 9
Pharisee, Φαρισαιος 5
place (n.), τοπος 5
place (vb.), τιθημι 41
place upon, επιτιθημι 41
poor, πτωχος 11
possible, δυνατος 11
power, δυναμις 31
powerful, δυνατος 11
practice, πρασσω 22
pray, προσευχομαι 23
prayer, προσευχη 8
preach, κηρυσσω 22
preach the gospel, ευαγγελιζομαι 23
prepare, ετοιμαζω 22
presbyter, πρεσβυτερος 5
present, παριστημι 43
present time, at the, νυν 37
price, τιμη 8
priest, ιερευς 31
prison, φυλακη 8
privately, κατ᾽ ιδιαν 16
proclaim, κηρυσσω 22
promise, επαγγελια 9
prophesy, προφητευω 13
prophet, προφητης 10
pure, καθαρος 12
pursue, διωκω 13
put on, ενδυω 13

question, ερωταω, επερωταω 40

race, γενος 29
raise, raise up, εγειρω 3; ανιστημι 43
rather, μαλλον 33
read, αναγινωσκω 13
rebuke, επιτιμαω 40
receive, παραλαμβανω 13; δεχομαι 23
reckon, λογιζομαι 23
recognise, επιγινωσκω 13
rejoice, χαιρω 13
release, απολυω 13
remain, μενω 3
remaining, λοιπος 11
repent, μετανοεω 4
repentance, μετανοια 9
rest, the, λοιποι 11
result that, with the, ωστε 20
resurrection, αναστασις 31
return, υποστρεφω 35
reveal, αποκαλυπτω 22
revelation, αποκαλυψις 31
reward, μισθος 6
rich, πλουσιος 12
right (hand), δεξιος 12
righteous, δικαιος 12
righteousness, δικαιοσυνη 8
rise, ανιστημι (intrans.) 40
river, ποταμος 5
rock, πετρα 9
round, περι 16
rouse, εγειρω 26
rule, αρχω 23
ruler, αρχων 28

Sabbath, σαββατον 7
sacrifice, θυσια 9
saint, αγιος 12
salvation, σωτηρια 9
same, αυτος 15
sanctify, αγιαζω 22
Sanhedrin, συνεδριον 7

Satan, Σατανας 10

save, σωζω 3

saviour, σωτηρ 28

say, λεγω 3, 25; φημι 44

scribe, γραμματευς 31

Scripture, γραφη 8

sea, θαλασσα 9

season, fitting, καιρος 6

seat, καθιζω 22

second, δευτερος 12

see, βλεπω 3; θεωρεω 4; ὁραω 25, 40

seed, σπερμα 2ς

seek, ζητεω 14

seem, δοκεω 14

sell, ἀποδιδωμι 42

send, πεμπω 3; ἀποστελλω 26

send out, ἐκβαλλω 13

sergeant-major, ἑκατονταρχης 32

servant, διακονος 5; παις 28

serve, διακονεω 14

seven, ἑπτα 32

sheep, προβατον 7

shine, φαινω 35

show, δεικνυμι 44

shrine, ναος 6

sick, ἀσθενης 30

sign, σημειον 7

silver, ἀργυριον 7

similarly, ὁμοιως 33

Simon, Σιμων 28

sin (n.), ἁμαρτια 9

sin (vb.), ἁμαρτανω 25

sinner, ἁμαρτωλος 6

sit, καθιζω 22; καθημαι 34

sit at table, ἀνακειμαι, κατακειμαι 34

sit at table with, συνανακειμαι 34

six, ἑξ 32

slave, δουλος 6

small, μικρος 12, 33

smallest, ἐλαχιστος 33

so, οὑτως 33

so that, ὡστε 20

soldier, στρατιωτης 10

someone, something, τις, τι 30

son, υἱος 6

soul, ψυχη 8

sound, φωνη 8

sow, σπειρω 26

speak, λαλεω 4

specially, μαλιστα 33

spirit, πνευμα 29

stand, ἱστημι 43

stand beside, παριστημι 43

stand by, ἐφιστημι, παριστημι 43

star, ἀστηρ 28

steadfastness, ὑπομονη 8

still, ἐτι 37

stone, λιθος 5

strong, ἰσχυρος 12

stumble, cause to, σκανδαλιζω 22

stumbling-block, σκανδαλον 22

such, of such a kind, τοιουτος 37

suffer, πασχω 25

sufficient, ἱκανος 11

sun, ἡλιος 6

synagogue, συναγωγη 8

take, λαμβανω 3

take away, αἱρω 26

take hold of, κρατεω 14; ἁπτομαι 23

tax-collector, τελωνης 10

teach, διδασκω 13

teacher, διδασκαλος 5

teaching, διδαχη 8

temple, ναος 6; ἱερον 7

tempt, πειραζω 22

temptation, πειρασμος 6

ten, δεκα 32

test, πειραζω 22

than, ἠ 33

thank, give thanks, εὐχαριστεω 14

that (conj.), ὅτι 26
that (demon.), ἐκεινος 14
that (relat.), ὅς ἥ ὅ 18
the, ὁ ἡ το 8
then, οὖν, ἀρα 10; τοτε 37
there, ἐκει 37; preparatory 'there',
  Lesson 16
therefore, οὖν, ἀρα 10; διο 18
thing, p. 58
think, δοκεω 14
third, τριτος 11
this, οὑτος 14
(in) this manner, οὑτως 33
(by) this time, ἠδη 37
thousand, χιλιοι, χιλιας 32
three τρεις 32
throne, θρονος 5
through, δια 16
throw, βαλλω 3
throw out, ἐκβαλλω 13
thus, οὑτως 33
time, χρονος, καιρος 6
to, see Vocab. 16
today, σημερον 37
tomb, μνημειον 7
tongue, γλωσσα 9
touch, ἁπτομαι 23
towards, προς 10
tradition, παραδοσις 31
tree, δενδρον 7
tribulation, θλιψις 31
tribune, military, χιλιαρχος 32
trouble, θλιψις 31
true, ἀληθης 30
truly, ἀληθως, ἀμην 33
truth, ἀληθεια 9
turn, στρεφω, ἐπιστρεφω 35
twelve, δωδεκα 32
two, δυο 32

unbelieving, ἀπιστος 11
unclean, ἀκαθαρτος 11

under, ὑπο 16
understand, συνιημι 44
unrighteousness, ἀδικια 9
until, ἀχρι, ἑως 16, 26
upon, ἐπι 16

vessel, σκευος 29
village, κωμη 8
vineyard, ἀμπελων 28
virgin, παρθενος 6
voice, φωνη 8

wait upon, διακονεω 14
walk, περιπατεω 14
wander, cause to, πλαναω 40
warn, ἐπιτιμαω 40
water, ὑδωρ 29
way, ὁδος 6
we, ἡμεις 19
weak, ἀσθενης 30
weak, am, ἀσθενεω 14
weep, κλαιω 13
well, εὐ, καλως 33
what? of what sort? ποιος 37
when, whenever, ὁτε, ὁταν 26, 38
where, ὁπου 37
where? που 37
whether, εἰτε 39
while, ἑως 26
whither, ὁπου 37
who, which, whoever, ὁς 18; ὁστις
  30
who? what? τίς, τί 30
whole, ὁλος 14
why? τί 30
widow, χηρα 9
wife, γυνη 28
will (n.), θελημα 29
will, am willing, θελω 20; βουλομαι
  23
wind, ἀνεμος 6
wine, οἰνος 6

wisdom, σοφια 9
wise, σοφος 11
wish, θελω 20; βουλομαι 23
with, *see* Vocab. 16
witness, μαρτυρια, μαρτυριον 9; μαρτυς 28
(bear) witness, μαρτυρεω 4
woe, οὐαι 33
woman, γυνη 28; expressed without a noun, pp. 58, 92
wonder (n.), τερας 29
wonder at, θαυμαζω 22
word, λογος 5; ῥημα 29
work (n.), ἐργον 7
work (vb.), ἐργαζομαι 23
workman, ἐργατης 10

world, κοσμος 5
worse, χειρων 30
worship, προσκυνεω 14
worthy, ἀξιος 12
write, γραφω 3
writing, γραφη 8
wrong, do, ἀδικεω 14

year, ἐτος 29
yes, ναι 33
yet, ἐτι 37
you, συ, ὑμεις 19
young, νεος 12
young man, νεανιας 10
your, yours, σος 19; ὑμων p. 80
yourself, σεαυτον 19

GREEK INDEX OF WORDS GIVEN
IN THE VOCABULARIES

An index, rather than a general Greek–English Vocabulary, has been provided for two reasons. On the one hand, it encourages an effort of memory by making the meanings slightly less accessible. On the other, by directing the reader back to the vocabularies, it helps to impress *groups* of words on the mind.

This index covers all the words needed for the English–Greek exercises, but after Lesson 31 the student is expected to use a lexicon for the less common words in the Greek–English exercises.

The number after the Greek word refers to the Vocabulary in which it will be found. *p.* or *pp.* refers to the page or pages on which further information is to be found. When the **principal parts** of a verb are set out in full on pp. 227 f., the appropriate page reference is given in **heavy type**.

α- pp. 198, 201
'Αβρααμ 29
ἀγαθος 11, p. 131
ἀγαπαω 40
ἀγαπη 8
ἀγαπητος 11
ἀγγελλω 26, p. 227
ἀγγελος 5
ἁγιαζω 22
ἁγιος 12
ἀγοραζω 22
ἀγρος 5
ἀγω 13, p. 227
ἀδελφος 5
ἀδικεω 14
ἀδικια 9
αἱμα 29
αἱρω 26, p. 227
αἰτεω 4
αἰων 28
αἰωνιος 11
ἀκαθαρτος 11
ἀκολουθεω 14

ἀκουω 13, p. 227
ἀληθεια 9
ἀληθης 30
ἀληθως 33
ἀλλα 10
ἀλληλους 15, p. 62
ἀλλος 15, p. 62
ἁμαρτανω 25
ἁμαρτια 9
ἁμαρτωλος 6
ἀμην 33
ἀμπελων 28
ἀν 38
ἀναβαινω 25, p. 227
ἀναγινωσκω 13
ἀνακειμαι 34
ἀναστασις 31
'Ανδρεας 10
ἀνεμος 6
ἀνηρ 28
ἀνθρωπος 5
ἀνιστημι 43
ἀνοιγω 13, p. 227

ἀξιος 12
ἀπαγγελλω 26
ἀπαγω 13
ἁπας 32
ἀπεθανον 25
ἀπερχομαι 23
ἀπιστος 11
ἀπο 10
ἀποδιδωμι 42
ἀποθνησκω 13, p. 227
ἀποκαλυπτω 22
ἀποκαλυψις 31
ἀποκρινομαι 23,
  p. 111
ἀποκτεινω 26
ἀπολλυμι 27, 44,
  p. 228
ἀπολυω 13
ἀποστελλω 26, p. 228
ἀποστολος 5
ἁπτομαι 23
ἀπωλομην 27
ἀρα 10

GENERAL INDEX

In the case of the various forms and uses which have already been collected in the Summary, reference is made to the page number of the Summary only. This number is given in **heavy** type and the individual items are not repeated here.

Abbott-Smith, G. 191
Ablative 45, 207
Abstract nouns 4; with article 35
Accents viif., 23, 51, 72 n. 1, 105, 121
Accidence 8
Accusative 9, **244**
Acrostic 218
Action: linear, punctiliar, state of completion 54, 96ff., 139f.
Action ending in -σις 219 n. 1
Active voice 11
Adjective clauses 13f., 73; adjectival participle 151
Adjectives 2, 5, 47f., 50, **230f.**, **246**
Adverb clauses 13f., 151f.; adverbial participle 151f.
Adverb-prepositions 79 n. 1, 206
Adverbs 2, 7, 131f., 221f., 224
Adversative clauses 14, 152
Agent 69f.
Alexander the Great 17
Alphabet 17ff.
Anacolouthon 204
Antecedent 5, 72f.
Aorist 96ff., **232ff.**
Apodosis 166
Apostrophe 22, 199
Apposition 9, 13, 40 n. 1
Aramaic 156, 197
Arian controversy 202
Arndt–Gingrich–Bauer 191
Article 2, 30, 40, **245f.**
Asyndeton 200, 204
Attendant circumstances 153
Attic dialect 17
Attributive use of adjectives 6, 48
Augment 53, 97
Auxiliary verbs 10, 27, 156

Bauer, W. 191
Blass–Debrunner 35 n. 1, 192
Breathings viii, 21

Byzantine period 17

Capitals 18f., 21, 24
Cases 9, 64, **244f.**
Causal clauses 14, **248**
Classical Greek 16, 62 n. 1
Clauses, definition of 1; *see also* Adjective, Adverb, Noun
Collective nouns 4, 127 n. 1
Commands **247**
Comparative clauses 14; particle 222
Comparison of adjectives and adverbs 6, 8, 130ff., **231**
Complement 7, 9, 13, 35
Complex sentences 13
Compound verbs 54f.; prepositions after 212
Concessive clauses 14, 152
Conditions 152, 166ff., **249**
Conjunctions 2, 200
Consecutive or consequence clauses 14, 85, **248**
Construction according to sense 127 n. 1
Contracted verbs **236ff.**
Contraction, rules of 29, 83 n. 1, 171
Co-ordinate clauses 13
Crasis viii, 209
Cursives 17

Dana, H. E. 192
Dative 9, **245**
Declensions **229ff.**
Deliberative subjunctive 163
Demonstratives 4, 5, 57f.
Dentals 89, **234**
Dependent (Indirect) commands, questions, statements, 14, **249**
Deponent verbs 93, 212
Diaeresis 22
Dialects 17
Digamma 195, 222

265

GENERAL INDEX